Shakespearean
Afterlives
TEN CHARACTERS WITH A LIFE OF THEIR OWN

Shakespearean
Afterlives

TEN CHARACTERS WITH A LIFE OF THEIR OWN

JOHN O'CONNOR

ICON BOOKS / TOTEM BOOKS

Originally published in the UK in 2003 by Icon Books Ltd.

This edition published in the UK in 2005
by Icon Books Ltd., The Old Dairy,
Brook Road, Thriplow, Cambridge SG8 7RG
E-mail: info@iconbooks.co.uk
www.iconbooks.co.uk

This edition published in the USA in 2005
by Totem Books
Inquiries to: Icon Books Ltd.,
The Old Dairy, Brook Road, Thriplow
Cambridge SG8 7RG, UK

Sold in the UK, Europe, South Africa
and Asia by Faber and Faber Ltd.,
3 Queen Square, London WC1N 3AU
or their agents

Distributed to the trade in the USA by
National Book Network Inc.,
4720 Boston Way, Lanham,
Maryland 20706

Distributed in the UK, Europe, South
Africa and Asia by TBS Ltd., Frating
Distribution Centre, Colchester Road,
Frating Green, Colchester CO7 7DW

Distributed in Canada by
Penguin Books Canada,
10 Alcorn Avenue, Suite 300,
Toronto, Ontario M4V 3B2

This edition published in Australia in 2005
by Allen & Unwin Pty. Ltd.,
PO Box 8500, 83 Alexander Street,
Crows Nest, NSW 2065

ISBN 1 84046 643 X

Typesetting by Wayzgoose

Printed and bound in the UK by Clays, Bungay

JOHN O'CONNOR, formerly Senior Lecturer in English at Westminster College, Oxford, is a writer and editor whose recent publications include an account of Shylock on stage and screen in *The Merchant of Venice: New Critical Essays* (Routledge), a new edition of Marlowe's *Doctor Faustus* (Longman) and *The Pocket Guide to the English Language* (Cambridge University Press). He is series editor for the Longman Shakespeare, and has also written a number of plays for children. John O'Connor lectures in Shakespeare in Performance and spends most of his free time acting and directing with Oxford-based theatre groups.

STANLEY WELLS is General Editor of the Oxford editions of Shakespeare. His book *Shakespeare: For All Time* comprehensively surveys Shakespeare's life and career, his techniques as a writer, and many aspects of the afterlife of his plays.

Contents

Acknowledgements

I owe a great debt of thanks to the actors and directors who have generously given of their time to be interviewed: Sinead Cusack, Alexandra Gilbreath, Henry Goodman, Sir Derek Jacobi, Josie Lawrence, Adrian Noble and Philip Voss; and also to Rabbi Julia Neuberger for discussing Shylock with me.

For comments on draft material, profound thanks to my wife Sue, who read everything first; to my editor Duncan Heath for his encouragement and ideas; and to Dominic Oliver, whose knowledge and understanding have been invaluable.

Some of the material in Chapter 4 originally appeared as part of a doctoral thesis; for his advice on that, and for his continued inspiration, I owe much to Professor Stanley Wells.

Finally, this book could not have been written without the resources of the library of the Shakespeare Institute, Stratford-upon-Avon, where I have greatly valued the expertise and interest of James Shaw and Kate Welch, keeper of the wonderful collection of Shakespeare newspaper cuttings.

Foreword

From early times, readers and spectators of Shakespeare's plays have revelled in his capacity to portray characters who seem to transcend the works in which they appear, acquiring an individuality that gives them a life of their own. King Charles I, scribbling in a copy of the Second Folio, altered the title of *Much Ado About Nothing* to the names of its best-known characters, Beatrice and Benedick (later to be the title of an opera by Hector Berlioz). In the first detailed criticism of Shakespeare, of 1664, Margaret Cavendish, Duchess of Newcastle, wrote that 'one would think he had been transformed into everyone of those persons that he hath described', and even that 'he had been metamorphosed from a man to a woman, for who could describe Cleopatra better than he hath done, and many other females of his own creating'. The metaphor in 'creating' prefigures the attribution of god-like powers to the writer which lies behind David Garrick's 1769 praise of him as the 'god of our idolatry'. Alexander Pope, in the preface to his edition of the Complete Plays, claimed that 'every single character in Shakespeare is as much an individual as those in life itself'. In the theatre, the plays were frequently adapted to throw as much emphasis as possible on individual characters, as in Colley Cibber's version of *Richard III*. And when Sir Henry Irving played Shylock, the whole of the last act of the play – in which he does not appear – was often omitted. Perhaps the best-known 18th-century essay on Shakespeare is Maurice Morgann's study of Falstaff, who is reported to have seemed to Queen Elizabeth I to be so real a character that she asked Shakespeare to write a play – *The Merry Wives of Windsor* – showing him in love. Since that time Falstaff has been the subject of many paintings, operas, orchestral compositions, novels and poems.

Innumerable books have used characters from the plays as stepping stones to new fictions. Mary Cowden Clarke's three-volume *The Girlhood of Shakespeare's Heroines* (1850–2) cleverly extrapolated details from the plays to create fictional biographies of the characters leading up to the first line they spoke in their play. Much more recently, John Updike did something similar in his novel *Gertrude and Claudius*. The 19th-century actress Helena Faucit wrote eloquently on *Shakespeare's Female Characters* (1892), dedicating her book to Queen Victoria. Robert Nye's novel *Falstaff* (1976) fleshes out the character in a rambunctious piece of fiction. And, as John O'Connor discovered in interviews generously given by well-known actors of the present, a rather similar process lies behind the thinking of many modern performers as they explore the motivation of the characters they are playing, seeking imaginatively to deduce information not given by the text which may help them to bring the words to life. How long has Shylock been a widower? Did Hamlet fancy his mother, or she him – or both? Did he sleep with Ophelia (as he visibly does in Kenneth Branagh's film)? Did Lady Macbeth ever give suck? Was Antonio in love with Bassanio? Though audiences may never know what answers the actors find to such questions, posing them may help performers to flesh out their roles with vivid three-dimensionality.

In our own time, many of Shakespeare's characters have become stereotypes for particular kinds of personality or behaviour: the amorous office boy as a Romeo, the domineering wife as a Lady Macbeth, the grasping usurer as a Shylock, the over-emotional neurotic as a Hamlet. And in popular culture, in television series and comedy shows, in pop songs and advertisements, in newspaper reports of scandals and of political events, Shakespearean characters are regularly invoked as handy points of reference that will be meaningful even to people who know little or nothing of the plays in which they originate.

In the 1930s, an academic strain of criticism drawing heavily on character study and most notably represented – sometimes misrepresented – by A. C. Bradley's great study *Shakespearean Tragedy* (1904) came under attack, particularly in an essay by L. C. Knights called 'How Many Children Had Lady Macbeth?' which parodies the titles of some of Bradley's appendices that pose unanswerable questions such as 'Where was Hamlet at the time of his father's death?'. Somewhat in parallel, theatre productions influenced especially by the work of Granville Barker have encouraged emphasis on the totality of the play considered as a poetic drama rather than on the psychological interpretation of its central roles. Such theory and practice have had healthy results on both criticism and performance, but they run the risk of encouraging a stultifying austerity which places the fertility of Shakespeare's abundant imagination in an over-rigid straitjacket. It is a glory of the creative imagination that it stimulates wit in other men (as Falstaff recognised), and in this racily written, intriguingly organised, entertaining and informative book, John O'Connor draws on a vast range of material ranging from early and recent theatrical performance, through film, to modern journalism and popular culture in his demonstration of the constant mutations that Shakespeare's favourite characters have undergone over the centuries from his time to ours.

STANLEY WELLS

Introduction

THE ACTRESS: 'On pretty well every level and in every area of society – be it in literature, be it in advertising, be it on a sauce bottle, be it on whatever – you find Shakespeare. And used, I mean, in such a constant and pervasive way that it's astonishing. And the expectation is that people will immediately be able to identify something because of that Shakespearean reference.'

THE INTERVIEWER: 'You can show a young man in black holding a skull —'

THE ACTRESS: '— And everybody knows it's Hamlet! Now that's astonishing! I love it!'

That's Sinead Cusack talking excitedly about Shakespeare.[1] And in that brief snippet you have my two reasons for writing this book. I started out wanting to explore some of the extraordinary afterlives that Shakespeare's characters have enjoyed, because I was fascinated by their ability to turn up in fields as diverse as psychoanalysis and cigar ads. But I wasn't far into the initial thinking before I realised that any examination of a given character's continued existence and varied incarnations would be damagingly incomplete if it failed to embrace the extraordinary world of Shakespeare performance. So the chapters that follow are also an unabashed celebration of actors, directors and production teams – the people in whose hands lies the responsibility for keeping Shakespeare alive and well in each succeeding generation.

Browsing the other day through the fascinating collection of Shakespeare-related newspaper cuttings in Stratford's Shakespeare Institute, I came across the following from the London *Evening Standard* of February 1937:

Shakespeare is Now a Serial

SHAKESPEARE has suffered the final indignity. Something stranger than tweed-suit costumes, chromium settings, bizarre back-cloths has befallen him. 'Romeo and Juliet' has been rewritten by a woman novelist as a serial in an American newspaper.

This is a piece from the last chapter but one, the reader being kept on the tip-toe of expectancy as in the old silent-film days when the heroine Elaine used to finish each 'Exploit' dangling over the edge of a cliff:

And so throughout the night the road from Mantua to Verona echoed to galloping hooves, as Romeo, the poison in his pocket, rode to take his place beside Juliet in her tomb, and as Friar John, the messenger who might have saved him, returned to Friar Lawrence.

Will Friar John overtake Romeo on the road? Or will Romeo reach Juliet's tomb before she can be saved? Don't miss tomorrow's concluding chapter!

The reporter mischievously goes on:

Why not 'Macbeth'?

'Macbeth' has plenty of what fiction pundits call 'drama, suspense, passion and conflict interest'. I recommend a footnote: 'Look out for tomorrow's instalment! It's packed with thrills! Uncanny adventure on battlefield: did the forest move? Macbeth, at bay, in blood-tingling all-in bout with the intrepid Macduff!'

The cutting caught my eye for a number of reasons. First, it's a charming thought that this journalist – writing in 1937 – believed that serialising Shakespeare in a newspaper for a popular audience was any kind of indignity at all, let alone the ultimate one. What would he have made of Hamlet's appearance in a Carling Black Label advertisement, I wondered, or Richard the Third's on a *Morecambe and Wise* Christmas Special? Second, it's clear that he is writing for a readership that is still unused to the idea of Shakespeare being performed in modern dress: 'tweed costumes, chromium settings, bizarre back-cloths'.* Then, leaving aside what we might deduce from the writer's need to identify the perpetrator as a '*woman* novelist', it is amusing to note that his satirical jibe at the urgent, hyped-up questions ('Will Friar John overtake Romeo …? Or will Romeo reach Juliet's tomb …?') is a pretty accurate prediction of the ways in which Shakespeare is commonly advertised today, as witness the Royal Shakespeare Company's blurb for its 2003 *The Taming of the Shrew*:

> Petruchio also has a reputation, as a wild boy.
> Will he take Kate on? … and who will tame who?[2]

Regarding a novelistic serialisation of *Romeo and Juliet* as an 'indignity' implies a mind-set that places strict demarcations between 'high' and 'low' culture. Given his problem with a serialised *Romeo and Juliet*, it's interesting to speculate on how he might have coped with *West Side Story*, let alone the 'Kung hop actioner' movie *Romeo Must Die*,[3] or a whole world of *R and J*-inspired pop lyrics, which include The Reflections' 'Our love's gonna be written down in history / a-Just like Romeo and Juliet' and Mark Knopfler's 'There's a place for us, you know the movie song, / When you gonna realise, it was just that the

---

* The writer's reference to 'bizarre back-cloths' suggests the designs created for the Russian Theodore Komisarjevsky's productions at Stratford in the 1930s.

time was wrong, Juliet?', a particularly interesting lyric for observers of intertextuality, in that its reference to *West Side Story* makes it a spin-off from a spin-off.[4]

However much our 1937 journalist would have struggled with the appearance of the star-cross'd lovers in pop, he would surely have revised his definition of 'the final indignity' when confronted with the appearance of Hamlet's 'To be, or not to be' in *Star Trek*:

> KLINGON GENERAL CHANG: You have not experienced Shakespeare until you have read him in the original Klingon.
>
> KLINGON: Tak Pah, Tak Beh.
>
> ALL: [*laughter*]*[5]

For many people, the Klingon *Hamlet* is 'the final frontier'. And yet it is with spin-offs such as this – as well as the representation of Shakespeare's characters in 'high' culture, 'popular' culture, and out and out 'Schlockspeare'[6] – that this book is largely concerned.

Its intended audience is that 'great Variety of Readers' first addressed in 1623 by Shakespeare's actor friends John Heminges (or Hemminge or Heminge) and Henry Condell when they collected together and published his plays in an edition which we know as the First Folio. These readers are people who have an interest in Shakespeare and enjoy watching the plays on stage and screen, but do not profess to be experts. And I am acutely aware that this 'great variety of readers' entertains an equal diversity of views on what a Shakespeare character *is* and how we can think about them.

There are many people, for example, who see Shakespeare's characters as – if not actually 'real' people – then certainly figures whose

---

* *Star Trek* aficionados and fantasy linguists can find the complete 'Klingon *Hamlet*' at www.kli.org/stuff/Hamlet.html

personalities and biographies can be discussed and speculated upon as though they were indeed flesh and blood human beings. On the eccentric fringe of this group sits Dickens's Mr Curdle in *Nicholas Nickleby*, who

> ... had written a pamphlet of sixty-four pages, post octavo, on the character of the Nurse's deceased husband in *Romeo and Juliet*, with an enquiry whether he really had been a 'merry man' in his lifetime, or whether it was merely his widow's affectionate partiality that induced her so to report him.[7]

With his portrait of Curdle, Dickens is gently mocking a tradition of Shakespearean character criticism which had been going strong since the end of the 18th century. Inspired by Bard-phenomena such as the Shakespeare Jubilee of 1769, organised in Stratford-upon-Avon by the great actor David Garrick, and the success of John Boydell's Shakespeare Gallery and its widely disseminated engravings of scenes and figures from the plays (see Chapter 6), a plethora of books had appeared with titles such as *A Philosophical Analysis and Illustration of some of Shakespeare's Remarkable Characters* – this one published in 1774 by a Scottish academic, William Richardson.[8] In such a reading of character, Kate and Petruchio's love-life could be speculated upon in essentially the same way as Nelson's and Lady Hamilton's: all four became equally real people with equally debatable histories. Well might our lyricists write: 'Our love's gonna be written down *in history* / a-Just like Romeo and Juliet.'

This 'Romantic' approach to Shakespeare's characters persisted well into the 20th century. But it was notably attacked in 1933 when the critic L. C. Knights penned an essay satirically entitled 'How Many Children Had Lady Macbeth?'. Knights's argument (which I will return to in the Lady Macbeth chapter) was, broadly speaking, that to conceive of Shakespeare's characters as though they were real people was to be guilty of misunderstanding Shakespeare's art, an art which concerned itself with the creation of 'dramatic poems'.[9] And, while critical theory has moved a long way since the 1930s, a consensus view has persisted among academics in recent decades that it is both naïve and wrong to think of Shakespeare's characters as though they were anything very much more than the sum total of the words on the page, literary products of the 'social energy'[10] which circulated in the Early Modern era in which Shakespeare lived and worked.

This view is all very well for scholars. The problem is that the 'great variety' of the theatre-going, movie-watching public resolutely refuse to accept it. And they do so because they have seen Derek Jacobi's Prospero or Sinead Cusack's Cleopatra or Claire Danes's Juliet. And nobody is going to convince them that they haven't seen a version of reality which helps them make sense of their own existences.

The actors I have spoken to and read about while researching this book leave me in no doubt that there is indeed a kind of 'biographical reality' in Shakespeare's characters. Or rather that there are many realities which have to be explored and analysed before a Hamlet or a Cleopatra can come truly alive on stage. And that, while it might not be the academic's concern to speculate on how many children, if any, Lady Macbeth might have had, it unquestionably *is* the actor's. Which, in turn, by a kind of theatrical osmosis without which theatre is sterile and mechanical, makes it the audience's concern too.

Facing this particular question of Lady Macbeth's children, Harriet Walter wrote: 'Every production has to find a solution. Scholars' concerns lie elsewhere.'[11] And we, the audience, are an essential part of that production. Finding a solution is as crucial to us as it is to the actor. We collaborate with her, endorsing her conviction that, having in a very real sense 'become' Lady Macbeth, the actor's flesh-and-blood reality is passed on to the character. We know intellectually that Harriet Walter isn't actually Shakespeare's Scottish Queen. But it's a knowledge we happily subdue as part of our contract with the actor and the production of which she's a part. It's an important manifestation of what the poet Coleridge famously termed 'a willing suspension of disbelief'.[12]

It is therefore a fundamental premise of this book that, in all contexts outside the narrowly academic, it is perfectly proper to theorise on whether Kate has become 'a shrew' because she misses a mother's love (as actress Josie Lawrence does in Chapter 8);[13] or to surmise that Shylock might be smothering his daughter in oppressive love because he is recently widowed (Henry Goodman and David Calder in Chapter 4); or to worry what might befall Prospero on his return to Milan (Derek Jacobi in Chapter 9).

But, having argued for this reality, the question then becomes: Whose Kate are we talking about? Whose Shylock? Whose Prospero? Because every one of these characters is genetically unstable. Watch the videos of Olivier's 1944 *Henry V* followed by Branagh's 1989 version, and you watch two completely different kings, even in those scenes when they are speaking the same words in apparently similar cinematic contexts. But this inherent instability of Shakespeare's characters – self-evident when we think about the multiplicity of actors' and directors' interpretations – is just as striking when you move outside the theatre. Take Romeo. In Shakespeare's play, he is a boy who has two girlfriends, the second of whom he marries and loves so deeply and faithfully that he kills himself believing she has died. It is unthinkable that, had he survived, he would quickly have 'moved on' and formed a new relationship. And this image of monogamous fidelity has been widely reinforced in – to name a selection of the most famous instances – the Prokofiev ballet and Tchaikovsky overture, the music of Bellini, Berlioz and Gounod, in *West Side Story* and in the Baz Luhrmann *Romeo + Juliet*. And yet, despite that army of positive image-builders, from Shakespeare to Sondheim, what is 'a Romeo' in

7

today's popular consciousness? He is a bit of a lad with the ladies (not always successful – sometimes a 'failed' or an 'ageing' Romeo); or, more darkly, he is an irritating harasser (the 'office Romeo', or the KGB agent taking advantage of women as a 'Romeo spy'). It seems that, however often an agreed basic interpretation of the character might be reinforced in performance or the study, once these characters start to live in the popular consciousness, they begin to take on a life of their own. Or rather a number of lives, determined by the vagaries of each succeeding generation's preferences and prejudices. Once upon a time, Shylock might have been a comic figure of fun; then he was a villain; latterly a victim. And those radical changes have taken place despite the fact that, allowing for the cuts made by particular directors, he has continued to speak precisely the same words.

The point is that the *idea* of 'Shylock' has changed through the centuries, not least because the resonances of the concept 'Jew' have changed – when Disraeli came to prominence, for example, and – obviously – after the Holocaust. And these changes are totally consistent with the ways in which individual words have changed in meaning since Shakespeare's actors first uttered them. To take an example from Shylock's play, consider what Portia says when she dismisses her failed suitor, the Prince of Morocco:

A gentle riddance. Draw the curtains, go.
Let all of his complexion choose me so …[14]

Now, an Elizabethan audience had the option of believing that she was alluding, not to his African skin colour, but to his disposition or temperament, the psychological mix formed by the *complex* of humours within him. Today's audiences, largely unaware of the earlier meaning, are frequently shocked by Portia's casual racism. The line is often cut in performance or delivered in such a way as to suggest that Portia doesn't really mean it unkindly. My point is that the words spoken by the characters self-evidently cannot always be said to have an intrinsic, unchanging meaning established by the writer; and no more does the idea of 'Portia' or 'Shylock'.

Developing this line of argument, and proposing that Shakespeare has actually been influential in shaping the ways in which we think about ourselves, Terence Hawkes wrote:

> ... for us, [Shakespeare's] plays have the same function as, and work like, the words of which they are made. We *use* them in order to generate meaning. In the twentieth century, Shakespeare's plays have become one of the central agencies through which our culture performs this operation. That is what they do, that is how they work, and that is what they are for. Shakespeare doesn't mean; *we* mean *by* Shakespeare.[15]

All this is to demonstrate that defining what a Shakespeare character *is*, and agreeing upon the ways in which it is proper to speak about them, is no easy matter. And it is further complicated by the fact that Shakespeare himself didn't have a consistent view of what 'a character' was either, a point elucidated by director Adrian Noble when I interviewed him in London's Haymarket Theatre:

> 'Shakespeare's attitude towards character shifted and changed during the course of his life, I would say. If you look at his approach to character in, let's say, the *Henry VI* plays, pretty early stuff, almost everybody speaks in verse, almost everybody's thoughts are roughly iambic. Which means that almost all the characters have a very strong pulse in their language. The same is true of *Titus Andronicus*, *Richard III*, all those early plays. And you could say therefore that maybe they're all rather similar. Because whether it's the Duke of York coming on or Queen Margaret coming on or Clarence coming on, they all think through to the end of the line,

they very rarely have a full stop, or a change of thought in the middle of the line. And in a way one can't resist that. One must deduce from that that Shakespeare was trying to create a world that has this energy, this pulse, this life coursing through it. And all the characters are infused with that particular blood group, and you then make your distinctions within that blood group.

'Now when you get to the middle plays, to *Henry V*, for example, you get Henry's mates, that wonderful rabble he has: Pistol, Bardolph, Nym, Mistress Quickly. Some of them have virtually nothing to say and some of them are gas-bags. And they are so delineated in such a precise and brilliant way. Now get to *Cymbeline* or *Pericles*, and you won't find that there. They're not created in the same way in those late plays. Shakespeare gives you the corner of a piece of pottery from which you have to create the rest of the picture. Here's a bit of vase and here's a man with a sword drawn … And you have to extrapolate out from that fragment he gives you of one small character – one little comment – "Oh, interesting, you said that?" – and you extrapolate out from it. He doesn't give you all the details …

'So he didn't have a consistent view of character, I don't think. And character is always subject to the greater dramatic purpose, it seems to me. And actors need to understand that, either instinctively or intellectually. It's crucial.'[16]

Noble's point is echoed by John Morrish, reviewing a book called *The Bard on the Brain*:

In the great tragedies, starting with *Hamlet*, characters are imbued with a self-aware, questioning type of consciousness, new in drama. A few years on, though, and he seems to have changed his mind. Now he gives us Leontes, in *The Winter's Tale*, whose moods and motivations are both instantaneous and unfathomable. Was he depicting a different type of mind? Did he decide that the mind was unknowable after all? Or was he just in a hurry?[17]

So, if Shakespeare's characters are unstable because they can be interpreted in so many different ways, unstable because '*we* mean *by* them', and unstable because they fulfil different functions at different stages in the dramatist's career – where does all this leave the much-vaunted idea that they are 'universal', that his plays are, in the words of his fellow-playwright Ben Jonson, 'not for an age, but for all time'? Well, again you will tend to get one answer from the academics and another from actors and directors. Academics generally dislike and reject the notion that Shakespeare's plays represent an unchanging and universal picture of human nature. They argue, for example, that when people talk about 'human nature' they too often unthinkingly base their observations on male, white European heterosexual attitudes, and that their idea of 'universality' ends up by marginalising disadvantaged groups, at worst denying them their humanity. Sitting at home, reading a Shakespeare play, I can sympathise with that viewpoint.

In the theatre, on the other hand … Here is director Nicholas Hytner talking on BBC Radio 4's *Start the Week* about his production of *Henry V* which had just opened in the National Theatre:

'What you find is that a really good artist finds in his time and in his place phenomena that never change. That a leader dragging his country into a war which has dubious justification is going to find similar things going on, whatever time, whatever place. It's a play that always seems to be about a war that's just happened, or is happening, or is about to happen.'[18]

Hytner isn't concerned, as scholars might be, that 'war' means something very different to us from what it meant to a Londoner in Shakespeare's time, and different again from what it meant to a

Warwickshire farmer, or to a Scot or a Spaniard. For him, enough has remained unchanged in the actions of war-leaders and those urging them to battle, for Henry's French campaign to seem forever fresh, endlessly making connections with current conflicts. In that sense, the characters planning, fighting and arguing about the war – the young Henry, the persuasive Archbishop, the sceptical, challenging Williams – are, in any common use of the term, 'universal'.

As a further argument for Shakespeare's universality, consider the following report from *The Guardian*:

> The Bard boom knows no bounds. Far away from the millennial fanfares of the BBC, across the tempest-tossed seas in Buenos Aires, Shakespeare is all the rage.
>
> Free adaptations are popular, ranging from rock opera style glossy musicals to offbeat versions on the fringe, with black blocks for sets and puppets for protagonists. *The Winter's Tale* is being performed in the capital for the first time, one of some 25 Shakespeare theatre productions scheduled for the city. And among the films coming from the US are *Titus*, with Anthony Hopkins, *O*, the high-school version of *Othello*, and a couple of *Midsummer Night's Dream*s. It may be the centenary of Borges's birth, but even Argentina's most esteemed man of letters cannot compete with Big Will.[19]

So, if he isn't universal, what could millennial Argentina have found in Shakespeare? It seems to me that if the emotions experienced by Shakespeare's characters – love, hate, jealousy, loss – are those that have been experienced by people throughout history and regardless of geography, and if the same can be said about the actions they perform – killing, stealing, kissing, betraying – then it is quibbling to reject 'universal' as an epithet for the characters themselves.

But universal or not, most actors and directors who have worked with Shakespeare's plays will tell you that there is something about his characters which is unique, however difficult it might be to pin down precisely what it is. Adrian Noble prefaces his own definition with an account of his approach with actors:

'My approach is almost entirely based upon the words that they say. I will say to the actors that your character is what you say, you are defined by the language you use, the vocabulary you employ. Because it seems to me that if you try and contemplate the words the character says, if you try and just think about the vocabulary that character uses, then you'll get nine tenths of who they are. You'll find, for example, that some characters – Juliet, for example, uses an enormous amount of metaphor, a huge amount of metaphor in her language; another character uses absolutely no metaphor whatsoever. Now that defines who you are much more than where you went to school and what sort of love life you had. Somebody who thinks in metaphors is a particular kind of human being. Somebody who has a very small vocabulary is another kind of human being. So that's how I start. The fascinating thing about Shakespeare is, firstly, that almost all his characters are articulate; there are very, very few who aren't – even Dull in *Love's Labour's Lost* is actually articulate. He doesn't decide to say much, but what he has to say he says with extraordinary economy of language and accuracy. And so a Shakespearean character is actually rather a wonderful thing to live with – they are unlike other creatures because they have this extraordinary ability to communicate. And because they have an extraordinary ability to create their own world, they can carry a cosmos around with them – you know? They can carry their own world where they go. But that's partly – no, largely – because of the way Shakespeare conceived his drama. Things like scenery, things like location, social context, political context, all of that is expressed through what people say. You know, they carry it around with them in a rather curious way – like a snail carries its house on its back, a Shakespeare character carries that whole reality around with them. It's extraordinary. Chekhov's characters don't do that at all.'

Noble's idea that almost all Shakespeare's characters are articulate would provoke strong responses in some quarters. No, they will argue, it's Shakespeare who is articulate, not his characters. But again – and forgive me for revisiting a familiar theme – that's a scholar's viewpoint. Sit in the stalls and listen to Sinead Cusack's Beatrice (or Harriet Walter's or Emma Thompson's), scrapping it out verbally with Derek Jacobi's Benedick (Nicholas Le Prevost's, Kenneth Branagh's), and Adrian Noble's point is spectacularly made. In the heat of battle, it is the lovers who are articulate; a writer's verbal dexterity is only notice-able if it is forced or missing.

However, there is one distinction between the characters and their creator which is unquestionably worth making. It arose recently in some newspaper correspondence following an article by Gary Taylor.* Prompted by the imminence of Nicholas Hytner's National Theatre production of *Henry V*, and musing on Henry's post-victory claim that 'God fought for us',[20] Taylor wrote:

> No one in the play contradicts this claim. God must enjoy frying the French. If our illegal invasion of Iraq appals you, blame Shakespeare …
>
> For centuries, this bellicose poet has saturated the conscious-ness of the English-speaking empire …
>
> Shakespeare has been shaping anglophone perceptions of the world for more than four centuries. During those centuries, the

* Among other things, Gary Taylor is a General Editor of the *Complete Works of William Shakespeare* (Oxford University Press, 1988).

English-speaking people have been more aggressive and expansionist than anyone else on the planet. Is that because God fought for us? Or because Shakespeare thought for us?[21]

It was an extraordinary train of thought, promptly and fittingly answered by Hytner himself:

Gary Taylor's characteristically provocative claim ... that 'the English-speaking people have been more aggressive that anyone else on the planet' because Shakespeare 'thought for us' rests on the assumption that Henry V speaks for Shakespeare. In my experience, once a playwright hands a play over to actors, its characters speak only for themselves. I'm currently rehearsing *Henry V* at the National Theatre, and as ever it's impossible to know what Shakespeare thought. So Henry V will speak for himself, and audiences can decide whether they agree with him or not.

Nicholas Hytner, National Theatre, London[22]

Hytner's letter was accompanied by another in which the writer pointed out that what Taylor had forgotten to mention was:

... that Shakespeare also makes pretty powerful poetry out of the devastation of war ... that *Henry V* questions the legality of Henry's enterprise, compares expansionist leaders with dubious motives to thieves committing larceny on a grand scale, and devotes a good many lines to the moral confusions behind the glorious rhetoric: a topical play.[23]

And, accompanying both letters was a cartoon showing a luvvie director getting cross with an actor playing Henry (who is wearing a 'Not In My Name' T-shirt), insisting: 'Look, Jeremy, unless you go once more unto the breach, it just isn't the same play.'[24]

I don't want to labour this point, and I will be returning to it in

Chapter 9. But it's surprising how often people will tell you that a thought uttered by a character must be Shakespeare's opinion – failing to take into account that it's not uncommon to hear several different opinions voiced by equally authoritative characters, each of which contradicts all the others.

So. What *is* a Shakespeare character? How should we think about them? Are they 'universal'? What does the 'meaning' of a Shakespeare play mean? How do actors and directors go about creating a Shakespeare character? These were some of the questions I set myself when embarking on this book. And I came to realise that, in endeavouring to answer them, I should need a very particular structure.

I had decided from the outset that I should devote a chapter to each chosen character (or, in one case, pair of characters); and that each chapter should have at least two strands running through it. One strand would be a summary of the character's performance history, the other a commentary on his or her 'afterlife' – Henry the Fifth in management training, Hamlet in Freud, Cleopatra in *Carry On Cleo*, and so on.

I then realised that a third strand would be needed: one which would help to remind the reader who the character was and what they did. This strand would consist of retelling the key moments of their story (*the Christians come to Shylock … he offers the bond … he is destroyed by the loss of Jessica* … and so on). It then occurred to me that, as I retold each scene, I could describe a different actor's performance of it, or a representation of it in a different medium. For example, I would open the Shylock chapter by describing the scene in which he offers the bond – but as it was performed by Bob Peck in the 1996 version for Channel 4; when I came to the moment where Shylock enters bewailing the loss of Jessica, it would be as Warren Mitchell performed it for the BBC in 1980; his rejection of Antonio would be based on a 1795 painting by Richard Westall … and so on.

After retelling each episode, I would then home in on a feature of that particular actor's performance and use it as a springboard for the other two strands. For example, in retelling the story of Hamlet, I relate the episode in which he visits his mother in her 'closet', but describe it as it is performed in the Zeffirelli film by Mel Gibson with Glenn Close. I then link back in the performance history to Olivier's similarly 'psychoanalytic' Hamlet and both lead me on to Freud and his use of Hamlet to explain the Oedipus complex – one of the character's best known 'afterlives'.

While I was researching the book, I also conducted a number of interviews with leading Shakespearean actors and directors: Sinead Cusack (one of our most experienced performers who has fascinating things to say about Kate and Cleopatra); Alexandra Gilbreath (in the forefront of the younger generation of RSC actors); Henry Goodman (whose award-winning Shylock was one of the finest Shakespeare performances of the 1990s); Sir Derek Jacobi (one of our genuinely great Shakespearean actors, the most brilliant Hamlet of his generation); Josie Lawrence (who came to play Kate and Beatrice from the world of stand-up comedy and *Whose Line Is It Anyway?*); Adrian Noble (Artistic Director of the RSC from 1991 to 2002); and Philip Voss (an RSC stalwart, notable for his Malvolio, Menenius, Ulysses and Shylock). These interviews provide original and unique personal perspectives, as well as voices different from my own.

My criteria for selecting characters have been relatively straightforward. I wanted to focus on those who were most vividly in the popular consciousness. When I asked academics who were the most important Shakespeare characters, their list almost invariably had Falstaff near the top, and Lear and Iago in the first half-dozen. When I asked friends and acquaintances who enjoyed watching Shakespeare, but had never studied the plays since school, they gave me Romeo and Juliet, Hamlet, Henry the Fifth, Cleopatra, Shylock, Richard the Third, Lady Macbeth and Kate 'the Shrew'. Prospero I have added for three reasons. First, because he is one of the best examples of how Shakespeare helps to shape the ways we think of ourselves as social beings – the sense in which we can be said to 'mean by Shakespeare'. Second, because he is the one Shakespeare character traditionally associated with the playwright himself, the magician's renunciation of his art commonly taken as an expression of the dramatist's retirement from the theatre. And third, because – I have to admit this – Sir Derek Jacobi was in the middle of playing the character at the Old Vic, and the great man agreed to give me an interview.

This book is not designed to be encyclopaedic. It is not an exhaustive and definitive catalogue of all the spin-offs from the Prince of Denmark, the music based on the Verona lovers, the political caricaturing inspired by the Scottish Queen. It claims to be nothing more than a series of personal reflections on the ever-expanding universe of Shakespearean afterlives. But it is informed by the thesis that these frequently eccentric reincarnations and spin-offs have the power to tell us something new and unpredictable about both Shakespeare's characters and ourselves.

I began this introduction with an actress, and I will end with one. This is Alexandra Gilbreath, an RSC Hermione, Juliet, Rosalind and Kate, concluding an hour's animated chat about Shakespeare's characters on the roof terrace of the Swan theatre, Stratford. Her speculative fantasy expresses both the actor's and the writer's hopes and fears:

'I hope he's not turning in his grave. I hope that ... You know, sometimes I think, we have our little conversations, and I hope if he's out there somewhere, or looking down on us from that church, he's thinking, "Yeh, that's *all right* ..."

'And I guess he'd have liked the continuation of challenging people's psyches, emotionally and intellectually, and the fact that we still love to sit and talk about it. I hope he'd say "Good one! Good! *That's a result!*"'[25]

CHAPTER 1

Romeo and Juliet

'It is Shakespeare all over, and Shakespeare when he was in love'
William Hazlitt, *The Characters of Shakespeare's Plays* (1817)

The Prologue: Enter Chorus

A television appears in the centre of a black screen. It is on, but all we can see and hear is interference. Then it flickers into life with a picture of a national network news reader, and, flashed up behind her, an image of a fractured wedding-ring and the caption STAR-CROSS'D LOVERS. Her tone is serious and urgent ...

> *'Two households, both alike in dignity*
> *In fair Verona where we lay our scene,*
> *From ancient grudge break to new mutiny,*
> *Where civil blood makes civil hands unclean.*
> *From forth the fatal loins of these two foes*
> *A pair of star-cross'd lovers take their life*
> *Whose misadventured piteous overthrows*
> *Doth with their death bury their parents' strife.*
> *The fearful passage of their death-marked love*
> *And the continuance of their parents' rage,*
> *Which, but their children's end, nought could remove,*
> *Is now the two hours' traffic of our stage ...'*

Suddenly, before the TV anchorwoman can quite complete her report, our ears are bombarded by dramatic choral music, and the camera violently crash-zooms in to a blurred image resolving itself into the street of a major city, seen from above. Flashing from one shot to another, the music growing in intensity, we barely register the caption IN FAIR VERONA, the opening shot in an impressive montage of —

an enormous statue of Christ atop a vast church, an urban skyline with two great commercial tower-blocks bearing the names MONTAGUE AND CAPULET, screeching car-tyres, a deafening police helicopter, a street riot, the statue again, injured police, the helicopter, a final zoom in on the statue, before cutting to —

a grainy photograph of that last image of Christ which, as the camera pulls back, is seen to be the focus of a newspaper spread – it's the Verona Beach Herald – featuring pictures and brief biographies of the leading members of the two warring families.

'Two households …' – a new voice we will later identify as that of the Friar (or 'the Priest' as he is in this version of the story), repeats in voice-over the news reporter's heavy words, as further images assail our senses – 'Both alike in dignity …' – flames give way to a newspaper headline: MONTAGUE v CAPULET – 'in fair Verona …' – caption, through more flames: IN FAIR VERONA – 'where we lay our scene …' – another aerial shot of the police chopper – 'From ancient grudge break to new mutiny …' – a night scene of armed police responding – 'Where civil blood makes civil hands …' – newspaper headlines dramatically proclaim: ANCIENT GRUDGE, NEW MUTINY, CIVIL BLOOD intercut with shots of rioting, armed response, the beleaguered Chief of Police (Captain Prince), magazine covers showing the street riots, and finally, as the voice says '… unclean' – a single gunman.

'From forth the fatal loins …' – the Montague parents look anxiously out

of a limousine window – 'of these two foes ...' – now a shot of the Capulets – 'A pair of star-cross'd lovers take their life ...' – and the caption which spells out these final words has a Christian cross in place of the 't' in take ...

This astonishing opening to Baz Luhrmann's brilliant 1996 film *William Shakespeare's Romeo + Juliet* is both iconoclastic in its aggressively modern Miami-esque setting, MTV speed-editing and disorienting camera-work; and deeply traditional in its theatrical foregrounding of the Chorus's opening speech. While not by any means the first interpretation to give the story a modern urban backdrop, Luhrmann's film unusually highlights the pervasive influence of the Catholic Church – here represented by the towering statue of Christ which looms constantly over the city. But it is, of course, the Montague–Capulet feud which will destroy the lovers, and it is this conflict and its terrible repercussions which visually dominate the opening sequence, as images flash before us of LA-style street riots, followed by reaction shots – as they arrive on the scene of the latest flare-up – from 'Ted Montague', Mafia-boss 'Fulgencio Capulet' and their two wives.

In constructing this introductory collage, Luhrmann has created an outstandingly cinematic representation of a device – the Chorus – patently designed to suit the conditions and conventions of the Elizabethan playhouse. But he has done more than that. He has also tapped into the popular modern understanding of what the Romeo and Juliet story is all about: a boy and girl from different social groups whose love is thwarted by the mistrust or hatred that exists between their two communities. And that meaning is so widely shared by people who have never seen or read Shakespeare's play that a newspaper sub-editor can head up a story 'Romeo and Juliet lovers face life in jail'[1] in total confidence that readers will understand exactly what to expect.

In that particular story, from Pakistan, the source of division was ethnic – the Romeo was a Pathan, the Juliet a member of the Mohajir majority; and we find a similar context implied by this preview of a BBC television programme, *Forbidden Love*: 'Love on the run: tales of British Romeos and Asian Juliets.'[2]

Those stories represent one classic type of 'Romeo and Juliet situation': young lovers suffering because they come from different ethnic or religious communities.

Another paradigm sees the couple as connoting defiance in the face of oppressive convention; and in this incarnation they are commonly evoked in stories about rebellion against forced marriage, such as this from New Delhi concerning Humaira Khokhar and her husband Mahmood Butt: 'A woman whose defiant marriage has turned her and her beloved into a Pakistani version of Romeo and Juliet, is now facing the full might of the country's legal system ...'[3]

That story was followed up six weeks later by: 'Pakistan's "Romeo and Juliet" yesterday glimpsed a possible happy ending ...' And it is significant that the lovers are no longer 'a Pakistani version of ...' but 'Pakistan's "Romeo and Juliet"', with all that the reference implies.

Class divide can also create the right environment for impossible young love, and it was no surprise when Kate Winslet's Rose and Leonardo DiCaprio's Jack in *Titanic* were dubbed 'this Edwardian Romeo and Juliet'.[4] Less seriously, a teacher writing about a school trip in which 'their' boys had to be kept apart from 'our' girls, could report that: 'By the end of the week we were patrolling what resembled a set for a Shakespearean remake. Juliets hung from balconies while prospective Romeos blew kisses ...'[5]

However, it is a fairly safe prediction, with increasing generation-gap difficulties within immigrant communities throughout the West, unremitting tension between Jews and Arabs in the Middle East, and the general fall-out from 'the war on terrorism', that an increasing number of Romeo and Juliet stories will be sectarian, along the lines of this one from the war in Bosnia:

> ... of a young Serb and his Muslim girlfriend who had been flashed across the world's media as the Romeo and Juliet of the war. They had been trapped in Sarajevo but believed they had been given safe passage from the city so they could find a place to be together. In fact, they were double-crossed and killed by sniper fire as they left. They died in each other's arms.[6]

In media parlance, a 'Romeo and Juliet' couple are essentially any young lovers thwarted in one way or another by a divided or oppressive society. But there are further ingredients which can turn a story into a classic Romeo and Juliet scenario. One is horrifyingly present in that story from Sarajevo: namely, the threat, or actuality, of violent death. It also existed in two of the examples quoted above: the 'Pakistani Romeo and Juliet' report, where Sultan Khan, a leading Pathan, had commented that 'Tradition demands that the girl should be killed ...'; and the BBC television programme:

> ... strong on the affecting stories of Pakistani Juliets such as Shazia, kept prisoner in her own home, and Zena, told by her brother that she and her boyfriend were 'walking corpses' ...

In each of those 'Romeo and Juliet stories', violence was a key ingredient; and it is at the heart of 'Star-cross'd Romeo falls foul of Mafia', a report from Rome which begins:

> In what the Italian press yesterday dubbed a 'Mafia version of Romeo and Juliet', a 17-year-old boy has been murdered after falling in love with the niece of the boss of a rival clan and vowing to marry her.

'This is a replay of the rivalry between the Montagues and the Capulets', said *La Repubblica*. 'It is a case of impossible love between two young people from irreconcilable families.'[7]

Describing a perfect example of art following life, which then follows art, the report went on:

It is said the tragedy could have been drawn from the recent film version which places the 'Star-cross'd lovers' in a modern gangland setting in 'Verona Beach'.

The article was illustrated by a still of Leonardo DiCaprio and Claire Danes in the Luhrmann movie.

This story in turn introduces a further ingredient of the classic Romeo and Juliet set-up: the powerful and overbearing patriarch. Here, the 'capo' (actually the girl's uncle) was Orazio Trubia, head of the powerful Trubia clan, and had himself arranged the boy's murder. Shazia and Zena, the Juliets in the BBC film, had been imprisoned by their fathers in their own homes; while the father of Humaira Khokhar, referred to above, who had so opposed the match that he instituted charges of kidnapping, was an influential member of the Punjab Provincial legislature. And, just to increase the parallels with Shakespeare's play, some stories even have a Paris figure – the suitor preferred by the girl's father – as was the case with the 'Pakistani Juliet', whose '… family had opposed the marriage, wanting her to marry her cousin …'.

Act 1, scene 1: 'In sadness, cousin, I do love a woman'

Walking slowly and dreamily up the cobbled street, holding a flower, Romeo pauses for thought …

SC.	FT.FRMS.	ACTION	SOUND
16.	148.6	Low Angle LS BENVOLIO seated on wall, reading a book….	BENVOLIO: 147.9 148.6 Good morrow, cousin.
17.	158.10	LS ROMEO seated on step, legs crossed, looking upward L.	ROMEO: 156.11 158.6 Is the day so young?
18.	161.6	BENVOLIO as shot 16	BENVOLIO: 160.1 160.7 But new struck nine.
19.	181.7	MCS ROMEO seated against stone wall, facing L. PAN DOWN & L/R. As he lies on back, flowers in L. hand.	ROMEO: 161.11 181.1 Ay me! Sad hours seem long.

When we first meet Romeo (here portrayed by Leonard Whiting in the 1968 Franco Zeffirelli film),[8] he has yet to meet Juliet. The love for which he pines is that of 'the fair Rosaline', a character not given an appearance in Shakespeare's script, but who is useful in helping to construct a picture of a Romeo as an infatuated and inconstant boy in the throes of nothing more than 'Young men's love', which 'lies / Not truly in their hearts but in their eyes'.[9] And this initial impression of Romeo, slightly ridiculous, mildly disparaging, is the one that has endured in the popular consciousness. For, despite attaining some kind of tragic apotheosis in the arms of Juliet, Romeo considered alone has not proved to be an impressive figure. In fact, it is a curious phenomenon that, while media references to 'Romeo and Juliet lovers' are almost invariably intended to evoke sympathy, 'a Romeo' is an altogether different bucket of ducats. Whereas 'a Juliet' is very much a character to be taken seriously – often abused and imprisoned, always bullied and oppressed – 'a Romeo' is frequently little more than a figure of fun.

'Romeos' seem to fall into three main categories. Category one Romeos are absurdly love-sick, impetuous and soppy; as witness the following:

Romeo of The Week
The representative of the German motoring organisation who said, after a study of Britain's contra-flow system, 'I think your roadworks are brilliant … I would like to marry the daughter of the man who makes your traffic cones.'[10]

And, from an agony column, the advice that:

A young teenager who tells you he wants to spend his life with you after five minutes' acquaintance is lying (Romeo excepted).[11]

The second and largest category, however, invokes 'Romeo' as a failure, often because some romantic scheme has gone comically wrong, as in this story in which two firemen arranged an assignation with two nurses, only to find that their blind dates were firemen as well:

Romeos say 'no way hose, eh?'
… Both failed Romeos are being coy although [one] is promising revenge …[12]

Other examples of Romeo the bungler include:

Roses wilt for jilted Romeo
Almost 1,500 roses, the last one delivered on a horse, failed to persuade an Italian woman to go back on a decision to break off an

engagement, the Italian news agency, ANSA, said yesterday.

Roberto's doomed attempt to win back Alessandra took place near the northern city of Verona, where Shakespeare staged his tragedy Romeo and Juliet. – Reuters, Rome.[13]

And, for a particular kind of romantic let-down, we find:

Romeo rams find surfeit of sex doesn't pay
Sheep show how macho males do not always live up to their image, writes Roger Highfield.[14]

Still part of the 'failure' category, a man might be called 'a Romeo' because he embodies some romantic or sexual aspiration which is in itself ridiculous. In that case the name might be enhanced by some pejorative prefix such as 'would-be-' or 'ageing-', as in 'Mel mocks the ageing romeos', an article about movie-star Mel Gibson's refusal to be cast romantically opposite much younger actresses (in which he cites, among others, the 40-year age-gap between Sean Connery and his co-star Catherine Zeta Jones in *Entrapment*).[15]

The third Romeo category moves the name into the serious territory of sexual harassment and exploitation. Here a Romeo might be at best tolerated:

Avoid the office Romeos
… The office Romeo is often looking for attention, or just plain bored …[16]

at worst a pariah:

Office Romeo sues ex-lover for slander over rape 'fantasy'
… He was a ladies' man …[17]

and frequently an unscrupulous charmer:

The detective who became a 'Romeo spy'
… the Mitrokhin archive revealed how a policeman was recruited by the KGB to seduce lonely female officials …[18]

The term is, of course, *de rigueur* if the harassers in question are Italian, as in 'Buzz off, you Romeos',[19] a travel article about troublesome 'Latin lovers' in Naples.

This curious dichotomy of attitude – in which 'a Romeo and Juliet', or 'a Juliet' on her own, can evoke sympathy of tragic proportions while 'a Romeo' is at best indulged, commonly mocked or disparaged – is hard to explain. The worst that can be said of Shakespeare's hero is that he is immature and impetuous and has appalling luck: he hardly seems to have deserved such a bad press at the hands of popular usage.*

Act 1, scene 5: 'Did my heart love til now?'

A singer and orchestra perform the velvety 'Loving You'. Its wistful longing accompanies the whole sequence …

In an attempt to clear his head of the effects of a tablet that Mercutio has given him, Romeo retires to the washroom and dunks his head under the cold tap. The place is an ostentatious display of Capulet wealth, and Romeo, now more alert, is taken by the vast aquarium which stretches the length of the room, separating the men's from the women's areas, stocked with the most extraordinary and exotic corals and tropical fish … But, as he stares, one small splash of colour is not a coral – it is an eye, then a face – a girl's, who has herself been absorbed in the aquarium and gazes in

---

*We might, of course, be witnessing a return to the pre-Shakespearean attitude to the lovers. In Shakespeare's sources, especially Arthur Brooke's 1562 poem, *The Tragical History of Romeus and Juliet*, the sympathy is with the parents, and the lovers' deaths are seen as righteous punishment for their disobedience.

from the other side. They smile at each other, she looks away, then back at him, and they laugh …

'Madam, your mother calls!' It is Juliet's Nurse, who hastens her charge back into the vast dance-hall, pursued by Romeo, already in love with this beautiful creature. Who is she? How has he never seen her before?

Led by the hand to her waiting date, the handsome and eligible Paris – 'A man, my lady! (from her encouraging Nurse) – 'Such a man!' (from her besotted mother) – Juliet accepts the invitation to dance …

But the romantic atmosphere is jolted: Tybalt (dressed as Mephistopheles) has spotted the intruder and has to be restrained by Lord Capulet (particularly repulsive as Emperor Nero). As master of the house, Capulet angrily asserts, he is not going to be told who he can and cannot entertain – besides, the gate-crashing Montague is Romeo, 'And, to say truth, Verona brags of him to be a virtuous and well-governed youth' … So Tybalt is obliged to bite back his anger. But the incident has bred a bitter resentment which will surface later with devastating consequences …

Meanwhile, Juliet is dancing with Paris (who is trying a little too hard with some exaggeratedly romantic moves), but repeatedly glances over to where Romeo stands watching her, and coyly smiles –

'Did my heart love til now?' he asks himself; 'Forswear it sight! For I ne'er saw true beauty till this night.'

What is so clever in Luhrmann's transference of Shakespeare's story to present-day not-quite-Miami is that the modern allusions are rarely allowed to be merely decorative or self-conscious. While it might seem obvious to turn the Capulet ball into a drug-fuelled fancy-dress rave for the Verona Beach glitterati, the presentation of Paris – to take just one example – as 'Dave Paris, *Time* magazine's Bachelor of the Year', and his arrival at the party dressed as a NASA astronaut (Neil

Armstrong?), is a witty interpretation of a character who is so often relegated to the role of 'blocking device'. In Shakespeare's script, Paris doesn't play any part in this sequence at all (though Capulet has invited him). Luhrmann's decision to include him – and have him dance with Juliet while her attentions are on Romeo – perfectly establishes his future status as well-meaning gooseberry. But better still is having him kitted out in a white space-suit. For, not only is it perfectly 'Dave Paris' – exactly the kind of elaborate fancy-dress costume that such a celebrity would choose if he wanted to give himself an aura of manly glamour; its inflexible bulk also makes it very difficult for him to dance closely and elegantly with Juliet. And in his attempts to do so we have to sympathise as he misreads her smiles and barely suppressed giggles (in fact, reactions to Romeo's eye-contact) for coyness and girlish embarrassment. So that his fate from this point on – to misunderstand Juliet's responses – is foreshadowed by this apparently innocuous faux-pas of choosing a costume that makes him appear both gauche and superficial.

The soundtrack too is selected with a sensitive ear. The beautifully sung 'Kissing You' is a perfect accompaniment to the lovers' first meeting; while the song to which the androgynous Mercutio wildly and brazenly struts his stuff (Harold Perrineau, in a performance enhanced by a sequinned bikini top and bubbly wig) is 'Young Hearts Run Free', simultaneously one of the great disco anthems of its time and a lyric with obvious resonances for the relationship which is about to unfold.

Luhrmann's reinterpretation of the Romeo and Juliet story was inspired and innovative. Skipping from one genre to another – Spaghetti western to *Miami Vice*, Busby Berkeley to pop video; whirling his characters through a neon club-land hosting strip-joints called Mistress Quickly, Midnite Hags and Bound of Flesh; and employing the kind of disorienting camera work more usually associated with police dramas like *NYPD Blue* – Luhrmann displayed a postmodern eclecticism and cinematic style which justifiably earned the description 'hyperkinetic'. But in placing his characters in a contemporary ambience, the Australian director wasn't of course doing anything new. There have been numerous modern settings for this play, including Michael Bogdanov's 1986 version for the RSC in which Tybalt entered driving a bright red Alfa-Romeo, and Mercutio entertained the guests at the Capulet ball with an impressive riff on his electric guitar.[20]

Modern settings of Shakespeare can be both liberating and illuminating. Placing Romeo and Juliet in a context of turn-of-the-century gangland violence and decaying social structures might seem an obvious thing to do; but, speaking personally, I experience a much more profound sense of waste watching the ruin of Luhrmann's young Americans, and maybe come closer to understanding the horror that Shakespeare's audiences felt watching boys clumsily carve each other up with swords, than I ever do with a traditional setting of the play. It's something to do with the fact that stage and screen sword-fighting almost inevitably has a whiff of the heroic and swash-buckling about it, not least because such a combat has to be skilfully choreographed if it is to meet the dual criteria imposed by aesthetics and safety. But the ensuing display of virtuosity – I'm thinking about the magnificent opening fight scene in Zeffirelli's 1968 film – serves to mask the horror of what's actually going on, to the extent that the Prince comes across as a bit of a spoilsport for stopping it. I feel sure that a parent watching the Montague–Capulet fights in the 1590s would be shuddering at the all-too-familiar sight of boys mutilating each other and bleeding ingloriously to death in dirty London alleyways; not admiring a balletic display of heroics, as it can so easily be for a century that has grown up to think not of sword-*fighting* but sword-*fencing*, in which the sword is endowed with romantic and 'heritage' connotations along with the doublet and the flagon of sack. Giving boys guns – or, as in the 1986 Bogdanov version, flick-knives and bicycle-chains – helps us to see their brawling for the messy, destructive business it actually is.

There is, of course, a problem in giving the rioting in this play a modern spin: namely that Shakespeare's script is full of quite specific references to swords. Take the opening scene. Within the first 80 lines, the word 'sword' is used four times (including Capulet's 'Give me my long sword, ho!' and his wife's disparaging reply 'A crutch, a crutch! Why call you for a sword?'), and 'blade' once, and there are additional expressions to indicate that people 'draw', are 'drawn' and wield 'naked weapons'. So that, for anybody contemplating setting this play in the modern world, the inclusion of up-to-date ironmongery is a bit of a problem. Shakespeare simply wrote this play for swords, not guns. And it isn't just a question of props: there are plot inconsistencies too. I remember speaking to one of the actors in the Bogdanov *Romeo and Juliet*. I asked her whether the cast had experienced any difficulty in transferring the setting from the Renaissance to the mid-1980s. She thought for a moment and replied: 'Well, yes … When the lovers are separated by exile, it did occur to us to wonder – why the fuck doesn't she just *ring* Romeo?'

You can never solve all of these attendant problems, but Luhrmann circumvents most with elegance and wit. It's easy to understand, for example, why a modern-day Juliet might nonetheless be hemmed in by Elizabethan-style restrictions, when you see her as the only daughter of a possessive and violent Mafia boss, a child allowed out only to visit the priest for confession. (I could also imagine a convincing version of the play in which a modern Juliet was placed in a culture which imposed severe restrictions on its women – though such an interpretation would require sensitive handling.)

The role of the Friar also makes sense if you play him as the Priest in a society that is dominated by its observance of Catholicism – a dominance symbolised in Luhrmann's film not only by the frequent shots of the Christ statue that towers over the city streets, but also by the plethora of kitsch Catholic imagery. I have tried teaching this play to teenagers for whom 'a friar' is the fat guy in *Robin Hood*. Pete Postlethwaite's tough and tormented hard-drinking community priest – who wears a Hawaiian shirt under his cassock and has a huge celtic cross tattooed on his back – makes a kind of sense of the character that is so often lacking in this story, and helps me for one to understand why Elizabethans might have placed him, rather than the lovers, at the moral heart of the play.* At the same time, this priest's man-of-the-kids cool has some worrying features: his casual preparation of drugs in front of his confirmation class daringly parallels the moral ambiguity of Shakespeare's Friar.

The Chorus too is given a radical new meaning when viewed as the anchor-woman authority whose calm, unemotional commentary on the events suggests a degree of control and social order which, from our perspective on the world of Verona Beach, is plainly a delusion. She represents the management of news for a society in which order and authority have clearly disintegrated into anarchy and random violence, thereby transforming Shakespeare's Chorus into a device which invites us to contemplate the ways in which the Romeo and Juliet story is mediated for each generation that experiences it.

But back to the problem of the swords ... Luhrmann's solution is delightfully simple. When, after a thrilling opening-scene stand-off on a petrol station forecourt, the peace-maker Benvolio cries 'Put up your swords!', Luhrmann gives us one of his trademark crash-zooms onto the gun brandished by Romeo's cousin: and, where we might expect

---

*'It is probable that Shakespeare's audience would have taken the observations of the Friar more seriously than we do, and that their sympathy with the lovers would not have prevented them from accepting the Friar as the voice of wisdom.' (T.J.B. Spencer, Introduction to the New Penguin edition, first published 1967, p. 8.)

to read 'Smith and Wesson', this firearm bears the brand-name 'SWORD 9mm Series S'. And the convention is speedily reinforced when Capulet, at the wheel of his car, cries 'Give me my long sword!' and reaches for an extended-muzzle version – again, clearly identified by its trademark name, LONGSWORD – fixed to the face of his dashboard. In this way, 'sword' is elegantly translated into SWORD, a make of gun, the brand-name evoking all the deadly craftsmanship of its Toledo ancestor.

Act 2, scene 2: Enter Juliet, above

The scene is at the heart of Shakespeare iconography: the balcony, the boy climbing up from below, the girl standing gazing up at the stars, as yet unaware of his presence …

'O, Romeo, Romeo, wherefore art thou, Romeo …?'

But this time it is a strangely masculine voice and the accent is distinctly London. This is boxer Frank Bruno – his counterpart climbing the trellis-work, the comedian Lenny Henry. Everybody knows the scene and everybody can quote the famous line (even if they tend to think that 'wherefore' means 'where'). But this moment is unique in Shakespeare, as far as I am aware, in that you could remove the characters altogether, and people would still be able to tell you which play they were watching. Why? Because there's a balcony. Shakespeare doesn't specify where Juliet is standing – there's no mention of a balcony at all. But his architectural imprecision hasn't prevented this particular structure from being a *sine qua non* of an infinity of visual representations – so much so that a newspaper article reviewing a new and unusual version of Shakespeare's play can be headed 'Never mind the balcony'.[21] A boy in tights wooing a girl could be anybody. Add a balcony and they're unquestionably Romeo and Juliet. If you go to

34

Verona, you can visit 'Juliet's balcony', but it's a rather apologetic structure and so placed as to make the ascent of any prospective Romeo hazardous, to say the least. But, along with Elsinore and Ann Hathaway's cottage, it's become part of the Shakespeare industry tourist trail.

Frank Bruno and Lenny Henry can have their fun with this moment not only by virtue of its iconography (the relative positions of the lovers, their youth, the iconic balcony ...) but also thanks to the familiarity of the text; for, as a scene 'full of quotes', this one is almost in the *Hamlet* league: 'Romeo, Romeo ...', 'what's in a name', 'a rose by any other name would smell as sweet', 'parting is such sweet sorrow' – the familiar lines mount up. And interestingly, although they derive from a serious scene in one of Shakespeare's tragedies, these quotations are commonly used for comic effect; so that, for example, a newspaper article on light pollution can be headlined: 'What light through yonder window breaks?'[22] Like Frank Bruno performing Shakespeare, the comedy derives from the incongruity – in this case between the romantic, 'high culture' context of the original and its use as an introduction to something mundane and technological. With Bruno, we were asked to laugh at the cultural chasm between the 'uneducated' boxer's stilted delivery (comically implying 'I don't understand this, it's not part of my world ...') and our conventional understanding of what 'the Shakespeare experience' (Johnny Gielgud, 'the verse', men in codpieces ...) ought to be like.

A similar kind of thing happens in this extract from an episode of *Hancock*, in which Tony-as-thespian is auditioning for the part of Hamlet in a 'British Arts Council tour of Tanganyika':

TONY: Hush, what light from yonder window breaks? 'Tis Juliet, and the sun is in the West —

VOICE: Mr Hancock, the play is *Hamlet*.

TONY: *Hamlet?* Is it? I was distinctly told *The Merchant of Venice.* I'm terribly sorry. *Hamlet* is a different cup of tea, of course ...[23]

Like the Frank Bruno scene, it works partly because of the incongruity – Hancock is in his familiar persona of an out-of-work ham actor pretending to be 'cultured'; but the writers know that, in order for the incongruity to be apparent to us ('us' being, in this instance, a prime-time television audience), we will have at least a nodding acquaintance with this famous line from Romeo's speech.

So much a part of *popular* culture have parodic versions of this scene and these characters become, in fact, that a Shreddies ad on television can show Romeo attempting to woo Juliet and succeeding only after her rumbling tummy has been silenced by a bowlful of the appropriate breakfast cereal;[24] and a chocolate bar can invest in a half-page colour advertisement which shows the product bearing the name *TOBLEROMEO* and the caption: 'JULIET. GIVE ROMEO A 'TO MY LOVE' VALENTINE'S TOBLERONE.'[25]

Act 3, scene 1: 'O, I am fortune's fool!'

Romeo and Juliet has inspired more ballets than any other Shakespeare play, and most have used the score composed by Sergei Prokofiev for a version first staged in 1938. Pamela Mason describes the moments in choreographer Kenneth MacMillan's 1965 version of the ballet (with Rudolph Nureyev and Margot Fonteyn as the lovers), following Romeo's killing of Tybalt:

> MacMillan dispenses with the Prince's entrance here, focusing instead on Lady Capulet's grief at Tybalt's death. Her violent grief makes Romeo's attempts to explain futile and Benvolio rushes him away leaving a tableau of agonised loss which Lord Capulet can do nothing to assuage. He stands on the upper level looking

down at his wife rocking Tybalt's corpse. Also looking down is a bedraggled, maimed beggar. He symbolises the world's frailty generally but more precisely the particular cruelty and inadequacy of Verona.[26]

In one way it seems perverse to take a Shakespeare script and remove the words. But MacMillan's choreography and Prokofiev's music distil the emotional power of the story in such a way as to allow Nureyev and Fonteyn to become genuinely Shakespeare's lovers, rather than some pale imitation: a quintessence rather than a dilution.

Modern dance too has mined a rich vein of material from the lovers' story. In Rennie Harris's 'hip-hop opera' *Rome and Jewels*, for example,[27] the 'two warring families become rival gangs who waste each other through violence and do battle in street dance competitions; the Monster Q's are identified by the bravura spins and acrobatics of break dance/B-boy, while the Caps dance group perform sequences of hip-hop.'[28] With the conviction that 'rappers are the only ones who come close to Shakespeare' and that 'his stuff was originally for hookers and drug-dealers', Harris's production mixed a little Shakespeare with current black street vernacular. And, while some might question the choreographer's restricted definition of Shakespeare's audience, the main thrust of *Rome and Jewels* – that, when Romeo falls in love, he begins to question 'all the ignorance and the sexist stuff' – seems to me a valid line of interpretation.

As a snapshot of the wide variety of afterlives that a character like Romeo has had over the centuries, it is worth looking back at the 'high culture' of the Nureyev–Fonteyn ballet, and then listening to Rennie Harris describing what Shakespeare and his writing means to him today. Comparing Shakespeare's language with 'ebonics' (sometimes called 'black English'), Harris says:

The language that Shakespeare used was the same thing. It was the language that was used by the common people. To call someone a 'strumpet' and to call someone a 'whore' – it's no different. Shakespeare had a rhythm and a tone that is like black culture ... The truth of the matter is that he wrote for everyone.[29]

A creation like *Rome and Jewels*, of course, opens up a big can of Shakespearean worms ...

Some people will rejoice that Shakespeare can still seem immediate and relevant in this way, and celebrate Shakespeare's continued impact on people as diverse in background and upbringing as Rudolph Nureyev and Rennie Harris. Others will feel disappointed that Harris could not have found an inspiration for his choreography closer to home – say, from the rich tradition of African-American story-telling; and will see *Rome and Jewels* as further regrettable evidence of white cultural imperialism. As you might expect, I'm in the rejoicing and celebrating camp; but I do see the other argument.

Geographically closer to (Shakespeare's) home, though still a world away culturally, the French-Albanian choreographer Angelin Preljocaj set his version of the lovers' story in a modern totalitarian state. Preljocaj's parents had been Albanian dissidents who had fled to France only two weeks before he was born; so that, throughout his childhood he experienced what it was like to be split between two cultures and maintain two sets of loyalties. This meant that his first action on being commissioned to create a new version of *Romeo and Juliet* was to rush off and re-read George Orwell's *Nineteen Eighty-four*, a logical move when your vision of the play is that of lovers punished under a dictatorial régime. Describing his irresistible attraction to Orwell's dystopia as a setting for his dance, he said:

I thought of a world, like some European state, where everyone was under surveillance, under control. I liked the contrast between this very deep and sweet love and this very hard, cold political situation. I thought it would make the love story even more fragile.[30]

Entranced, on re-reading Orwell's book, to find that his heroine was called Julia, Preljocaj decided that 'it seemed a sign', and his own version of Juliet evolved into the daughter of a Ceaucescu-style dictator, while Romeo became a homeless drifter.

Adopting a similar line to Rennie Harris, Preljocaj explained why he believed that *Romeo and Juliet* had taken on a new relevance for a wide variety of cultures by the end of the 20th century.[31] The eastern bloc, he argued, might have disintegrated, but other contexts had emerged as ripe breeding grounds for all manner of Romeo and Juliet tragedies:

I've read all these stories – like about a Serbian guy and a Bosnian girl … Romeo and Juliet will always be modern because there will always be conflict between people …

This conflict was classically portrayed in the most famous of all Romeo and Juliet spin-offs, *West Side Story*. Both the source of division and the Juliet figure's tragic innocence are embodied in this brief exchange between the Puerto Rican gang-leader Bernardo and his younger sister Maria, when he upbraids her for having danced with 'an American', Tony (the son of Polish immigrants):

BERNARDO: Did you know that he was one of them?

MARIA: No, I only saw *him*.
('…'Tis but thy name that is my enemy. / Thou art thyself …')

The idea for the musical came in 1949, when, as Leonard Bernstein recalls in his log for 6 January:

… Jerry R [Jerome Robbins, director and choreographer] called today with a noble idea: a modern version of *Romeo and Juliet* set in slums at the coincidence of Easter–Passover celebrations. Feelings run high between Jews and Catholics. Former: Capulets; latter: Montagues. Juliet is Jewish. Friar Lawrence is a neighborhood druggist. Street brawls, double death – it all fits.[32]

Originally called *East Side Story* – the working title was changed when it was recognised that the notorious tenements on Manhattan's East Side had been demolished, and that gang warfare had moved west – composer Leonard Bernstein's collaboration with lyricist Stephen Sondheim and librettist Arthur Laurents had its New York première on 26 September 1957, ran for nearly two years and has never gone totally out of fashion, even if its choreography and script can these days seem dated. Described by an early influential review as 'a profoundly moving show … as ugly as the city jungles and also pathetic, tender and forgiving',[33] *West Side Story* was turned into a film in 1961 and earned an Oscar for Best Picture. Few media phenomena testify more eloquently to the enduring power of Shakespeare's young lovers to be re-fashioned by succeeding generations, for varied cultures, in changing media and in different forms of artistic expression.

Act 5, scene 3: 'The lady stirs …'

John Philip Kemble and Sarah Siddons in the 1780s; Henry Irving and Ellen Terry in the 1880s; John Gielgud (alternating with Laurence Olivier) and Peggy Ashcroft in the 1930s … Then, in a play-within-a-film at the end of the postmodern 1990s, Joseph Fiennes and Gwyneth Paltrow …

INT. THE CURTAIN THEATRE. STAGE. DAY
'JULIET' wakes up with a start

> VIOLA AS JULIET
>
> … Where is my lord?
> I do remember well where I should be,
> And there I am. Where is my Romeo?

INT. THE CURTAIN THEATRE. AUDITORIUM. DAY

> NURSE
> *(involuntarily)*
>
> Dead!

INT. THE CURTAIN THEATRE. STAGE. DAY

> VIOLA AS JULIET
> What's here? A cup clos'd in my true love's hand?
> Poison, I see, hath been his timeless end.

INT. THE CURTAIN THEATRE. STAGE. DAY
'JULIET' takes 'ROMEO'S' dagger

> VIOLA AS JULIET
> … O happy dagger
> This is my sheath. There rust, and let me die.

She stabs herself and dies. The 'inner curtain' closes over the tomb.

INT. THE CURTAIN THEATRE. STAGE / AUDITORIUM. DAY
HIGH ANGLE on audience and stage. 'THE PRINCE' played by WABASH is having the last word.

> THE PRINCE
> For never was a story of more woe
> Than this of Juliet and her Romeo.

The end. There is complete silence. THE ACTORS are worried. But then the audience goes mad with applause.

INT. THE CURTAIN THEATRE. THE INNER CURTAIN / STAGE. DAY

The inner curtain opens, but WILL and VIOLA are in a play of their own … embracing and kissing passionately, making their own farewell.

HENSLOWE is too stunned and moved to react at first. Then he looks at the audience and the penny drops. It's a hit.[34]

Shakespeare in Love[35] has been an extraordinary phenomenon. Made for $25 million, the film quickly grossed $100 million in the United States, a further $190 million throughout the rest of the world, and collected seven Oscars and a Bafta, including Best Film/Best Picture from both academies. Its appeal derives from a treasury of comic and romantic sources, but is grounded in the Romeo and Juliet relationship at its heart, between Joseph Fiennes's Will Shakespeare and Gwyneth Paltrow's Viola De Lesseps. The film cleverly exploits our knowledge of the Romeo and Juliet story three times over: *thematically* as a model for the central characters' star-cross'd love (he is poor and married, she is rich and destined for another); *structurally* in its cast of characters – the young lovers, the oppressive father, the nurse, the rich rival suitor …; in its plot, which includes a dance at which the lovers meet, followed by a balcony scene; and in its dialogue (Will cries 'O, I am fortune's fool!'); and (*iconically? biographically? narratively?*) as the play that Shakespeare is struggling to write and the actors struggling to stage, its working-title *Romeo and Ethel the Pirate's Daughter*, its storyline needing a kick-start from the rival playwright Christopher Marlowe:

MARLOWE
Romeo is Italian … Always in and out of love.

WILL
Yes, that's good. Until he meets …

MARLOWE
Ethel.

WILL
Do you think?

MARLOWE
The daughter of his enemy.

WILL
(thoughtfully)
The daughter of his enemy.

MARLOWE
His best friend is killed in a duel by Ethel's brother or something. His name is Mercutio.

WILL
Mercutio … good name.[36]

In the climactic scene, all three strands merge, when Viola steps in to play Juliet to Will's Romeo in the play's triumphant opening performance, only an hour after the moment at which her marriage to the appalling Lord Wessex (he hates the theatre, dammit!) has sealed their separation for good.

Also featuring *Romeo and Juliet* as a play-within-a-play is *Shakespeare's R & J*, Joe Calarco's thrilling reworking of the story for New York's Expanded Arts Theater, which, from its opening in 1997, became New York's longest-running *Romeo and Juliet* ever.[37] Working with an all-male cast, adapter-director Calarco sets his version in a repressive Catholic boys' school. Discovering a copy of Shakespeare's play, four adolescent boys at first leaf through the script, giggling at Mercutio's smutty puns and sorting out the sexy bits. But, once they begin to act it out, they become totally absorbed, and involved in the action in a way that, for Calarco, recalls the hysterical girls in Arthur Miller's *The Crucible*:

> It made me realise that Romeo and Juliet is about a similar kind of madness – the sexual hysteria of young people raised in a repressive and violent society … Suddenly the all-boys school, with its mixture of religion and militarism, seemed a perfect fit.[38]

Describing her response to the performance, *Guardian* drama critic Lyn Gardner wrote:

> There is a strange alchemy at work: it is as if the audience shares the boys' sense of discovery. Even watching a performance under the strip lighting in a New York rehearsal room I suddenly felt as if I were seeing and hearing Shakespeare's play for the first time. The mix of pugnacious energy and adolescent vulnerability creates just the right emotional landscape for Romeo and Juliet. And because the boys are so interested in what will happen next, you are too.[39]

Gardner's response is consonant with the *New York Times* reviewer's impression of an early performance:

> The production is spare, disciplined and bursting with the kind of energetic life and erotic tension you don't often find in other *Romeo and Juliets*.[40]

Calarco's play is just the kind of messing about with Shakespeare that many people hate. But for me, versions like this so often unlock new meanings, or refreshingly express known ones, in ways that more traditional and 'faithful' renditions by major established companies – somewhat depressingly – don't get anywhere near.

Russell Jackson lists both *Shakespeare in Love* and *West Side Story* as Shakespeare 'off-shoots'.[41] This seems to me to be a reasonable term for works which, while clearly based on *Romeo and Juliet*, do not actually feature Shakespeare's Romeo or Juliet as their central characters. In that sense, we might distinguish 'off-shoots' from 'adaptations' – works which, however different from Shakespeare's stage play in style or medium of artistic expression, nonetheless have characters at their heart who are recognisably Shakespeare's Romeo and Juliet in name and characteristics.

Romeo and Juliet 'off-shoots' have been as wide-ranging in setting as in quality. They include Joan Lingard's Belfast novels, beginning with *The Twelfth Day of July* (Protestant boy, Catholic girl);[42] the Opera Factory's *Julia* (Jewish Julia/Juliet, Arab Ahmed/Romeo);[43] plays such as *Prem* (Hindu Prem/Juliet, Muslim Rashid/Romeo);[44] and the movie *The Punk and the Princess* (aimless London punk Romeo, rich American Juliet), a dire version which includes a sword-fight with pool cues.[45] As a contemporary screen spin on Shakespeare's story, *The Punk and the Princess* is much less fun than a more recent *R and J* spin-off, *Romeo Must Die*.[46] This is a hybrid of martial arts (notably 'wire-fu' – a Hong Kong 'wire-suspension technique') and black gangsta gunplay, described by *Variety* as 'a Kung hop actioner', in which Verona is translated to Oakland Bay and the balcony scene consists in our hero tapping on a window and saying 'Hi'. Following the *West Side Story* tradition, the Andrew Lloyd-Webber/Ben Elton collaboration *The Beautiful Game* (its title a partly ironic use of Pele's famous description of football) transposes the story to 1969 Belfast.[47] The Romeo figure is a talented young Catholic footballer, and Mercutio an innocent friend brutally killed by a gang of Protestants, in a dance-musical which inevitably earned the (not wholly affectionate) nickname 'Bogside Story'.

Among the many *adaptations* – versions which actually feature Romeo and Juliet by name – some of the most enduring have been the classical ballet, based on music by Prokofiev, the Tchaikovsky overture, and the operatic and symphonic versions by Bellini, Gounod and Berlioz.

Vincenzo Bellini's opera *I Capuleti e i Montecchi*, though now regarded as one of the Italian composer's masterpieces, was a great disappointment to the French composer Hector Berlioz when he attended a performance in 1831, a year after the opera's Venice opening. This was not only because Bellini had followed Italian tradition in having Romeo played by a woman, but because there was —

> ... no ball at the Capulets', no trace of Mercutio, no garrulous nurse, no grave and tranquil hermit, no balcony scene, no sublime soliloquy for Juliet as she takes the hermit's phial, no duet in the cell between the banished Romeo and the disconsolate friar, no Shakespeare, nothing ...

Describing the opera as '... a botched piece of work, mangled, disfigured, *arranged* ...', Berlioz asked:

> And in the music, where was the double chorus of Montagues and Capulets, where the passion of the two lovers, the great orchestral outbursts, the vivid instrumental patterns, the new and searching melodies, the bold progressions lending colour to the scene, the unexpected modulations? Where was the musical drama, the dramatic music, that such poetry should give birth to?[48]

What Berlioz had failed to acknowledge was that Bellini's story was based not on Shakespeare, but on his Italian sources, notably the *Novelle*, a collection of prose romances written by the courtier, priest and soldier Matteo Bandello between the 1550s and 70s. However, clear in his own mind about the shortcomings of Bellini's version, Berlioz returned to France determined to compose his own opera. (The story goes that, when he had seen the Irish actress Harriet Smithson play Juliet in 1827, Berlioz had vowed not only that he would marry her, but that he would base his greatest work on Shakespeare's play.)

In keeping with all adaptations, including the reviled Bellini's, Berlioz's *Roméo et Juliette* cuts some scenes from Shakespeare's play and adds others. His most interesting addition derives from the fact that he appears to have been working from a version of the story based on the actor-manager David Garrick's popular revival (which had opened at Drury Lane in 1748 and would hold the stage for 97 years, not being finally displaced until the late 1800s). Among Garrick's revisions was a climactic moment revived by Baz Luhrmann in his 1996 film, in which Juliet awakes before the poison drunk by Romeo fully takes effect. Describing Charles Kemble's and Harriet Smithson's performance of these moments some 30 years later (see Figure 3), Berlioz wrote:

> [Romeo] dashes upon the funeral couch, snatches the beloved body from it, tearing the veils and the winding-sheets, and brings it to the front of the stage where he holds it upright in his arms. Juliet gazes languidly around her with dim eyes, Romeo calls her by name, hugs her in a distraught embrace, smooths away the hair which is hiding her pale forehead, covers her face with mad kisses, is carried away with gusts of convulsive laughter; in his heart-rending joy he has forgotten that he is about to die. Juliet breathes. Juliet! Juliet![49]

In Berlioz's work (which the composer himself actually called 'a choral symphony'), neither Romeo nor Juliet has a singing role. But his compatriot Charles Gounod more than made up for this disappointing deficiency in his own *Roméo et Juliette*; and nowhere more tellingly than in the final passionate moments between the two lovers. In Gounod's floridly Victorian 1867 opera, Roméo sings a highly emotional lament of regret and farewell over what he believes to be Juliette's lifeless body, beginning with the words 'O, my wife, my dearly beloved ...', and then, as she awakes, the doomed couple get to protest their love at length before expiring in each other's arms. As one modern critic observed: 'This is altogether more satisfying, when duets are what the public wants.'[50]

Ironic or not, that reviewer's comment actually touches on a real point. Why does Shakespeare have Romeo die before Juliet awakes? Why deny us a final moment between the two lovers? Garrick's answer to these questions was to effect an 'improvement' to the ending – in which Juliet wakes in time for Romeo to rejoice (if only briefly) that she is alive. It was an addition which has been frequently echoed, if not actually revived, in any number of modern productions since.

I know that many people regard this kind of tampering as anathema. My own view is that, if you're reconceptualising a four-centuries-old script conceived for daylight performance on an Elizabethan amphitheatre stage as a screenplay for a contemporary mainstream movie, you have not merely a right, but a duty, to make some fundamental changes. And I for one think the Shakespeare world would be a lesser place without the moment when the camera focuses on Claire Danes's lovely, innocent features and her eyelids flicker into consciousness, just as Romeo brings the deadly phial to his lips …

CHAPTER 2

Henry the Fifth

'A very favourite monarch with the English nation'
William Hazlitt

Act 1, scene 2: 'We are no tyrant, but a Christian king'

Darth Vader. The smoke billowing around his feet and the fiery back-glow beyond the massive doors creating that familiar black silhouette ... But this isn't Star Wars, it's Shakespeare, and the figure striding towards us is not the embodiment of the Dark Side, but the King, Henry the Fifth. Forget Darth Vader, but don't forget his potential for terror, as Henry's courtiers, many of them older men, one his uncle, respectfully incline their heads as he passes. This is all about medieval kingship, power and dynasty.

He reaches the dais, sits and throws off his cloak. Silence falls and we see him for the first time. And what we see is an adolescent Little Lord Fauntleroy: a (slightly pimply) boy in blue velvet, sitting back in a huge throne, a world too big for his slight frame.

But don't be misled. The voice, when it comes, is that of neither a sinister despot nor a nervous adolescent. It is wary, knowing and a touch threatening.

'Where is my gracious lord of Canterbury?'

Sub-text: I don't trust him, I know he's up to something, and you people had better know that I know he's up to something.

Canterbury scurries in, accompanied by the Bishop of Ely. We know, and Henry probably guesses, that these dodgy prelates are about to make the King an offer. Namely that, if Henry blocks the parliamentary bill which threatens to deprive the Church of half its wealth, they will bankroll a military campaign in France. So first they have to persuade him to go to war ...

While these early moments from Kenneth Branagh's 1989 film of *Henry V*[1] are about as dramatic and suspenseful as you can get, the opening scenes of the play on stage are notoriously difficult to pull off. After a cracking opening speech by the Chorus – 'O for a muse of fire ...!' – we have a mysterious conversation between the Archbishop of Canterbury and the Bishop of Ely, followed by a court scene in which the Archbishop spends over 60 lines explaining the ins and outs of the ancient law which allows Henry to claim the French throne, and another 40 describing the habits of the honey-bee. Until we get to the Dauphin's insulting gift of tennis balls, it can make for extremely unriveting theatre. Except that at the centre of it all sits Henry. And a good production will make us ask a number of very tricky questions of this 'mirror of all Christian kings'. Does he know that it's in Canterbury's and Ely's interest to convince him to make war on the French? He isn't stupid or ill-informed, so he must do. But, if he does know, how sincere is he when he asks the Archbishop: 'May I with right and conscience make this claim?' It's like Hitler asking Krupps whether it's a good idea to invade Poland.

The cornerstone of Kenneth Branagh's interpretation was that Henry possessed 'a genuine humility in relation to God',[2] and his performance on film does bear that out. But this was not the view taken by the 19th-century essayist and critic William Hazlitt. In *The*

Characters of Shakespeare's Plays (1817), while acknowledging that Henry is 'a very favourite monarch with the English nation', Hazlitt declares that the King 'seemed to have no idea of any rule of right or wrong, but brute force, glossed over with a little religious hypocrisy and archiepiscopal advice', and that Canterbury 'gave the King *carte blanche*, in a genealogical tree of his family, to rob and murder in circles of latitude and longitude abroad – to save the possessions of the church at home'. Highlighting aspects of Henry's behaviour which have increasingly troubled modern audiences, he goes on: 'Because his own title to the crown was doubtful, he laid claim to that of France …'[3]

Act 1, scene 2: 'Now are we well resolved …'

The cabinet meeting convened to sell this dubious war has broken up, the fat dossiers prepared by Canterbury having done their work. But Henry's ministers return, now in army combat gear, 'well resolved'. Except for the anti-war dissenters. These – Scroop, Cambridge and Grey – are still in their civilian suits. They look the dissident outsiders – the traitors – they plainly are.

Nicholas Hytner's 2003 National Theatre production of *Henry V* was, according to its director, deliberately timed to draw parallels with the then jingoistic mood of the government as it first justified and then embarked upon the invasion of Iraq. But he could not have dared hope that the public justifications for the war by British government ministers would so uncannily echo those offered by Canterbury to Henry. 'A play about a charismatic young British leader sending his troops to war in a cause of dubious international legitimacy will be interesting', he said – with laudable understatement.[4]

Hytner's completely modern setting – in which Henry's pronouncements are delivered to reporters, Falstaff appears on a home video, and Bardolph zaps TV channels (preferring the snooker to the King's call to arms) – was throughout ironic and satirical. Michael Billington commented:

> ... at no point does [Hytner] let Henry off the hook. The embedded TV journalists dutifully fail to record the king's more savage threats to the citizens of Harfleur. Henry himself shoots his old mate Bardolph, at point-blank range, for his church-robbing. Most tellingly of all, when Henry gives the infamous order, 'Then every man kill his prisoners', the soldiers mutinously refuse until that arch disciplinarian, Fluellen, comes along and does the job for them.[5]

And it is when the invaded French watch Henry's subtitled speeches on their television screens, as he threatens their women with rape, that a frightened Princess Katharine decides she had better learn the English names for parts of the body.

Explaining his decision to give the production a modern setting, Hytner said:

> You use the interaction between the play and the world we live in to illuminate both ... It's a play that always seems to be about a war that's just happened, or is happening, or is about to happen ...
>
> There is a lot that feels familiar. We play it in modern dress as a modern parable. It's nevertheless about the invasion of France by a king called Henry the Fifth. It's not about the invasion of Iraq by an elected prime minister. But it is extraordinary to see how the entire first act of *Henry V* is taken up with the backroom dealings that the King has to get involved with in order to provide himself with a watertight reason for going to war.
>
> Shakespeare always sees the other side. He can see that Henry was an extraordinarily charismatic, heroic, determined figure. He

can also see that, in order to get himself to that position, he had to get involved with really dirty tax deals with the Church …[6]

In one extraordinarily funny and pointed moment, Adrian Lester's disguised Henry bumps into Pistol as he tours the camp the night before Agincourt: 'What is thy name?' asks Pistol. 'Harry le Roy', replies the King. 'LEROY?!' exclaims Pistol delightedly. The audience roar with laughter at this: both actors are black. Hytner likens the moment to Blair winning a vote in Brixton. But not all Henry's followers regard him as 'a lad of life, an imp of fame'. Court, Bates and Williams, those representations of the ordinary soldier whose cynicism always comes as a refreshing breeze, are by no means convinced by the King's justifications for leading them to war. Scoffing at his sophistry, they almost walk off in disgust when he dares to bring God into the argument.

Some people had concerns that Hytner's parallels were forced and distorting. Others found it profoundly disturbing to leave the National with Henry's rhetoric echoing in our ears, only to switch on the television and hear our Prime Minister asking us:

> [Am I to] tell our allies that the very moment of action, the very moment they need our determination, that Britain faltered?

… and concluding, in a statement redolent of all the self-importance of Henry's 'Tell you the Dauphin I am coming on …':

> I will not be a party to that course.[7]

Act 2, The Chorus: 'Now all the youth of England are on fire, / … and honour's thought / Reigns solely in the breast of every man'

Henry's three old companions from his wild teenage years, Pistol, Bardolph and Nym, take their leave of Mistress Quickly. They are going off to war and might not meet again. But the poignancy of the leave-taking is not prolonged; for, no sooner have they turned their backs on the inn, but they break into a raucous and enthusiastic chant of "Ere we go, 'ere we go, 'ere we go ...!', the England football supporters' rallying cry, their fervour enhanced by the sudden and violent din of football rattles and the unfurling from above of union jacks, Saint George's flags, the Welsh dragon, red-white-and-blue bunting, and an enormous banner which boldly proclaims the British army's determination to 'FUCK THE FROGS!'.

To the strains of 'And did those feet ...?' the Chorus enters, carrying a placard bearing the infamous Argie-hating Sun newspaper slogan 'GOTCHA!' ...

That was how the English Shakespeare Company portrayed the English army's less than heroic departure for France in their 1986 production.[8] In ways that foreshadowed Nicholas Hytner, director Michael Bogdanov saw Shakespeare's histories as 'plays for today, the lessons of history unlearnt', and described Henry as waging '[a] war of expedience, ruthless manipulation, bribery and corruption ...'.[9] Part of a generation which had grown up with Vietnam, rather than the D-Day landings, Bogdanov could not see Henry's story as heroic:

> Imperialism encourages jingoism. So the Falklands. So Agincourt. 'Fuck the Frogs'. The banner hung out by the send-off crowd at Southampton ... grew out of the desire to bridge nearly six hundred years of this same bigoted xenophobic patriotism ... The Last Night of the Proms, the troops getting the blessing at Portsmouth, football fury, all combined in my mind to produce this image one afternoon late on a Saturday ...[10]

Bogdanov's was an iconoclastic interpretation which would probably have interested Hazlitt, but was completely at odds with the Henry of popular consciousness: Henry as national hero; Henry representing the plucky island race standing firm and ultimately triumphant against overwhelming odds; the Henry who is part of the heritage industry and who looked extremely at home in the 2002 flag-waving Last Night of the Proms.* Looked at in this way, and given his present iconic status, it is difficult to conceive of a time when Henry did not live in the popular imagination as an embodiment of all that was finest in English heroism.

Yet, strange as it seems, *Henry V* does not appear to have been an especially popular play in the years following its first performance in 1599, for in the early 17th century there is evidence of only a single court performance, in January 1605.[11] In fact, it was not until the 1730s that the play really started to make a theatrical impact. When it did – in one of those pleasant ironies, given the play's male-dominated cast – it was at the request of the Shakespeare Ladies' Club, a circle of aristocratic women who petitioned theatre managements to stage more of the Bard's work.[12]

But while the play itself struggled for recognition, its hero seemed already to have established himself as one of Shakespeare's more popular creations. For, when in 1741 a monument was unveiled to the playwright in Westminster Abbey, the characters chosen to accompany the full-length marble statue of their creator were Richard the Third and Henry the Fifth.[13]

If Henry had a place in the hearts of theatre-goers by the 1740s, then the remainder of the 18th century served only to confirm his status as the English king who satisfyingly thrashed the French. During this period of serial Francophobia, and particularly during the Seven Years' War with France (1756–63), the play was performed regularly, and, if any actor from that period can be said to have made the part

---

*Accompanying William Walton's *Henry V Suite* (see below, pages 59–60), actor Sam West performed some of Henry's speeches.

of Henry his own it was John Philip Kemble. Kemble's Henry (first performed in 1789) was at the heart of a production which, with explicit topicality at a time when the threat of invasion was ever-present, played up the patriotic angle for all it was worth, even as far as donating box-office receipts to the Patriotic Fund. *The Times* opined that the production worked 'to convince our Gallic neighbours that in the midst of all their triumphs they are but mere mortals', a message reinforced by Kemble himself, who concluded at least one perform-ance with an 'Occasional Address to the Volunteers'.

It is interesting to speculate on the audience response to that address in 1803. Who did they feel they were they listening to? Having just witnessed a performance in which 'the character [of Henry] well accorded with the animated tone and manly ardour of that superb actor', were they being addressed by the manly and ardent Kemble, the m. and a. Henry, or a fusion of actor and character facil-itated by the special political circumstances that prevailed?

Another example of this productive confusion of identities is Frank Benson, whose heroic Henry first appeared in 1897 at Stratford and was revived on numerous occasions in the three decades that fol-lowed, a period which, of course, embraced both the Boer War and the Great War. A surviving photograph of Benson's Henry is a pleasing reminder of his interpretation. The armour, the heraldic standard, the pose: all connote heroism, patriotism and piety – three essential qual-ities for the Edwardian English gentleman; and it is no surprise that *The Times* described his performance on Boxing Day 1914 as 'marked with an unwonted fervour', adding: 'Evidently he felt himself not merely playing the stage part, but delivering a solemn message.' This must be almost inevitable for any actor playing Henry at a time when the country is engaged in a bloody war, a factor which makes per-forming him quite different from performing Macbeth or Richard the Third. Whether he likes it or not, the actor will be 'delivering a solemn message', a message which for Benson was a staunchly patriotic one. Perhaps the only Shakespearean character who shares with Henry this unasked-for responsibility is Falconbridge in *King John*, whose rousing 'This England never did, nor never shall, / Lie at the proud foot of a conqueror ...' cannot avoid making a connection with a patriotic wartime audience.

Emma Smith catalogues some of the many ways in which the play, and the figure of Henry in particular, was repeatedly conscripted as part of the war effort in the early decades of the 20th century. She recalls one 1916 audience at the Theatre Royal Nottingham 'filled with men in hospital blue'; a 1915 film entitled *England's Warrior King* featuring men from the Royal Scots Greys and accompanied by readings from the play; and the actress Fabia Drake in 1919 performing scenes from the play to an audience of 400 ANZAC soldiers awaiting repatriation. But it was to be in the Second World War that the play really came into its own as a stirring evocation of the bulldog spirit ...

Act 3, scene 1: 'Once more unto the breach ...'

A black cannon is dragged desperately up the shingle beach to aim at the single gap in a wall of chalky cliffs. We have little leisure to admire the distant view of hills and fir-trees, for a rabble of men-at-arms bursts through the gap, seemingly at flight from some unseen enemy, fleeing perhaps back to the temporary security of the beach and their moored ships. They are pursued by a figure on horseback who, even before removing his helmet, is clearly the King. Quite apart from the royal heraldry, if we happen to recognise it, his whole bearing (not to mention his shining armour and the splendid white horse that he bestrides) tells us unambiguously who he is. Reining in his mount, and removing his helmet, he rapidly appraises the situation and rides to and fro among his men, sword aloft, gathering them to him ...

'Once more unto the breach, dear friends, once more,
Or close the wall up with our English dead ...'

There is a pause while he gains their full attention, and a strange silence
falls, to be broken only by his almost subdued:

'In peace, there's nothing so becomes a man
As modest stillness and humility ...'

Reminding them of their heritage as true-born Englishmen, this King
exudes confidence; this is a leader men will follow anywhere. And, on a
climactic cry, he rears up his magnificent grey, turns and leads his men
back into battle, their shouts echoing his war-cry over and over —

'God for Harry, England and Saint George! ... God for Harry, England
and Saint George! ... God for Harry, England and Saint George! ...'

Laurence Olivier's 1944 film, from which this scene comes, was famously introduced by a dedication 'To the Commandos and Airborne Troops of Great Britain, the spirit of whose ancestors it has been humbly attempted to recapture in some ensuing scenes'. At the time of its first showing, uppermost in audiences' minds would have been the retreat of the British forces from Dunkirk, the Battle of Britain and, most recently, the D-Day landings. Less than two years later, it would be shown in Berlin to 1,800 students and schoolchildren, *The Times* of the day reporting that: 'Before each performance a short address is being given by an officer of the education section of Military Government, which regards the film as useful material for German re-education.'[14] But, for now, the film's opening, with its panoramic sweep across Elizabethan London, powerfully evoked the capital's spirited resistance to the Blitz, and the film as a whole celebrated a hard-won and deserved victory against overwhelming odds, by an army that was not just physically more resilient but morally superior as well, while throughout serving to reinforce the mythologising of England's hero-king.

When Churchill, in the darkest days of the war, had proudly cele-brated 'the British airmen, undaunted by odds, unwearied in their constant challenge and mortal danger ... turning the tide of world war by their prowess and by their devotion'; and had famously concluded that 'Never in the field of human conflict was so much owed by so many to so few',[15] there were clear echoes of another army, facing terrible odds, whose leader had lifted their spirits by calling them 'We few, we happy few, we band of brothers ...'. Olivier was not merely acting the role of Henry, he was speaking up for himself as a patriotic Englishman serving his country in wartime.

This fusion of actor with role can easily happen with Henrys, especially in time of national crisis (see Kemble and Benson above), and is dramatically illustrated by the fact that Olivier did most of his own stunts. Thus we could see the actor-director taking risks along-side his cast in much the same way as Henry does with his band of brothers, prompting us to ask who exactly it is we are watching bat-tering the French Constable in a dangerous and thrilling horse-back combat – the character (heroic Shakespearean warrior-king) or the actor (famously just come from service in the Fleet Air Arm)?

If the character of Henry was to a large extent reflected in the identity of Olivier the actor, then the actor himself was closely identi-fied with the film's music. Olivier and the composer William Walton were not only professional colleagues but close friends. The music critic Christopher Palmer has written:

> It is more than coincidence that those paying tribute to Olivier after his death wrote of the physical excitement he generated; of his voice now of clarion resonance, now of gentle mellifluousness; of his instinct for startling body gesture; of his virility, heroism

and romance, and the vulnerability, the femininity thereby concealed, or complemented; of his presence, his magnetism; more than coincidence that all these qualities are precisely reflected in Walton's music ... It epitomises Walton's affinity with Olivier's Shakespeare – larger-than-life, romantic, chivalrous, great-hearted and highly coloured.[16]

Restructured as a piece for speaker, orchestra and chorus, the *Henry V Suite* has been popularly recorded by Sir Neville Marriner, with Christopher Plummer reading the speeches.[17] And, whether performed by the Choristers of Westminster Cathedral and the Orchestra and Chorus of the Academy of St Martin in the Fields, as it was in 1990, or by the BBC Symphony Orchestra at the Last Night of the Proms in 2002, the combination of Walton's *Henry V Suite* and renditions of the text by leading classical actors leads to an interpretation both of the play and the character which is unlikely to be troubled by ambiguity.

But it would be a mistake to suppose that the effect of Henry's 'Once more unto the breach' exhortation has always been to stiffen the sinews and conjure up the blood. Indeed, the text itself offers every opportunity for Henry's rousing exhortation to be undermined, given that one of its immediate effects is to send the cowardly Nym and Pistol running off in the opposite direction, needing to be chivvied up by an angry Fluellen:

NYM: Pray thee, corporal, stay. The knocks are too hot ...
FLUELLEN: ... up to the breach, you dogs! Avaunt, you cullions![18]

Building on Shakespeare's seemingly endless capacity for reinterpretation, a profoundly questioning tone is found in David Jones's *In Parenthesis* (1937), where the more ambiguous aspects of Henry's speech are powerfully evoked by men in the trenches of the Great War as they prepare to 'go over the top'. Recalling the Shakespearean hero-king's encouragement —

> Disguise fair nature with hard-favoured rage.
> Then lend the eye a terrible aspect.
> Let it pry through the portage of the head
> Like a brass cannon …[19]

the men in Jones's book reflect that:

> — it will be him and you in an open place, he will look into your face; fear will so condition you that you each will pale for the other, and in one another you will hate your own flesh. Your fair natures will be so disguised that the aspect of his eyes will pry like deep-sea horrors divers see, from the portage of his rigid type of gas-bag —[20]

Act 3, scene 3: '… hot and forcing violation'

The scene is reminiscent of a Bosch hell. Unidentifiable black figures scurry frighteningly through a Passchendaele landscape of craters and mud before a backdrop of ruined town walls and a fire-red, smoke-filled sky. Their leader who follows, sweating and filthy with the grime of war, turns back to face the town gates and issues a most terrible ultimatum. He threatens rape and indiscriminate murder if the Governor of Harfleur refuses to open his doors, promises that infants will be spitted upon pikes, venerable old men's most reverend heads dashed to the walls – and these threats are supported by a spitting and screaming delivery that leaves no one in doubt as to the sincerity of the man's intentions.

The look of relief which suffuses his face when the Governor yields is of a man who knows that he will be spared the horror of having to carry out his threats.

Kenneth Branagh's 1989 film performance, described here, cannot be compared with Olivier's in 1944, because this was a scene that Olivier decided to cut. And it's easy to see why. Nowhere else, not even in the poetry of the Great War, is there such a remorselessly uncompromising picture of the violence of war as it affects civilians; and this was not something that a 1944 audience needed, or wanted, to be reminded about. In the years following the Falklands conflict, however, the public mood was very different; and Branagh strains every sinew to show that, far from being a romanticised piece of jingoism, Shakespeare's *Henry V* has some things to say about war which are very ugly indeed.

Moreover, the differences between Branagh's and Olivier's approaches to this part of Henry's story are epitomised, not so much in what choices the two directors made concerning the text, but in the visual representation of the siege of Harfleur. Olivier's battle is spotless, with even the common soldiers sporting clean tunics which rival Henry's gleaming armour, glinting in the sunshine and reflecting the clear blue sky. Branagh sets the siege at night and it is, from start to finish, a filthy, infernal business.

But, if there is a similarity between Olivier and Branagh at this point, it can be seen in their two Henrys' shared athleticism. Both men look terrific on their white chargers, both demonstrate their horsemanship by reining and rearing, twisting and turning in the saddle, and you wonder why they don't just vault the walls of Harfleur and be done with it.

This link between Henry and athleticism has been a longstanding one. Since Edwardian schoolboys read 'Once more unto the breach …' alongside Sir Henry Newbolt's *Vitai Lampada* ('Play up, play up and play the game …'), early 20th-century Henrys were consistently praised for their manly sporting vigour and physical prowess. Lewis Waller, for example – an actor who 'never merely stepped upon the stage but hurtled upon it' – 'climbed upon a great mass of fallen masonry [at the siege of Harfleur] and stood there, quivering, virile, sword in hand, a thing of force and strength, panting to regain his breath. He radiated power'; his was an interpretation of 'complete masculinity'.[21]

But a quality such as manly athleticism is easily parodied; and Max Beerbohm mercilessly exposed Frank Benson's attentions to physicality when he drew parallels with a cricket match:

... Every member of the cast seemed in tip-top condition, thoroughly 'fit' ... The fielding was excellent and so was the batting. Speech after speech was sent spinning across the boundary, and one was constantly inclined to shout 'Well *played*, sir! Well played *indeed*!'[22]

The style of this parody was especially apt for an actor who had a reputation for engaging young cast-members whose ability to deliver Shakespearean verse was of less account than their ability to deliver a few useful overs before tea. As Sally Beauman recalls:

So well known was this foible that when he once wired an actor, 'Can you play Rugby tomorrow?' the actor wired back 'Yes', and arrived the next day with his boots, to discover that Benson meant the part of Rugby in *The Merry Wives of Windsor* for which he urgently needed a word-perfect replacement.[23]

But this was not simply eccentricity. Benson took physical fitness very seriously, and his advice that the young actor should practice physical technique as conscientiously as a concert pianist practices scales is followed, albeit in modified form, by many actors today, especially if they are playing a role as physically demanding as Henry the Fifth.

Act 3, scene 6: '… if your majesty know the man'

When the Welsh captain Fluellen tells him that one of his men is to be hanged for robbing a church – 'one Bardolph, if your majesty know the man' – Henry's face betrays his agony at the dreadful realisation that he will have to sanction the death of an old friend: more than that, a close companion of his adolescence. He stares, devastated, as the wagon carrying the condemned man creaks into view, Bardolph's face bloodily betraying the beating that he has already received at the hands of Exeter's men; and, as the noose is placed roughly around the man's neck, Henry's thoughts go back to a moment, not so many years before, when he was still Prince Hal and could afford to pass his hours in the company of the very bass-strings of humanity …

Exeter looks to Henry to give the order, which he does with an almost imperceptible nod, and, as the cart is violently wrenched from under the bewildered and betrayed petty thief, Bardolph's feet skip and jerk in the air. As he struggles in vain for breath, a discordant and harsh fanfare of crows breaks out to accompany his grotesque dance …

Despite all the losses sustained in the campaign so far, this is Henry's most terrible moment, and starkly illustrates the tortured conflict between King and man, a conflict embodied in the tears that well up – for Bardolph and himself – while he publicly underlines his firm resolve that all such offenders will be so cut off …

This account of a determining moment in Henry's campaign, based on Kenneth Branagh's 1989 film version, introduces two afterlives of Henry, both of which are unlikely and unpredictable. The first sees Henry as an embodiment of modern masculine emotionalism; the second as a model for management training.

Writing in September 1997, only a few days after the funeral of Diana, Princess of Wales, Lisa Jardine saw in Branagh's Henry the perfect example of a fascinating modern phenomenon: the expression of manly emotion. More particularly, his performance on film vividly illustrated the way in which that kind of emotion is captured by the camera and advertised to the world. Comparing Branagh's Henry as he addresses his beleaguered troops with Olivier's stirring and unflinching hero-king of 1944, she writes:

> This Henry hesitates; his lip trembles slightly; his eyes, turned directly towards us, are moist, and fill with tears as he speaks. We feel the inner turmoil of royal grandeur versus common humanity. We understand that the King already grieves for the life of every soldier who will fall, even as he rousingly promises a glorious victory for his country in the battle to come.
>
> Here is a Henry for the late 20th century, a king whose manliness resides both in his dignity and in his compassion, his capacity to be moved as each of us is moved. Manly tears have become almost a diagnostic feature of this modern kind of masculine sensibility. Not the act of openly weeping, but the tear that can only be seen in the camera close-up, that sits unacknowledged in the corner of a man's eye, or lies for a moment on his cheek, as we are told one did on the cheek of a Welsh Guard bearing the coffin of Diana, Princess of Wales, into Westminster Abbey last Saturday.[24]

In Professor Jardine's article, Henry's expression of emotion, as portrayed by Branagh and captured in close-up for the benefit of cinema audiences, is likened to Prime Minister Tony Blair's, when he gave his televised public statement immediately after Diana's death. Both showed a simple understanding of 'the requirements of the new-style, camera-friendly masculinity' in which what is now required of the speaker is that 'his true and genuine inner feelings are given external manifestation'. As such, the Branagh–Blair behaviour is in stark contrast to Buckingham Palace's stiff upper lip and decorous observance of protocol in their public response to the royal tragedy.

Henry, then, has enjoyed contrasting afterlives: as the embodiment of manly 'play up and play the game' athleticism (as portrayed by Benson, Waller and Olivier) and also of the new-man touchy-feely emotionalism so much a feature of Branagh's passionate king.

But if the modern world is all about men who willingly display their emotions, it is also about performance-targets, mission statements and corporate strategy. So it should come as no surprise to learn that Henry has enjoyed yet another incarnation in the world of management training …

When Kenneth Branagh had first played Henry with the RSC (in 1984), he had gained a great deal of helpful publicity by interviewing Prince Charles on the rigours and responsibilities of royal leadership. Though Charles has never been in the position of having to agree to the execution of a former friend like Bardolph (at least, not as I write), he has unquestionably been faced with some tricky management decisions, and it is this aspect of Henry that interests Richard Olivier. Olivier, son of Sir Laurence, is a former theatre director – he directed *Henry V* at the Globe in 1989 – who now runs workshops to show business-people how Shakespeare can help them improve their leadership skills. His first book, *Shadow of the Stone Heart – A Search for Manhood*,[25] was about coming to terms with his famous father (interestingly, another problem faced by Henry as Prince Hal) and he has worked with the US men's movement guru Robert Bly.[26] Olivier's 'Theatre of Leadership' seminars, which claim to use 'mythodrama' and creativity to release people's potential, include 'Vision and Regeneration in *The Winter's Tale*' and 'Justice, Mercy and Risk in *The Merchant of Venice*'. But he has a particular interest in the figure of Henry the Fifth, as famously interpreted by his father. For Richard Olivier, Henry's story throws a clear light on modern business practice: 'When you look at the metaphors that people use in business, they are all about war – or sport. The sales director might say: "They killed us" or "It's a battlefield out there". The managing director says: "We have to fight for our share of this". We need to change the metaphors, or at least supplement them with metaphors to do with peace, growth and gardening …'[27]

Olivier places great emphasis on Henry's vision (his 'mission statement') and has described his workshop approach to the character in his second book, *Inspirational Leadership*, subtitled *Henry V and the muse of fire: Timeless insights from Shakespeare's greatest leader.*[28] Writing, for example, about the execution of Bardolph in a section headed 'Managers solve problems – leaders manage dilemmas', the former director observes:

> The Robert K. Greenleaf Center for Servant Leadership in America identified four 'Right versus Right' dilemmas. These are the leadership issues for which there is no simple answer; one could find different reasons to answer either yes or no. The leader has to make a choice – rather than a simple decision.[29]

He goes on to describe these four dilemmas under the headings: 'short term vs long term'; 'individual vs community' ('… Do we decide to enhance the life or prospects of one extremely talented individual, or do we share the available resources among a group?'– he offers the National Health Service as an example); 'truth vs loyalty' and 'justice vs mercy', concluding:

> All four of these dilemmas are reflected in the 'Bardolph decision'. On this occasion Henry chooses long term, community, truth and justice …

Olivier rounds off the section with a case study of 'Sarah', a senior manager in a TV production company who was unwilling to confront a member of staff with his incompetence, describing how in one workshop —

> We role played her metaphorically putting on some 'armour' and summoning up some Warrior energy to brave the first meeting. After this, Sarah realized what she had been avoiding and why. It was a lesson in the occasional need to wear a leader's face, rather than a personal face – and was a similar struggle to the one [Henry had to go through].[30]

Speaking at the 2002 Oxford Literary Festival, Richard Olivier described Henry the Fifth's journey as 'a great project led from start to conclusion by the same person', a venture which reaches crisis point the night before the Battle of Agincourt, when Henry 'provides visible leadership', his lieutenants 'want a strategy meeting', he discovers that the common soldiers are 'blaming it all on the management', he 'takes all that on board … and gets back to his core values …'.

Reinterpreting Henry's story in management-speak will no doubt offend, amuse or illuminate, according to our standpoint. But, whatever the reaction, it is a striking example of the way in which Shakespeare characters have taken on lives that their creator could not have dreamed of.

CHAPTER 3

Cleopatra

*'The triumph of the voluptuous, of the love of pleasure and
the power of giving it'*

William Hazlitt

Act 1, scene 1: 'If it be love indeed …'

*Already deep in earnest dialogue with another of Antony's followers, Philo
sets the scene for us. To this Roman – and we suspect that he speaks for the
rest of the army – Cleopatra is the lustful gipsy who has transformed the
triple pillar of the world into a strumpet's fool. Inviting us to verify for
ourselves the validity of his condemnation – 'Look where they come …' –
he instructs Demetrius, 'Take but good note … behold and see …'.*

> 'But, you know, the first line Cleopatra has is "If it be love indeed,
> tell me how much". Now, what woman – *what woman!* – has not
> said that? And it's always when they're fragile. And, you know, I
> call it the cry of the mistress – it's not the cry of the wife. And I
> thought – of course, she's a *mistress*. Never to be forgotten – she's
> not a wife, she's a mistress …'

I am sitting opposite Sinead Cusack in her Oxfordshire home. She has
made a pot of tea and is telling me about her approach to Cleopatra,
a role she has just played with the Royal Shakespeare Company.[1] She is
passionate, beautiful, and ever on the point of laughter; and, sitting there

with my little tape-recorder, I know what Dolabella feels like in Act 5, the minor Roman who arrives on Caesar's business and falls immediately and comprehensively under the Egyptian Queen's spell. She goes on:

'And also I do think the play is about a love affair in decline. Because really you get one scene and then Fulvia's death, and from that moment the world is in trouble. Their relationship, you know, bleeds out on to a world stage and the world falls. Amazing. And those first two lines – "If it be love indeed ..." – and I thought – oh, so *that's* the reason the whole shape of history was changed [she laughs at the simplicity of the solution] – it's because she was a mistress and she had no certainties.'

Cleopatra the mistress. It's a powerful and convincing insight, and was brilliantly exploited by the actor when she came to perform the role in Stratford and London. But it was a perception that was arrived at only after a great deal of exploration and research by an experienced performer who confesses to having turned down the part on two previous occasions because she felt 'intimidated' by it. And why?

'Well, why I was so intimidated was the iconography of Cleopatra. To me, the iconography is so great, you know, in art, in literature, everywhere you look ... Cleopatra is there, one of the greatest icons that we have ever had ...'

And it isn't difficult to see what she means ... There is, for example, the image of the Egyptian queen in a 1918 advertisement for Palmolive shampoo that appeared in the fashion magazine *Vogue*, where Cleopatra's mythic sexuality and hedonism are exploited in order to sell 'The modern evolution of an ancient luxury – the perfect blend of the precious oils Cleopatra prized ...'.

Or take these contributions from the *Guardian*'s 'Pass Notes', occasioned by the discovery by archaeologists of a palace in Alexandria:[2]

Pass Notes

No 915: Cleopatra

Age: Cannot wither her, nor custom stale her infinite variety.

Come again? Oh, you're so prosaic. Born 69 BC; lived 39 eventful years …

A beauty then? The world's first supermodel, according to legend. Plutarch, Rome's pop biographer, gave her a good write-up; Caesar adored her and dedicated a golden statue in the temple of Venus to her; and Mark Antony was prepared to die for her. But the bas-reliefs are rather stylised and the paparazzi were working with chisels, so it's largely hearsay.

She was horribly manipulative of course? Male writers (Plutarch, Shakespeare, Shaw) thought so, but it cuts both ways. Feminists now claim her as one of their own: strong-willed, sexually dominant, politically adept.

What's the key question? Did she or didn't she try to seduce the emperor Octavian after Mark Antony fell on his sword, in order to have one more go at being Rome's empress?

And the answer? Probably not. She'd had enough and lost the man she loved ('Shall I abide / In this dull world, which in thy absence is / No better than a sty?').

Liked: Roman generals, barges, roses, flute music, fishing, hairdressers, the colour purple.

Disliked: Younger brothers (disposed of at least two of them), the shopping malls of Rome — much preferred the East End (via Syria).

A useless bit of celluloid history: Cecil B. De Mille had her portrayed campily by Claudette Colbert in 1934; Vivien Leigh played her as Scarlett O'Hara in a gold wig in *Caesar and Cleopatra* in 1945; Elizabeth Taylor wore even more eye shadow than the original in *Cleopatra* in 1963 ('the biggest asp disaster in the world', according to one critic).

Not to be confused with: The Duchess of York.

Most likely to say: 'Give me my robe. Put on my crown. I have immortal longings in me.'

Least likely to say: 'Mark, guess what. *Hello!* are offering us half a million sesterces for the barge shots. But Maximus Cliffordius says hold out for more.'

'Pass Notes' strikingly represents much of what 'Cleopatra' means these days; and the meanings are derived partly from Shakespeare, partly from the broader picture we have formed from history and legend: not only the quotes about infinite variety and immortal longings, but also the image of Cleopatra the seductress, trying it on with every powerful Roman who came her way; and Cleopatra the hedonist, temptingly luxuriating on her purple-sailed, flute-propelled barge, an image reinforced, modified and popularised by the advent of moving pictures. As *Guardian* drama critic Michael Billington puts it:

> Part of the problem, of course, is the movies: Hollywood has implanted in our minds a stereotypical image of Cleopatra. The vamp in the snake head-dress. The busty number wearing the horns of Hathor ...[3]

Warming to her theme of the Cleopatra myth, Sinead Cusack goes on:

> 'But, you see, what was very interesting was that Shakespeare had bought into all the iconography. And my view was that Octavius Caesar was arguably one of the greatest spin-doctors of all time because what he put about in Rome – at that time had to be put out in Rome – was that this woman was a slut, a harlot, and beyond imagination beautiful. She wasn't; but this was put about, and that through her wiles and her magic she had seduced a great man to become an impotent fool. And my feeling at the end was that, yes, Shakespeare bought in completely to Plutarch ...'

L. Mestrius Plutarchus, known to us now as Plutarch, was born around 46 CE, which means that he lived through the reigns of the Emperors Claudius and Nero. His *Lives* of famous Greeks and Romans had a profound effect on Shakespeare and his contemporaries when it appeared in a translation by Sir Thomas North in 1579, and became a main source for *Antony and Cleopatra*. Although the indebtedness of

Shakespeare to North's Plutarch has frequently been commented on, it is only when you compare the script of Shakespeare's play with its source that you realise the truth of the observation that the dramatist must have had a copy of the *Lives* open on his desk as he wrote. And this is nowhere better illustrated than in Enobarbus's famous description of the lovers' meeting at Cydnus. It comes at the point in the story where, stunned by the news that his wife Fulvia is dead, Antony has rushed back to Rome, where, to patch up a dangerous rift with Octavius Caesar, he has offered to marry Octavius's sister, Octavia.

In a scene which might well appear in some future sequel to *Shakespeare in Love*, imagine the dramatist as he prepares to write the scene which follows – a conversation between one of Antony's followers, Enobarbus, and two Romans, Agrippa and Maecenas. He needs something that will help to express Enobarbus's profound cynicism about the proposed marriage to Octavia, something that will demonstrate the nature of Antony's obsession with the Egyptian queen. So he takes his copy of North's Plutarch off the shelf, props it open at his elbow, and reads —

> ... she disdained to set forth otherwise but to take her barge in the river of Cydnus, the poop whereof was of gold, the sails of purple, and the oars of silver which kept stroke in rowing after the sound of the music of flutes, oboes, citherns, viols and such other instruments as they played on in the barge ...

He likes the details of the poop (nicely nautical), the specific colour of the sails, the luxury of the gold ... But make that 'beaten' gold ... cut the 'citherns' but do something with the idea that 'the oars ... kept stroke' to the music ... And – yes, good idea – bring in the language of infatuation – 'love-sick ... amorous ...'. He reads North's description over again, thinks for a moment, dips his pen in the inkwell, ponders a moment more and then scribbles —

> The barge she sat in, like a burnish'd throne
> Burn'd on the water: the poop was beaten gold;
> Purple the sails, and so perfumed that
> The winds were love-sick with them; the oars were silver,
> Which to the tune of flutes kept stroke, and made
> The water which they beat to follow faster,
> As amorous of their strokes.

And so it goes on ... North's

> And now for the person of herself:
> She was laid under a pavilion of cloth of gold of tissue ...

is lifted almost wholesale, but expanded and worked on to become:

> For her own person,
> It beggar'd all description: she did lie
> In her pavilion – cloth of gold, of tissue —

And by lunchtime he has completed – with the assistance of L. Mestrius Plutarchus and Sir Thomas North (not forgetting a Frenchman, Jacques Amyot, on whose translation North's version was based) – one of the most memorable speeches in world drama, and a description by which so much of the Cleopatra iconography has been inspired.

Enobarbus's barge speech offers a fascinating lesson in the way that Shakespeare often used sources like North's Plutarch and the historian Raphael Holinshed. At first sight it is amazing how much the dramatist seems to have lifted directly from North: not only details such as the golden poop, purple sails and silver oars; but phraseology too. North provides 'And now for the person of herself ...': Shakespeare borrows it as 'For her own person ...'; North offers 'cloth of gold of tissue'; the playwright lifts the whole phrase unchanged;

North feels that he has to explain 'Nereides' in a parenthesis – ' (which are the mermaids of the waters)' – Shakespeare condenses the gloss to 'so many mermaids'. Sometimes the dramatist borrows the historian's rhythms – 'the poop whereof was gold' becomes 'the poop was beaten gold'; elsewhere he employs the same comparison – as, for example, in describing the attendant boys as Cupids.

But it is, of course, what Shakespeare adds to the description that enables it to transcend even Thomas North's vivid prose. As Jonathan Bate puts it, 'The genius is in the embellishment'. To take just two examples:

> Shakespeare takes the golden poop and the purple sails from North's Plutarch, but adds 'and so perfumed / That the winds were love-sick with them.' Where the historian has offered mere description, the dramatist adds reaction. He imagines the wind being affected by Cleopatra's aura …[4]

And, when he takes North's original phrase 'And now for the person of herself …', and reworks it somewhat ordinarily as 'For her own person', he doesn't leave it there, but adds 'it beggar'd all description', an expression so familiar to us today that we need to be reminded both of its original figurative sense (anyone attempting to describe her would expend their whole treasury of words) and the fact that Shakespeare was in all likelihood inventing the expression then and there, for this is its first recorded use.

Act 2, scene 2: 'Rare Egyptian!'

The procession, when it finally hits the screen, is not a disappointment. Trumpeters on white horses are followed by chariots, a volley of arrows, a sequinned-nippled belly-dancer, pole-vaulters, a cloud of doves released into the sky, whirling dervishes, tinily-bikini-ed dancers, and then, to the accompaniment of drums, cymbals and trumpets, an army of slaves appears, dragging a gigantic stone Sphinx ...

Between its paws sits Cleopatra and silence falls ...

Lucy Hughes-Hallett completes the description:

> Cleopatra, still enthroned, is carried down the monumental steps by black slaves. Caesar rises to greet her. She bows, her breasts looming large around the edges of her deeply cut bodice. The crowd roars and then a remarkable thing happens. The camera stays on Elizabeth Taylor's face, made up in the fashion of the early sixties' style with heavy eyeliner, false eyelashes and pale lipstick. And, as she catches Caesar's eye, Cleopatra winks.[5]

Elizabeth Taylor's Cleopatra in the 1963 film[6] is hardly Shakespeare's. This is Cleopatra the self-parodist, the most magnificent example of a lineage of vamps stretching back to Theda Bara and 'It-girl' Clara Bow, through Rhonda Fleming and Claudette Colbert.* And Taylor's parody is itself parodied beautifully a couple of years later in the Goscinny–Uderzo *Asterix and Cleopatra*. After her arrival at the palace building-site on a vast, slave-drawn golden sphinx, she looks down from her throne at the adoring Gauls ('There's no denying it, she does have a pretty nose!' ... 'A very pretty nose ...' 'Did you see her nose, Dogmatix?'), and says: 'Oh, don't stop! I'm just paying a quiet visit, incognito. Do go on.'[7] The Gauls' admiring references are an allusion to Blaise Pascal's 17th-century *pensée* that, if Cleopatra's nose had been shorter, it might have changed the face of the world: 'Le nez de

---

*These four Cleopatras appeared in movies in 1917, 1918, 1934 and 1954 respectively. According to publicists, Cecil B. De Mille is reputed to have offered Claudette Colbert the role with the question: 'How would you like to play the wickedest woman in history?' (Lucy Hughes-Hallett, *Cleopatra: Histories, Dreams and Distortions* (Bloomsbury, 1990), p. 269.)

Cléopâtre: s'il eût été plus court, toute la face de la terre aurait changé.'

But Elizabeth Taylor's extraordinarily elaborate and overblown first appearance does owe something to *Antony and Cleopatra* – in attempting to emulate Shakespeare, what director Joseph L. Mankiewicz had come up with was the Hollywood-spectacular version of Enobarbus's account of the rare Egyptian and the barge she sat in. He knew that, as entrances go, it's hard to beat ...

Act 2, scene 2: 'The barge she sat in ...'

... the camera pans over an expanse of desert, dotted with camels. We hear the first waca wacas of a rhythm guitar and then hear Joe Simon's craggy soul tenor singing the film's theme, 'Cleopatra, All I See Is Your Face'. Next, we hear a helicopter, and our confusion ends. Like Cleopatra from her barge, Cleopatra Jones (played by African-American Tamara Dobson), dripping in furs, emerges from the helicopter. On the authority of the CIA, agent Jones is on a mission to destroy this Turkish field of opium poppies and, by long-distance magic, clear the streets of Los Angeles of the 'shit' (heroin) that plagues it ...[8]

Cleopatra Jones is a spirited reworking of Shakespeare's play in which Tamara Dobson's CIA Special Agent Jones powers her way through the mean streets of Los Angeles, thanks to an impressive display of martial arts and weapon deployment, in an action movie that also alludes to the LA uprisings, the Black Panthers and the feminist movement. While none of Shakespeare's lines is quoted, there are clearly visual references to his version, and not least to the barge scene, which is played out in a variety of different ways:

Tamara Dobson has several arrival and departure scenes where she performs the pageantry of Shakespeare's queen, but here she performs them as an action hero. With each costume change,

Cleopatra's 'cloth of gold of tissue' is replaced by fur, kente cloth, or red leather. Cleopatra's barge is replaced by an airplane, a Corvette, a luggage belt, an escalator, a motor bike – indeed, whatever form of transportation is most readily available for the action at hand. If her onlookers are lulled by her beauty at first, they must pay immediately for their passivity. In one early scene, Cleopatra Jones sneaks into a crowded airport lobby on a luggage conveyor belt, and chops, karate kicks and shoots her unsuspecting enemies, all the while maintaining the jaunty tilt of her African beaded cap.[9]

There are also clear parallels between Cleopatra Jones and her Shakespearean prototype. As Francesca Royster points out, quite apart from her allure and love of luxury, she moves, as Shakespeare's queen does, between different embattled worlds, demonstrating her power to control the activities of one nation from the distance of another. At one point, Jones proclaims: 'My jurisdiction extends from Ankara, Turkey, to Watts Tower, baby' (and it will be noted that, taking account of the new – young, black and American – audience, the script explains where Ankara is, while assuming that LA's Watts will be more than familiar).

Cleopatra Jones is a perfect example of the way in which a Shakespeare character and the story that surrounds her can be transformed to meet the specific needs of a targeted modern audience and a completely alien genre. In this case, Cleopatra and the famous barge scene found themselves an unlikely afterlife in a blaxploitation film, located in Los Angeles alleyways and Turkish airstrips.

More predictable, and less seismic a culture shift, is Cleopatra's representation in mainstream painting, in which the barge description, in particular, became a popular inspiration for painters in the 19th century. In Lawrence Alma-Tadema's portrayal (Figure 7), for example, we view Cleopatra through an opening in the side of the vessel, thereby receiving the same impression as Antony, who approaches from the other side out of an exotic, sunlit world like some awe-struck voyeur. Looking our way, disdainfully ignoring her visitor, Cleopatra lolls on her barge in the dimness of her silken, rose-garlanded pavilion. 'Passive and mysterious as the Orient was supposed to be, [she] awaits the arrival of Antony, the vigorous European discoverer.'[10]

Portraying the same moment, and conveying a similar image of the queen in a painting from 1917, the American Maxfield Parrish places Cleopatra's barge against a deep blue night sky, spangled with bright stars. The queen herself, surrounded by delicate pale pink flowers and contrastingly bronzed and muscular oarsmen, is a picture of tantalising femininity.

These barge paintings by Alma-Tadema and Parrish give rise to two questions concerning the Cleopatra myth. The first is: how far do images of Cleopatra draw on Shakespeare's creation of the character, and how far do they arise from a pre-existing biography based upon history and legend? The second opens up issues of representation.

Knowledge of the play's performance history provides a partial answer to the first question. For it turns out that, although Cleopatra was a figure of great fascination during the Renaissance – witness a variety of paintings by, among others, Vasari, Michelangelo, Guercino, Guido Reni, Tiepolo and Pietro Ricci – there is no record of Shakespeare's play having been performed by the King's Men.* And when Cleopatra's story did reach the stage, it wasn't courtesy of

*However, as Michael Neill points out, the absence of a recorded performance does not necessarily suggest that the play was unpopular: records for that period are notoriously patchy, and the fact that there was no published edition of the play before the First Folio in 1623 'might just as well indicate that the King's Men regarded *Antony and Cleopatra* as too valuable a property to let out of their hands' (Introduction to the Oxford University Press 1994 edition of the play, p. 24). Anthony Davies takes the view that 'in all probability *Antony and Cleopatra* enjoyed

Shakespeare's play, but in a form designed to please the tastes of Restoration and 18th-century audiences. This was a period, remember, in which the Poet Laureate and playwright Nahum Tate was to give his 1681 *King Lear* a poetically just and happy ending – Kent, Gloucester and Lear all live, as does Cordelia, who marries Edgar – a version which, with some alterations, held the stage for a century and a half. It should come as no surprise, then, that John Dryden's Antony and Cleopatra play *All For Love* (probably first performed in 1677) took a moralistic view of the lovers' story, in which, as its author explained in a Preface, 'the chief persons represented were famous patterns of unlawful love; and their end accordingly was unfortunate'. When Shakespeare's own *Antony and Cleopatra* was finally revived in 1759, David Garrick's expensive production enjoyed only four performances and did little to restore faith in the play, so that subsequent revivals (by John Philip Kemble in 1813 and William Charles Macready in 1833) were actually commercially safer hybrids of Dryden's and Shakespeare's texts, which endeavoured, as the Preface to Kemble's version explained, 'to blend the regular play of Dryden with the wild tragedy of Shakespeare'. Credit for staging the first unadulterated (though cut) production of Shakespeare's play since Garrick, therefore, goes to actor-manager Samuel Phelps, whose Sadler's Wells *Antony and Cleopatra* opened in 1849.

What all that might suggest, then, is that Shakespeare's contribution to Cleopatra mythography is at its most evident only after the middle of the 19th century, when his play, rather than Dryden's, provided the script and the performances with which people were to become familiar.

its first performance late in 1601' (*The Oxford Companion to Shakespeare*, p. 15). There was certainly no performance of the play between 1701 and 1750, however (see Charles B. Hogan, *Shakespeare in the Theatre* (The Clarendon Press, 1952), vol. 1, p. 461).

The second major question posed by the two paintings concerns the portrayal of Cleopatra – and specifically her skin-colour. The question 'Was Cleopatra black?' has implications, not only for dramatic performance and the visual arts, but importantly for the whole question of non-white representation in Western culture. And it isn't easy to answer. Historically, Cleopatra wasn't an ethnic Egyptian, but a Ptolemy, descended from one of Alexander the Great's generals. Given that the Ptolemys were Macedonian in origin, and had maintained the royal tradition of their adoptive country by marrying siblings, the historical Cleopatra presumably looked very much like any other Mediterranean European of her time – a tanned Fulvia or Octavia, perhaps.

But this doesn't help with the more intriguing question of how Cleopatra seems to be represented in Shakespeare's play. Interestingly, within the first ten lines, she is described by the Roman Philo as a 'gipsy' with a 'tawny front' (forehead), while she later says of herself:

> Think on me,
> That am with Phoebus' amorous pinches black,
> And wrinkled deep in time.[11]

At first sight, the terms 'gipsy', 'tawny' and 'black' seem to suggest that Shakespeare has in mind a dark skin; but each of these phrases is problematic, and the most troublesome of all is 'black'.

'Black', as a descriptive term applied by Shakespeare to women, does not mean 'black-skinned' in our modern sense of the term: it means 'brunette', and is used of a woman whose colouring – skin, hair, eyes – are not 'fair'. In Shakespeare's lexicon, 'fair' is an antonym of 'black', and implies both 'fair-skinned' and 'beautiful' (a correlation which might have something to do with the fashion for beauty set by flatterers of the ginger-blonde Queen Elizabeth). Correspondingly, 'black' can imply 'unattractive'. We can see this 'black–fair' conflict played out most notably in *Love's Labour's Lost*, where 30 lines of bantering word-play between the King and Berowne turn on the contrast between 'fair' and 'black'.[12] It is also vividly illustrated, of course, in the group of Sonnets addressed to the so-called 'Dark Lady', the first of which opens with the line: 'In the old age black was not counted fair'.[13]

The point is, when Shakespeare wants 'black' to carry racial connotations, he always makes it abundantly clear, as we can see in both *Titus Andronicus* (below) and *Othello* (where Iago's description of Othello as an 'old black ram' is matched by Roderigo's cheap racial insult 'thick-lips').[14] So when Cleopatra describes herself as being 'with Phoebus' amorous pinches black', the most obvious meaning of the word is 'bruised' – as in '*black* and blue'.

And yet ... and yet ... As Janet Adelman explains:

It is nonetheless suggestive that Cleopatra attributes her color to sunburn: the theory that the blackness of Africans was caused by sunburn was widely debated in antiquity and the Renaissance ...[15]

The position is slightly clearer with 'gipsy'. According to John Dover Wilson:

Shakespeare's age could hardly have helped believing in a 'gipsy' Cleopatra. For the word is simply a popular form of 'gyptian' or 'gypcyan' which was the name given to the tawny-skinned nomads ... who began to wander about English lanes and commons early in the sixteenth century, and were supposed to come from Egypt.[16]

And as far as 'tawny' is concerned:

Cleopatra's 'tawny' skin is 'olive-coloured', like that of the 'tawny' gypsies in a favourite masque of James I's, *The Gypsies Metamorphosed*.[17]

In defining 'tawny', Richard Madelaine might equally have cited the stage direction for the entrance of Morocco in Shakespeare's *The Merchant of Venice* (in 2.1): 'Enter MOROCCO, a tawny Moor all in white …', and the fact that the Moor Aaron in *Titus Andronicus* calls his child by the white-skinned Tamora 'tawny', because it is 'half me and half thy dam'.[18] Both of these indicate that 'tawny' is a lighter shade than 'black', the word used to describe both Aaron and Othello. As a further light on the meaning, we might consider Henry the Fifth's threat to the French Herald —

> … if we be hindered,
> We shall your tawny ground with your red blood
> Discolour …[19]

— an image drawn from the language of heraldry, in which *tenné* is, according to Richmond Herald of Arms, 'orange or tawny'.[20]

From this evidence, it seems that, for Shakespeare's King's Men at least, the actor playing Cleopatra would have worn make-up out of the same pot as the one playing the prince of Morocco – in other words, a significantly lighter shade than Othello's or Aaron's black: quite probably a hue that would make the character look like an Arab, rather than an equatorial African. But the exact shade isn't important – as Janet Adelman concludes, 'to Shakespeare's audience, what probably mattered is that she was darker than they were'.[21]

None of this should be taken to mean, of course, that African-American or Afro-Caribbean actors should hold back from laying claim to the role. Quite the reverse, in fact; for, as Michael Neill observes:

> … it is a telling paradox of the play's stage history that, despite Shakespeare's clearly envisaging Cleopatra as a North African queen whose skin is either 'tawny' or 'black', there is no history of

black Cleopatras as there has been, since the triumph of Ira Aldridge in the mid-nineteenth century, a series of striking black Othellos.[22]

In fact, there have so far been only four major theatrical productions of *Antony and Cleopatra* featuring black actors as Cleopatra: Rosalind Cash (Los Angeles Theatre Center, 1987), Francelle Stuart Dorn (Folger Shakespeare Theater, 1988); Dona Croll (London's Tawala and Bloomsbury Theatres, 1991, an all-black production);[23] and Cathy Tyson (English Shakespeare Company, 1998).

Cleopatra was, however, played by a white male, when Mark Rylance elected to take on the role at London's Globe in 1999.

Act 2, scene 5: 'Some innocents 'scape not the thunderbolt …'

The poor man designated to inform Cleopatra of Antony's marriage to Octavia enters timidly, walks slowly, tremblingly forward and kneels before her. Surrounded by her inner circle – her two women, Charmian and Iras, Alexas and the eunuch Mardian – and unaware of the thunderbolt that is about to strike her, she encourages the frightened messenger to deliver his report, going so far as to chuck him under the chin when he informs her that Antony is now 'friends with Caesar'. Emboldened, he moves on to the gist of his tale:

> 'But yet, madam —'

She stops him. Irritated by his hesitation, and disturbed by his ominous tone, she struts away and sits on a stool. She does not like 'But yet' —

> 'But yet is as a gaoler to bring forth
> Some monstrous malefactor', she says.

And so it proves. Her reaction on hearing that her Antony is now 'bound' to Octavia 'for the best turn in the bed' (what is this man thinking of,

1. LOVERS FOR A NEW AUDIENCE: Leonardo DiCaprio and
Claire Danes in the 1996 Baz Luhrmann *Romeo + Juliet*.

2. THE PLAY-WITHIN-THE-FILM: Joseph Fiennes and Gwyneth Paltrow as
the lovers Will/Romeo and Viola/Juliet in *Shakespeare in Love*.

3. 'ROMEO ... HUGS HER IN A DISTRAUGHT EMBRACE': Charles Kemble
and Harriet Smithson as Romeo and Juliet from the performance at the Odéon,
Paris in 1827 which so impressed Hector Berlioz.

4. THE BOY KING: Kenneth Branagh as Henry the Fifth in the 1989 film.
5. D-DAY DEFIANCE: Laurence Olivier stirring the troops in his 1944 *Henry V*.

6. THE CRY OF THE MISTRESS: Sinead Cusack as Cleopatra
for the RSC in 2002.

7. THE ICONIC BARGE MOMENT: Cleopatra awaits Antony's
arrival in a painting by Lawrence Alma-Tadema.
8. CLEOPATRA AS BIMBO: Amanda Barrie as the Egyptian
Queen in *Carry on Cleo* from 1964.

9. 'I'LL HAVE MY BOND!': Richard Westall's 1795 painting of 'Shylock
Rebuffing Antonio' in Act 3, scene 3.

10. 'JESSICA, MY GIRL ...': Gilbert Stuart Newton's 1830 'Shylock and Jessica from *The Merchant of Venice*'.

11. 'IF THE AUDIENCE CAN LOVE HIM AND HATE HIM …':
Henry Goodman as Shylock in the 1999 Royal National Theatre
production, directed by Trevor Nunn.

*phrasing it like that – is he mad?) is swift and deadly. She erupts, flies from
her seat and grabs him by the hair, kicks him, drags him – still by his hair
– across the floor and finally, on 'Rogue, thou hast lived too long!', snatches
the man's own knife —*

*Unsurprisingly, he flees, pursued by the furious queen, like Antigonus
about to be consumed by the bear, and narrowly avoids the deadly weapon
as it flies from Cleopatra's hand, her aim luckily marred by her passion …*

*As Cleopatra paces distractedly in a circle, Iras returns from her own pur-
suit of the messenger to report, somewhat timidly, 'He is afeard to come …'*

This was how Glenda Jackson's Cleopatra took the news of Antony's
marriage in 1978. However, whatever the influences upon that particular performance might have been, we can be reasonably certain
that she did not base the interpretation on her earlier incarnation of
the serpent of old Nile …

Imagine her dressed sumptuously in eye-catching Egyptian dress,
beautifully made up, reclining on a chaise longue, and turning to us
to say: 'All men are fools. And what makes them so is having beauty
like what I have got.'

This was the actor's guest appearance on the *Morecambe and
Wise* 1971 Christmas Special. In their long television career the two
comedians made several forays into Shakespeare, one of the most
notable being their earlier performance of Antony's 'Friends, Romans,
countrymen' speech from *Julius Caesar*, described here by Derek
Longhurst:

> [Eric] enters on to a stage with Roman pillars, bearing Ernie in
> his arms and begins the 'Friends, Romans …' speech. Gradually
> the speech disintegrates as the body gets heavier, and a great deal
> of visual comedy is generated by the pair clutching at each other's
> cloaks and togas, Ernie being hoisted into a fireman's lift exposing

his underpants beneath the toga. Eric begins to 'forget' the lines – 'He was my friend – an' all that', 'the good men do lives after 'em – I'll tell you that' – and he has to be 'prompted' in comically loud stage whispers by 'the body' ('the slings and arrows of out-rageous fortune' / Ernie (hissed): 'That's *Henry V*'). Finally 'the body' carries off Mark Antony in a fireman's lift exposing his shoes and socks under a Roman costume ...[24]

This kind of Shakespeare parody can be traced back to the Victorian burlesques[25] and beyond, and Cleopatra has been an especially popular subject. A specific echo of Shakespeare's script ('I am dying, Egypt!') can be heard in this piece of vintage New York burlesque performed at the Minsky Brothers Follies for some years throughout the 1920s:

> ... Julius Cæsar, in a tin helmet, smoking a big cigar, catches Antony (the Jewish comic) on a divan with Cleopatra (the prin-cipal strip-tease girl) and wallops him over the bottom with the flat of an enormous sword. 'I'm dying! I'm dying!' groans Antony, as he staggers around in a circle, and Caesar and Cleopatra, the Roman soldiers and the Egyptian slave-girls break into a rousing shimmy to the refrain of 'He's dying! He's dying!' ...
>
> 'Bring me the wassup', says Cleopatra, and her slave-girl, kneeling, presents a box, from which Cleopatra takes a huge prop-erty phallus ...
>
> Cleopatra falls prone on her lover's body, and Caesar, with pathetic reverence, places on her posterior a wreath, which he waters with a watering-pot ...[26]

Evidently puzzled by the *wassup*, Edmund Wilson suggests that 'At some point in the development of the ancient act the word *asp* was evidently confused with *wasp* ...'. This may be so, but it seems to me that *wassup* is New York 'What's up?', an appropriate term for a dildo.

And while we're on the subject of the *wassup*:

Slender, shapely and sexily baring the flattest of midriffs, her pretty, triangular face framed by a wide semi-circle of black hair, cut short and straight at chin-length, eyes wide open and lips slightly apart, she reclines on the (obligatory) chaise longue and pauses …

'I've been thinking', she says.

Mark Antony's eyebrows lift in shock.

'You do?!' he exclaims.

When Amanda Barrie played Cleopatra to Sid James's Antony in the 1964 film *Carry on Cleo*[27] (opening credit 'based on an original idea by William Shakespeare'), it was as a naïve and childish, though wonderfully seductive, Queen of the Nile. Though the dialogue drew little upon Shakespeare's — it was mainly a parody of the Burton–Taylor *Cleopatra* from the year before – there were numerous plot references both to *Antony and Cleopatra* and to *Julius Caesar*, the most widely quoted being Kenneth Williams's cry as Caesar of: 'Infamy! Infamy!' (wait for it), '… They've all got it in fer me!' The closing credits stated that 'Whilst the characters and events in this story are based on actual characters and events, certain liberties have been taken with Cleopatra.'

But in fairness to writer Talbot Rothwell, his good-natured portrayal of Cleopatra as bimbo was less of a disparagement to Shakespeare's creation than had been the mean-spirited perversion of the Cleopatra story that had appeared on the London stage in 1898.

George Bernard Shaw's *Caesar and Cleopatra* was written in reaction against what he took to be Shakespeare's romanticising and 'deification' of love. Unable to see any meanings in Shakespeare other than those imposed by his own psychology, Shaw systematically strips Cleopatra of both intellect and sexuality and instead presents us with a pretty, empty-headed kitten, of whom the departing Caesar can say in the final scene of the play: 'What! As much a child as ever, Cleopatra! Have I not made a woman of you after all?'[28]

Carry on Cleo actually celebrates Cleopatra's power (albeit exclusively through sexuality rather than allure combined with wit and political acumen). But in Shaw's *Caesar and Cleopatra* she is desexualised, infantilised and mocked. It is difficult to forgive him for that.

Act 3, scene 13: 'I kiss his conquering hand ...'

With Antony's fleet routed by Octavius's in the devastating battle of Actium, Cleopatra admits entrance to an ambassador from the victorious Caesar, a man called Thidias. What is she up to? Is she changing sides, keeping her options open, or just seeing how the wind blows?

In this 1849 engraving,* a representation of Isabella Glyn's celebrated performance, Cleopatra looks unsettlingly like Queen Victoria. While the kneeling Thidias appears to be wearing a Roman toga and cloak, she is decorously attired as a 19th-century matron, regally averting her eyes from the messenger while simultaneously offering her hand to be kissed. Charmian and Iras look on, bemused, while, outside the door, a furious Antony, witnessing this act of treachery, has to be restrained ...

Sinead Cusack frowns and thinks carefully how to reply. 'Well', she says finally, 'this is a hugely complicated area, the area of Thidias ...'

It seems to me that there are often key points of interpretation for a Shakespeare character, where each actor has to make his or her own individual choice. An obvious example is Shylock's offer of the bond

*In the Theatre Museum, Covent Garden, London.

in Act 1, scene 3 of *The Merchant of Venice*: is it part of a genuine bid for Antonio's friendship; or a cunning ruse to entrap him? For me, a scene that acts as a touchstone to differentiate one Cleopatra from another is the one with Octavius's messenger, Thidias: is she stringing him along; or, as it can appear, actually hoping to dump Antony and make terms with Caesar? Sinead Cusack goes on:

> 'I talk about embracing the ambiguities in Shakespeare. It's what you've got to do. All those contradictions, you embrace them, you never try to iron them out, you allow that. You, me, our children – those contradictions are there all the time. Yes, play the inconsistencies, embrace the ambiguities. Now, with the Thidias scene, I think ...' [she pauses, searching for the right phrase] '... she's thinking *on the hoof.* I think what she wants to do is buy more time, buy time for *him.* And in my view of Cleopatra, she never for a second thinks that Antony will suspect her of perfidy. What she wants to do is persuade [Thidias], and thereby persuade Caesar, that she is compliant and understands that she now has to bow down and kiss his foot. And she hopes that by doing that she will buy more time for them to plan. And so that was the way that I played it ...'

And the ambiguity?

> 'Well, also the wonderful thing about Shakespeare is that when Thidias asks if he can kiss her hand, and she says, "Oh yes, Julius Caesar used to kiss that hand" – when she does it, she *enjoys* it, she *enjoys* that a young man wants to kiss her. She knows she can use her innate flirtatiousness – she knows she can use it and has done all her life. And she understood quite rightly as a very astute political woman, that an affiliation with Rome was in her best interest.'

She smiles.

> 'It's probably a bit like Tony Blair and George Dubya – thinking, you know, "We've got to get in there [into Iraq], because, if we're not in there at the carve-up, we're lost" – if you want to be a bit cynical. But Cleopatra certainly was cynical. And she knew that Rome was necessary for the well-being of Egypt. But what came from that fear was falling in love the way that she did. And so with Thidias she is once again doing what she's always done – I'll seduce the man. I'll seduce *them* into believing – Thidias first and then Caesar – that I'm compliant and that I'm going along with their notion of him as Emperor of the world and me as a little adjunct.'

Her interpretation is supported by the Jungian theorist Priscilla Murr, who says: 'It seems to me natural that [Cleopatra] would attempt to gain control of these Romans through "love".' In continuing his discussion of Adler's psychological theory, Jung writes: 'Have we not seen countless people who love and believe in their love, and then, when their purpose is accomplished turn away as though they had never loved?'[29]

'But', the actress concludes:

> 'the Thidias scene is one of the most difficult scenes for Cleopatra to play. And we did all sorts of experimentation with it – where she was actually intending betrayal of Antony, and her allegiance was now to where the power-base lay – and it wasn't with Antony. I mean, I've seen loads of Cleopatras and I know some of them take that view ... But I don't.'

Act 5, scene 2: 'Hast thou the pretty worm of Nilus there, / That kills and pains not?'

With Antony dead and Octavius Caesar on her doorstep, Cleopatra knows that death is a happy and wished-for alternative to a future of mockery

and scorn in Rome, living to see 'Some squeaking Cleopatra boy [her]
greatness i' the posture of a whore'. Enclosed in her monument, she sits on
her imperial throne, and an extravagant head-dress is placed upon her,
gold and azure, suddenly and dramatically bringing out the bright live-
liness of her hazel eyes, which are now fixed in a heavenward gaze as she
calls out to her Antony:

> 'Husband, I come:
> Now to that name my courage prove my title!
> I am fire and air; my other elements
> I give to baser life.'

And the camera recedes to reveal the full splendour of an Egyptian god-
dess enthroned like a Luxor statue. Then, lying on a sarcophagus-like
golden bed, she reaches out to the basket of figs and places the first serpent
under the folds of her dress …

Dying, she gives voice to one of the most shocking images in the whole of
Shakespeare: 'Peace, peace!' she cries —

> 'Dost thou not see my baby at my breast,
> That sucks the nurse asleep?'

The death of Janet Suzman's Cleopatra was the self-affirming act of a
powerful and independent woman refusing to be marginalised by
Octavius Caesar, and resolving to die rather than live on as an
Egyptian puppet in Rome. Suzman was a lithe and boyish Cleopatra,
rather than a voluptuous one, and less passionate than, for example,
Jane Lapotaire, whose final moments as Cleopatra (for BBC
Television)[30] are here described by Michael Scott:

> The fire of Lapotaire's performance is evident here as she pushes
> her shoulders and face forward, her eyes darting, her constantly
> moving head determinedly expressing her resolve. In her death,

however, she resumes the resignation and strength of her tragedy. The camera again closes to frame her as she quietly bares her shoulder and caressingly places the serpent over it and towards her breast:

> As sweet as balm, as soft as air, as gentle —
> O, Antony!

She breathes heavily in a moment reminiscent of sexual satisfaction with Antony:

> Nay, I will take thee too.
> What should I stay

— and to the left quietly sinks her head in death: eyes closed, mouth slightly parted.[31]

In keeping with Shakespearean Cleopatras before and since, Janet Suzman and Jane Lapotaire dramatically died after placing a poisonous asp on their breast – and this theatrical, iconic moment is wholly Shakespeare's. For, according to Plutarch, 'the aspick being angered withal, leapt out with great fury, and bit her *in the arm* ...'. It is Shakespeare who makes the creature bite Cleopatra's breast, and in so doing, creates one of the most famous moments in world drama, as well giving an opportunity for that final horrific image in which the snake becomes an innocent baby, injecting lethal venom where it should suck life-giving milk. As Jonathan Bate said, 'the genius is in the embellishment'.

In contrast to Jane Lapotaire's orgasmic performance, Isabella Glyn's 1849 Cleopatra is said to have died 'in a sort of sleep ecstasy', and it is difficult to see how 19th-century women could have performed Cleopatra with the kind of passion and eroticism we associate with the role today. Mrs Siddons, for example, is said to have refused the part when offered it in 1813 on the grounds that she would despise herself if she played it 'as it ought to be played'.[32] It is interesting to speculate on how she might have reacted to the moments leading to the climax of Frances de la Tour's performance in 1999, when the actress, preparing to receive her ceremonial robe and crown, removed her gown and stood gloriously stark naked in the centre of the Stratford stage. As the man said, how different from the home life of our own dear queen ...

Summarising a selection of Cleopatra death-scenes over three decades,* Keith Parsons writes:

> Judi Dench had shown a huge, embracing humour, but here was single-minded with an intensity of focus. Earlier in the play Clare Higgins had worn a series of wigs to suggest her consciousness of the image she presented to Antony and the world, but in the final scene all pretence and play-acting were stripped away ... In contrast, Janet Suzman's encounter with the 'rural fellow' [who brings the figs] permitted a humour which emphasised the strength of her decision. She underwent a robing ceremony that became a ritual transformation into the icon by which the story reverberates through the ages.[33]

So Keith Parsons brings us back to Cleopatra the icon, and the burden of the iconography brings us back to Sinead Cusack, here describing her reaction to being asked by director Michael Attenborough to play Cleopatra for the Royal Shakespeare Company ...

> 'I felt very intimidated. I'd been asked to play it once – twice – before, and on both those occasions I'd turned it down because I thought I couldn't do it. And with Cleopatra there were just so

*Judi Dench played Cleopatra at the National Theatre in 1987, Clare Higgins with the RSC in 1992, Janet Suzman with the RSC in 1972.

many vivid, vivid colours that I had to accommodate and bring out. And, you know, she was *awful*! She was cruel and capricious and dangerous and wily ... But at the same time there was an extraordinary energy and sparkle and sharpness and fun and warmth.

'Then I did a play called *Our Lady of Sligo*, which is about as far from *Antony and Cleopatra* as can be, and it was about a monster ... But, as you peeled away the various skins of this ... onion [she smiles at the image], you found the soft melting heart in the centre ... And I so loved playing it; and I learned so much from that because a huge variety of emotional understanding was required.

'So what I was interested in with Cleopatra was getting underneath all that iconography, and finding out what powered the woman, her heart and her mind ... And so, there was one drunken night where I actually collared Michael, rather than the other way round, and I said to Michael, after a couple of glasses of wine, I said, "Michael, listen. I think I'm ready to do Cleopatra now, and I think you might be the one to do it". I said, "I've got very, very strong ideas about Cleopatra ..."'

CHAPTER 4

Shylock

'A half favourite with the philosophical part of the audience'
William Hazlitt

Act 1, scene 3: '… seal me there / Your single bond'

The voice is deep and seductive.

> *'Three thousand ducats. 'Tis a good round sum.*
> *Three months from twelve; then, let me see the rate —* '

In the silence that follows, Shylock's chair creaks as he leans back and closes his eyes. Antonio notices that it is an expensive chair of carved oak, nicely upholstered in the finest Moroccan leather. But an acquired chair. This is no inherited heirloom; for Shylock is a man who has had to buy his own furniture. A man like the Renaissance merchant Antonio himself, in fact; a man very different from the young pampered Bassanio who sits next to him and opposite Shylock, hanging on the money-lender's every word … For upon Shylock's decision lies Bassanio's opportunity to woo a rich heiress and recoup some of the wealth that he has squandered with his Venetian friends.

Both men watch Shylock intently. Looking over their shoulders, we observe a man with sallow skin and dark, deep-set eyes. His turban, wrapped round beneath his chin, fails to hide the fact that he is unshaven ... And, though at present bereft of his gabardine, everything marks him out as alien. For Shylock is a Jew.

Impatient to conclude the deal and be gone, and possibly also feeling that the money-lender is milking this situation, Antonio prompts: 'Well, Shylock, shall we be beholden to you?'

It's difficult to know how Antonio expects him to respond here. Surely the merchant must know that, at some point in this bizarre encounter, Shylock will remind him of the shameful treatment that he, as a money-lender and a Jew, had suffered publicly at the Christian Antonio's hands. But it's unlikely that he will have anticipated the degree of bitterness with which Shylock recalls it. For Antonio had not merely insulted him on the Rialto, but had called him 'misbeliever, cut-throat, dog ...', had spat upon him, gobbed phlegm on his beard ... And now, after all this – and it would be laughable were it not so obscene – Antonio has the effrontery to come to Shylock for help!

Faced with this response, what does Antonio do? He can hardly deny the accusations, since they are patently true. And he isn't the type to apologise or find excuses. So he goes on the attack himself. All right, he says, so I've spat on you. And I'll spit on you again. If you want to lend this money, treat me as your enemy. That way, there will be no qualms about exacting the penalty if I can't repay you ... And (he seems to imply) I'm damned if I see why I should sit here and be lectured to by a Jew usurer!

Shylock mollifies ... Don't get so het up ... you're misunderstanding me, I want to be your friend ... Look, I'll lend you the money and not take a penny in interest – how's that?

This is a move the Christians have not anticipated.

Shylock follows up while they're still reeling – speaking rapidly and excitedly, he explains what he has in mind (and if we've been here before, it's the moment we're waiting for...): 'Go with me to a notary', *he says,*

'... *seal me there*
Your single bond, and, in a merry sport,
If you repay me not on such a day,
In such a place, such sum or sums as are
Expressed in the condition, let the forfeit
Be nominated for ...'

He pauses, as though struggling to pluck out of the ether the most absurd, random and arbitrary penalty he can conceive of, something that will demonstrate just how ridiculous and 'merry' this whole contract is ... Yes, he has it! The perfect joke penalty – you'll be amused by this, he seems to say ...

'... *an equal pound —*'

— his hand waves suggestively in the direction of Antonio's torso —

'Of *your fair flesh to be cut off and taken*
In what part of your body pleaseth me.'

He chuckles contentedly at the amusing absurdity of it all and sits back, happy that the Christians will jump at the chance to conclude such an obviously profitable deal and think him a good fellow into the bargain ... which Antonio does and Bassanio doesn't. (Though why he doesn't remains unclear – perhaps he mistrusts the money-lender; or maybe he doesn't like the idea of Antonio signing up to a bond which – even in jest – implies that he is willing to die for his young friend ...). At any rate (not an original pun: Shylock has used it earlier), the deal is agreed and the Christians make ready to depart.

As first-time observers we admit to a sense of unease on Antonio's behalf: apart from anything else, Antonio seems such a nice man, and we would hate to see him come to harm … Though his past behaviour to Shylock – well, there must be a reason for it, and this Jew looks plainly dishonest.

If, on the other hand, we've seen this business played out before, or simply know the story, then it's really just a question of sitting back in our own versions of Shylock's chair and watching things unfold. We know what will happen, but not precisely how.

As Antonio and Bassanio take the long march back to the door – Shylock's desk is at the far end of this spacious room – we precede them, as it were walking backwards like lackeys at some royal occasion. This allows us to see what they cannot: framed between their heads, Shylock once again leaning back in his expensive chair, his hands joined comfortably at the fingertips beneath his chin, his lips curled in a smile which confirms our fears that this cannot nor it will not come to good …

And, as privileged spectators, we also witness the money-lender's reaction after the bond is signed. We watch as Antonio's ring-seal plunges into the soft wax to the accompaniment of ominous soundtrack music, and as Shylock lifts the document to his eyes for a final scrutiny, eyes which then turn to focus on us … No smiling now, no jocularity … This is deeply sinister stuff …

Every time I watch this Shylock of Bob Peck's, in a production made for Channel 4 in 1996,[1] I am aware that I am seeing a Shylock brilliantly portrayed, but who is about as obviously villainous as you can get these days; and surprisingly so for an interpretation which, though aimed at a schools audience, did not take pains to make clear that Shylock is a Jew who happens to be bad, rather than a man who is bad because he's a Jew. In that sense it was a careless interpretation featuring a famously very careful actor. And Shylock is a character that we can not afford to be careless about.

I recall opening my newspaper not so long ago to three articles.

One reported on the latest spate of suicide-bombings in Israel and the reprisals against Palestinians in the West Bank. Another was a warning from Chief Rabbi Jonathan Sacks about the resurgence of anti-Semitism across Western Europe. The third was about the burning down of a synagogue in Marseilles.

Now, Shylock isn't directly to blame for any of this, and nor is his creator: anti-Semitism – or more correctly, anti-Judaism* – had already had a long and ugly history by the time Shakespeare put his Jew on the stage. But there are many people who believe that Shylock doesn't help; some that we should exercise restraint over where and how often *The Merchant of Venice* is performed; and a significant few who would prefer it if the play were quite simply forgotten about.

Shylock is unusual because he is the only Shakespeare figure that I can think of, about whom you will hear people say: 'I wish Shakespeare had not created this character.' Or, if they don't go that far, ask: 'Why did Shylock have to be a Jew?'; or 'Why must his Jewishness be so explicitly linked to his villainy?' It is a fairly straightforward matter to stage a performance of *Othello* which avoids giving the impression that all 'moors' are by nature credulous fools dominated by their passions. Less easy to send audiences away from *The Merchant* believing that they have watched a villain who just happens to be a Jew.

I have often wondered what Shakespeare's audience made of Shylock at the opening performance of *The Merchant of Venice*. Many, perhaps most, of the audience in the Theatre in Shoreditch that afternoon in the late 1590s would have been familiar with Christopher

*Strictly speaking, the term 'anti-Semitic' is an anachronism if applied to early Shylocks, since the phenomenon of despising Jews *as a race* (as distinct from despising them for their religion) did not appear until the 19th century. Hostility to Jews up to that time should, therefore, more correctly be termed 'anti-Judaism'. It is a satisfying coincidence that Sir Henry Irving's ground-breaking first performance of Shylock was in 1879, the year in which the German Wilhelm Marr first coined the term 'anti-Semitism'.

Marlowe's Barabas, the eponymous *Jew of Malta*, a thoroughgoing Machiavellian nasty who strolls around at night killing sick people 'groaning under the walls' and poisoning wells just for the hell of it – 'a very Jew', in fact, in the sense that young Gobbo intends the word.[2] They might also have had views about people who loaned out money at ruinous rates, recalling Barabas's boastful curriculum vitae:

> Then after that I was an usurer,
> And with extorting, cozening, forfeiting,
> And tricks belonging unto brokery,
> I fill'd the jails with bankrupts in a year,
> And with young orphans planted hospitals,
> And every moon made some or other mad,
> And now and then one hang himself for grief,
> Pinning upon his breast a long great scroll
> How I with interest tormented him.[3]

Many, if not most, would also have known about the trial of Rui (or Roderigo) Lopez, a Portuguese Jew who had converted to Christianity and who was accused by the Earl of Essex of attempting to poison Queen Elizabeth in his capacity as her physician. Still in popular memory when *The Merchant* opened, the trial was notable for the anti-Jewish feeling expressed by everyone present – even the judge called Lopez 'that vile Jew' – and, despite the attempts of the Queen herself to postpone his execution, Lopez was hanged in June 1594. (Interestingly, Elizabeth ordered that all of Lopez's property, confiscated when he was found guilty, should be handed back to his widow. We don't know her motives, but it would be nice to believe that she felt Lopez to have been unjustly convicted.)

In fact, no opportunity had been lost to spread anti-Jewish hatred in the years leading up to Shylock's first appearance on the London stage. During the Black Death, Jews had been regularly accused of poisoning water supplies, because – so the argument went – the Jews' superior hygiene and diet made them less likely to contract the plague. (And nothing changes much: this week's tabloid headlines are all about today's bogey men, the asylum-seekers, and their responsibility for importing the deadly SARS virus.) Even during the 14th to 17th centuries when Jews were largely absent from England (they were to be recalled by Oliver Cromwell), anti-Jewish stereotypes were constantly being reinforced in the popular imagination through church sermons and religious literature.

So what did that first audience make of Shylock? What were they expecting and what did they get? It would be lovely to know who played the part, but no records survive to give us any help at all – except, that is, for an anonymous poem discovered in the 1840s by the assiduous Victorian scholar, J. Payne Collier. This was a funeral elegy to the greatest of all Shakespeare's colleagues in the Chamberlain's Men, the actor Richard Burbage; and its discovery revealed that, along with all the great tragic roles – Lear, Macbeth, Othello ... – Burbage was indeed the actor who created the part of Shylock. The elegy reads:

> Heart-broken Philaster, and Amintas too,
> Are lost for ever; with the red-haired Jew,
> Which sought the bankrupt merchant's flesh,
> By woman-lawyer caught in his own mesh ...[4]

The discovery of this information came as no surprise to Victorian academics. As the most celebrated of the Chamberlain's Men, Burbage was always a likely candidate for Shylock, and it was a bonus to learn that he had played the part in a red wig.

The fact that the manuscript in which the elegy appeared turned out to be a forgery (Collier's enthusiasm had outrun his academic probity) does not, of course, invalidate the claim of Burbage as the first Shylock; but the volume in which Collier published his 'find' contains an interesting piece of surrounding text which goes some way to suggesting why the Victorians in particular might have readily accepted Burbage as the obvious creator of the role, and why they might have been led astray by their preconceptions of it. Collier writes:

> To the list of characters in plays by Shakespeare sustained by Burbadge [sic] we still have to add Lear and Shylock, so that we may safely decide that he was the chosen representative of all, or nearly all, the *serious parts* in the productions of our great dramatist.[5] [*My italics.*]

The significance lies in the categorising of Shylock as a 'serious' part. Collier was writing at a time when the two great interpreters of Shylock to date had been Charles Macklin and Edmund Kean, who had both played the part with utmost seriousness; while the Shylock of William Charles Macready, revived at Drury Lane only five years before the publication of Collier's book, had been 'abject, sordid, irritable, argumentative'.[6] Collier took it for granted that Shylock would always have been played by a 'serious' actor. Had he lived in the time of the comic Shylock Thomas Dogget (who played him in a farcical version of the play by George Granville, Lord Lansdowne in 1701, retitled *The Jew of Venice*),[7] he would presumably not have assigned the role to the Chamberlain's Men's leading *tragic* actor, but to one of their clowns.

The two outstanding comic actors in Shakespeare's company at the time when *The Merchant of Venice* was first performed[8] were Will Kempe and Thomas Pope. Kempe is known to have played, among other roles, Peter in *Romeo and Juliet* and Dogberry in *Much Ado About Nothing*, and might also have played Pistol.[9] Pope, like Kempe, was a senior member of the company – a 'payee' with Heminges in 1595, one of the seven 'sharers' in the Globe building costs four years later, and also a sharer in the Curtain. It has been speculated that he played Sir Toby Belch.[10] That either of these actors might have played the original Shylock, the other taking the role of Lancelot Gobbo (perhaps with Burbage as Bassanio) is, I would suggest, a plausible speculation, as too is the possibility that the role was taken by John Heminges.[11] It is certainly unwise to associate Burbage with Shylock on the presumption that the role demands tragic weight, however many 'serious' actors – Irving, Olivier, Redgrave, Gielgud ... – have since regarded the role as an obvious vehicle for their talents.

So it isn't likely that we will ever know who that first audience saw playing Shylock or, more interestingly, how he was performed, how the audience reacted and what they felt as they left the playhouse. But I would be amazed if they were not at the very least taken aback by the experience of hearing 'the Jew' – the Barabas, the Rui Lopez – requiring the Christians (on stage and off) to stop and consider that he bleeds, laughs and dies just as they do. It's my view that they would have given him a fair hearing; and that we should think very carefully indeed before concluding that Shakespeare's audiences engaged in the kind of crude pantomime booing and hissing at Shylock that we witnessed at London's reconstructed Globe in 1998.[12] I find utterly implausible the notion that an age which demanded the kind of sensitive and attentive looking and listening required for the appreciation of works of the subtlety of Hilliard's miniatures and Byrd's masses, might have performed one of its up-and-coming dramatist's more ambiguous creations in a red wig and a funny nose.

Simply to contemplate that image reveals the extent to which Shylock lives on in our consciousness – not least, because we are profoundly uncomfortable about him. From every audience that attends a performance of *The Merchant of Venice*, there will always be some people leaving the theatre entertaining the possibility that Shakespeare was an anti-Semite. It has often been observed, of course, and rightly, that this play was never designed to carry the weight of post-Holocaust consciousness. But what interests me is that audience anxieties about the potentially harmful effect that Shylock can have are by no means a new phenomenon born of modern sensibilities.

In 1775 a German visitor to England, Georg Lichtenberg, saw a performance of *The Merchant* at Drury Lane in which Shylock was played by the Irish actor Charles Macklin.* Macklin, known for his violent outbursts, was notorious for having killed a fellow-performer after an argument about a wig, and audiences appear to have seen some of this barely controlled danger in his interpretation of Shylock. In stark contrast to the almost farcical interpretation of the clown Thomas Dogget at Lincoln's Inn Fields at the beginning of the 18th century, Macklin's Shylock was striking in its ferocity, malice and vengefulness. Where Dogget played for laughs ('very Aspect-abund, wearing a Farce in his Face'),[13] Macklin's severe interpretation obliged audiences to confront the two questions that are still being asked about Shylock today: how far do you play him for sympathy; and is the play anti-Semitic?

Most observers agree that Macklin's portrayal of the Jew was not one to evoke audience sympathy. Garrick at the time referred to 'the extreme spite and bitterness' with which Macklin played his opening scene.[14] The actor and critic Thomas Davies, though, saw something else, and remarks that the interpretation 'made some tender impressions upon the spectators'.[15] What Davies seems to have witnessed, whether consciously designed by Macklin or not, were the beginnings of audience sympathy for Shylock.

There are several reasons why an actor might wish to endow Shylock with some sympathetic qualities, not the least important of

---

*Macklin opened as Shylock in February 1741. Confounding rehearsal run anxieties, the performance was an outrageous success and Macklin continued to play the part on and off for the next 48 years.

which is the awareness that Shylock's story is indissolubly linked with that of the suffering and persecution of the Jewish people as a whole. This consciousness, and the accompanying fear that the play can be seen as anti-Semitic, can be traced back to Macklin; and there are two elements of his performance which point to an embryonic sensitivity concerning the ways in which Jews should be played upon the stage.

The first lies in the care with which Macklin researched the role, visiting the Exchange and

> ... adjacent coffee-houses; that by a frequent intercourse and conversation with 'the unforeskinned race' he might habituate himself to their air and deportment.[16]

This does not, of course, imply a favourable stage portrayal: most of the contemporary evidence shows that it was not; but it does at least indicate an unwillingness merely to replicate a stale comic stereotype or deny the character individuality.

The second piece of evidence which might be said to demonstrate some unease over the ramifications of portraying an evil Jew, is found in a letter written by that German tourist, Georg Lichtenberg, who concluded:

> It cannot be denied that the sight of this Jew is more than sufficient to arouse once again in the mature man all the prejudices of his childhood against this race.[17]

What I find interesting in Lichtenberg's comment is his reference to the susceptibility of 'the mature man' to prejudice and hostility if Shylock is played in certain ways; and the perception that such feelings are inculcated in childhood. This brief statement demonstrates not only the deep-seated hatred which permitted generations of parents to use the figure of the Jew as bogey-man; but also, conversely, the awakening sensibility in thinking men and women that this was fundamentally wrong. Moreover, it is possible to see in Lichtenberg's careful phrasing ('It cannot be denied that ...') something which suggests that this is not merely a personal confession, but the beginnings of a serious debate upon the implications of restating and reinforcing this racial and cultural stereotype on the popular stage.

I have mentioned Macklin and Dogget not only because they come at the beginning of the recorded history of Shylock performance, but because they suggest two reasons why Shylock has been important to us since the 18th century. The first reason is cultural, or socio-political: namely, that Shylock obliges us to confront the issue of how non-Jews feel about Jews and how they treat them. The second is theatrical and lies in the simple fact that, as a stage character, he is ambiguous, protean and constantly re-interpretable. And this means that the major actors, from Edmund Kean to Laurence Olivier to Dustin Hoffman to Antony Sher, have clamoured to play him.

But there might be a third reason too. Jonathan Bate has argued that the growth of Bardolatry in the 18th century and the developing view of Shakespeare as the national genius went hand in hand with the need to define and distinguish 'Englishness', and that this need was felt most urgently during the intermittent conflicts with France from 1702 to the end of the Napoleonic Wars in 1815.[18] Bate does not mention Shylock in this context, but it seems to me that, if Shakespeare was indeed being seen in this way, then Shylock had a significant role to play at that time in representing the alien 'other', offering a set of behavioural and cultural characteristics in contrast to which audiences could form a definition of the English Christian gentleman. That Jews had long been viewed as an eternally unassimilated group is clear from writings such as those of the influential theologian Andrew Willet in 1590, who averred that, while a Scot might easily settle in Spain and his heirs become Spanish,

... a Jew, though, whether he journeys into Spain, or France, or into whatever other place he goes to, declares himself to be not a Spaniard or a Frenchman, but a Jew.[19]

And it is no coincidence that *The Connoisseur* of 1754 described Macklin as having made a study of 'the unforeskinned race' in order to imitate their 'air and deportment'. The choice of vocabulary is not arbitrary. The actor had sought to make his costume as authentic as possible (his research taught him that Venetian Jews at that time habitually wore hats, for example),[20] and he had made notes in his diary after perusing Josephus's history of the Jews.[21] Macklin's Shylock was clearly not an English coffee-house merchant, but studiedly alien – and his interpretation was to dominate the English stage until 1789, eight years before his death at the age of 98.*

Interestingly and perhaps predictably, it was only as the Napoleonic Wars were coming to an end – and the need to define and assert 'Englishness' presumably becoming less urgent – that a new, less alien Shylock appeared on the stage. This was Edmund Kean's, whose first performance of the character took place the year before the Battle of Waterloo.

Edmund Kean's interpretation is notable for two significant landmarks in the performance history of Shakespeare's Jew: the endowment of the figure with a degree of tragic grandeur; and the apparent response in the actor's portrayal to the changing moral sensibilities of the age. But Kean's was not only a bold and original conception; it was one which endowed the role with a star-vehicle status that it was never to lose.

The way in which interpretations of a particular role seem to be reflecting, in some manifestations, 'the spirit of the age', is always

*Macklin retired from the stage when he was 90, after his memory had failed when playing Shylock.

difficult to define and to identify in performance. I referred above to Georg Lichtenberg's misgivings concerning the stage portrayal of a villainous Jew. Four decades later we begin to see the effects on stage Shylocks of the growth of 19th-century liberalism. Kean's relationship to this burgeoning liberalism is hard to determine. But I find it significant that his biographer B. W. Procter concludes his account of the actor's Drury Lane success with an impassioned plea for an acknowledgement of Jewish suffering through the ages. Was Kean's interpretation motivated, if only in part, by compassion for Jews? John Gross is sceptical: 'He was an actor, on the look-out for dramatic opportunities: religious and social questions were of little if any account to him.'[22] And Gross may be right. But, whatever motivated the actor, the fact remains that Procter, writing in 1835, certainly made a connection himself between Kean's Shylock and the persecution of the Jews. In a section following on without pause from the account of Kean's performance, he writes:

> We confess that we sympathise somewhat with the revenge that rankled in the heart of Shylock. He was an ill-used and oppressed man. He suffered, individually, and as one of a people, on whom the world had been spitting its scorn for nearly two thousand years ...[23]

Whether Kean himself entertained these wider social and religious considerations seems less important than the fact that his was a performance which – if Procter is in any way typical – served to raise the audience's consciousness about Jews and Jewish persecution.

Kean's was therefore a Shylock for its time. For Jews were to be admitted to the Bar for the first time in 1820, to the Shrievalty in 1835 and to other municipal offices in 1843; and in 1848 Lionel Rothschild was the first Jew to sit in the British House of Commons.

Given that historical context, we might be forgiven for finding

Dickens's creation of Fagin perplexing. Fagin and Shylock have to be the two most famous Jews in English – perhaps world – literature; and we might recall the description that Dickens first published in 1837 of:

> ... a very old shrivelled Jew, whose villainous-looking and repulsive face was obscured by a quantity of matted red hair.[24]

Dickens was a keen theatre-goer and might have been an actor himself if things had turned out differently. But the Jew in *Oliver Twist* seems to owe little to Kean's dignified Shylock, which – given that the final performance was not until 1833 – Dickens must have had the opportunity to see. So perhaps we need to look elsewhere for the inspiration for Fagin ...

In 1839, two years after Fagin had first appeared in print, Dickens dedicated his new novel, *Nicholas Nickleby*, to another great 19th-century actor. This was his close friend William Charles Macready; and a copy of the new publication had been awaiting the actor as a gift on his return home from the theatre one evening.[25] The night in question was the opening performance of Macready's revived Shylock (he had first played him in 1823) at Covent Garden.

So here's a speculation. That Fagin was a dated portrayal, out of sympathy with its times, because he was based at least partly upon Macready's Shylock, described by G.H. Lewes as 'abject, sordid ...' and by the *Theatrical Journal* as '... a Jew wheedling, a Jew storming, a Jew affronting the whole state of Venice, but a Jew always triumphing some way or other ...'.[26]

Abject, sordid ... wheedling, storming, affronting ... Not bad words with which to describe Fagin.

Whether or not Macready's Shylock influenced Dickens, the popularity of Fagin with the reading public must surely in turn have helped to shape the Shylocks who appeared in mid-19th-century burlesques – that anarchic theatrical form once po-facedly described as 'the use or imitation of serious matter or manner, made amusing by the creation of an incongruity between style and subject'.[27] The burlesques demonstrated a commendable absence of respect for Shakespeare's creations. Rather like pantomime today, they revelled in cringingly awful puns and threw in topical and local allusions and hit tunes, revealing, as Stanley Wells has happily put it, 'Victorian society at its most unbuttoned'.[28] One burlesque playwright, for example, Francis Talfourd, has his Antonio declare at the end of the trial:

> There are two points though that I must insist on,
> You'll shave your face and look more like a Christian,
> And take your daughter to your arms again.

Shylock replies:

> Well, since you've got the upper hand it's plain,
> I must knock under – and I will, I swear,
> Receive my heiress and cut off my hair![29]

The pun in that last line is typical of this burlesque, which carried the title of *Shylock; or The Merchant of Venice Preserved. An entirely new reading of Shakespeare, from an edition hitherto undiscovered by modern authorities, and which it is hoped may be received as the stray leaves of a Jerusalem Hearty-Joke.*

In a later burlesque performed in America by Christy's Minstrels,[30] the trivialisation of the Jew's villainy is represented in the punishment inflicted on him at the end of the performance:

> *(They all rush after him, bring him back, crying out, 'Toss him in a blanket.' They get a large canvas and toss him in the air until.)*

CURTAIN

Burlesque, of course, can work effectively only if the audience knows the original that is being sent up. In the case of Talfourd's *Shylock*, it is clear that, not only did London play-goers know Shakespeare's plot, they were also expected to recognise the text. Thus the following exchange:

SHYLOCK
Pay thrice the bond and let the Christian go.

PORTIA
Your pardon, Shylock, not exactly so,
The law has yet another hold on thee:
Fair play's a jewel, as the Jew'll see!

Here, the characteristic *jewel / Jew'll* word-play is embedded in a script which echoes Shakespeare's lines 'Pay the bond thrice / And let the Christian go' and 'The law hath yet another hold on you …'.[31]

While I am not claiming too many conscious influences at work here, it is nonetheless possible to pick out one line of descent in which the stage Jew over the centuries becomes less menacing and more comic. Such a genealogy might begin with Judas in the mystery plays (the 'unreformed' Jew, traditionally played in a red wig), take a route through Marlowe's Barabas and Shakespeare's Shylock, throw up the Jew of the burlesques, and then in the 20th century produce the comic anti-hero of Lionel Bart's *Oliver!*, dancing off into the sunset singing 'I'm Reviewing the Situation'.[32] But perhaps we should see the burlesques as actually representing a collateral branch of the family; so that there are now two lines of descent after Edmund Kean: one through Henry Irving and the legitimate theatre; the other through Talfourd's … *Hearty-Joke*, Christy's Minstrels and Lionel Bart, in which Shylock's villainy converts to roguishness and his punishment, if any, is token.

Act 2, scene 5: 'Jessica, my girl …'

Every fibre of his being is telling him to stay at home tonight, for there is some ill a-brewing towards his rest. But he knows he has to go out – not just to seal the bond, but to 'feed upon The prodigal Christian'. Why is he going? He was so adamant with Bassanio that he would do anything – buy and sell with them, talk with them, walk with them and so following … but on no account would he eat or drink or pray with them. Yet here he is, dressing up to go out. And here is Jessica, his daughter, not daring to press him to go, lest he might suspect something – though her planned elopement with a Christian is not anything that could ever have entered his mind – let alone that she would decamp with the best part of his money and jewels, including the precious turquoise, given to him by Leah when he was a bachelor – a ring he would not have parted with for a wilderness of monkeys …

So he hugs her and tenderly strokes her hand and kisses her as he reluctantly instructs her to lock every door, unable to let her go, it seems, in his almost paranoid obsession that she should keep away from the windows to avoid any glimpse of the debauched Christians' scheduled masque.

This is an oppressive love, however, and fittingly exhibits itself in front of the black tower of Shylock's prison-like house. But, playing the part of wife and mother in this widower's household, Jessica wraps her father up in his overcoat – a service, we feel, that she has performed many times before – and hastens him on his way. The sincerity of these apparently loving actions is infected by our knowledge that she is desperate to get him out of the house. And it is difficult to have much sympathy for this teenage rebel, hard to feel that 'our house is hell', when, as her father finally makes to leave, she pulls him back – and, experiencing a flicker of conscience, in the knowledge that this would be his last glimpse of her – gives him the most peremptory peck on the cheek. Clearly unaccustomed to such spontaneous demonstrations of affection, he emits a surprised and touched 'Oh!', before himself placing his finger-tips tenderly on her cheek and departing ...

When Philip Voss and Emma Handy played out that scene in 1997, it was after a series of rehearsal discussions in which Voss had come to excuse Shylock's behaviour towards Jessica as deriving from the absence of a mother's moderating influence.

Talking to me four weeks into rehearsals and just under six weeks from the first public performance,[33] he says: 'I don't know how my constraints are affecting her.' (Like a lot of actors, he often lapses in discussion into a mode of speaking about himself as though he were the character.) '... I'm doing it for her own Jewish good. But I hope we've found a way of showing, even in a short scene, the complex and loving relationship that we have.' Enunciating his thoughts very carefully – Voss thinks everything through and keeps a neatly written notebook of ideas on his approaches to the parts he plays – he goes on:

'We've sort of worked out – or decided – that Shylock's wife died about five years before – making Jessica, I think, about thirteen. To explain how Jessica has come to loathe her father so much, you need a certain amount of time for his oppressive behaviour to have affected her to that degree. Because, I mean, I see Shylock as a perfectly nice man; I don't see anything wrong with him at all. The reason that Jessica hates him, I think, is because he is oppressive, because he is a widower, because he has lost his wife, and that she is the woman in the house and he has just demanded too much of her, both in her religion and domestically. And then in every way he has absolutely fed off her, I think. And, if she's that age, she just wants to get away – the house *is* hell, because it's no fun ...'

Interpretations like this imply a shallow, immature and thoughtless Jessica, far removed from many portrayals, especially those from earlier centuries. In paintings by Robert Smirke in 1795 and Gilbert Stuart Newton in 1830,[34] Jessica is saintly in her patient forbearance, hand virtuously on heart in the Smirke, eyes modestly downcast in the Newton, as she receives the household keys. There is a difference in the two Shylocks, however. The earlier picture represents him as a half-crouching figure, as though about to spring, with a Mephisto-phelean beard and leather-thonged walking stick. By 1830 he has mellowed into an image of portly prosperity, though the speck of brilliant white in the piercing eye suggests that he is almost seeing through his daughter's modest acquiescence (see Figure 10).

Seeing Shylock as recently widowed is one way in which actors flesh out this character's history. David Calder, who played him in 1993, said: 'I've thought about him a lot. He has, for instance, no wife. Well, I feel she can have only recently died – that throws an enormous light on the bond between Jessica and her father.'[35] Henry Goodman (1999) also felt that it was easy to see why such a man, mourning the recently dead Leah, would impose intolerable burdens upon his daughter.

When I meet Goodman during rehearsals in his dressing-room at the National Theatre, there is still much to be decided about his Shylock, and the uncertainty gives an edge of anxiety to his observations. Everything he says is highly charged with energy, intensity, passion. Goodman decides that Leah has died within the past year. Early rehearsals, he says, 'completely affirmed my sense that he's living on his own without his wife'.[36] Many actors have bemoaned the few lines given to them in which to portray Shylock's relationship with his child. But when it came to performance in the Cottesloe just four weeks later, such was the dramatic power of the scenes we were able to observe – Jessica being chastised and slapped one minute (as, according to one reviewer, 'a shocking but pathetic expression of his anxious love'),[37] caressed and sung to the next – that it was possible to imagine the whole daily existence in the Jew's household. For this Jessica (sensitively portrayed by Gabrielle Jourdain, with 'the air of a refugee child, bewildered by the two worlds to which she belongs'),[38] the house was 'hell', not because of specific ill-treatment, but because of the incessant demands upon her to be both wife and daughter to Shylock, preparing his food according to strict dietary laws and participating in the regular, and highly emotional, services for the dead Leah.

It is natural, therefore, that a Shylock with a love of such intensity should be utterly destroyed by the loss of Jessica; and we feel his loss all the more powerfully if we have seen him actually witness her elopement.

This is what happened in Gregory Doran's 1997 production, in which Shylock ran into the raucous and nightmarish carnival which had modulated grotesquely from the same masque that he had watched as an entertainment laid on for his meal with Bassanio and Antonio. Apparently coming home after leaving the Christians, Voss's Shylock stumbled unwittingly into the obscene and drunken cavortings of the Christians' street party. Attempting without success to avoid the lunging pigs' heads, the old man was jostled and pushed around the stage, until, at a point when the goading was at its height, the music stopped and he suddenly saw his daughter, dressed improperly in boy's clothes and carried high on her lover's shoulders. Screaming her name, he was dragged into his house and spun around as it revolved in a nightmare sequence which saw him thrown from one wall to another as his daughter made her escape.

After Act 2, scene 6: 'Fled with a Christian!'

If, however, you had been in the stalls of the Lyceum in November 1879, you would have seen the great Henry Irving perform a similar moment like this:

*The elopement of Jessica and Lorenzo was then effected, in a gondola,
which moved smoothly away in the canal, and the scene became tumul-
tuous with a revel of riotous maskers, who sang, danced, frolicked, and
tumbled in front of Shylock's house, as though obtaining mischievous
pleasure in disturbing the neighborhood of the Jew's decorous dwelling.
Soon that clamorous rabble streamed away; there was a lull in the music,
and the grim figure of Shylock, his staff in one hand, his lantern in the
other, appeared on the bridge, where for an instant he paused, his seamed,
cruel face, visible in a gleam of ruddy light, contorted by a sneer, as he
listened to the sound of revelry dying away in the distance. Then he
descended the steps, crossed to his dwelling, raised his right hand, struck
twice upon the door with the iron knocker, and stood like a statue, waiting – while a slow-descending curtain closed in one of the most expressive
pictures that any stage has ever presented.*[39]

That account was by the theatre historian William Winter, one of
many observers to have noted the dramatic potency of the moment. As
a piece of stage business designed to convey all Shylock's loneliness,
humanity and – looking ahead – feelings of deep betrayal, it could
hardly have been bettered. It was, as Winter described it, 'an apex of perfect pathos'.[40] Indeed, it was copied in so many later interpretations of
the play that, when Oscar Asche left it out at Stratford in 1915, one local
reviewer complained that he was not following 'the usual tradition'.[41]

Irving's Shylock had been inspired by his vision of a Jew on a brief
visit to Tunis in the summer of 1879. Recalling the incident later,
Irving said:

I saw a Jew once, in Tunis, tear his hair and raiment, fling himself
in the sand, and writhe in a rage, about a question of money, –
beside himself with passion. I saw him again, self-possessed and
fawning; and again, expressing real gratitude for a trifling money
courtesy. He was never undignified until he tore at his hair and

flung himself down, and then he was picturesque; he was old, but erect, even stately, and full of resource. As he walked behind his team of mules he carried himself with the lofty air of a king. He was a Spanish Jew, – Shylock probably was of Frankfort; but Shakespeare's Jew was a type, not a mere individual: he was a type of the great, grand race, – not a mere Houndsditch usurer. He was a man famous on the Rialto; probably a foremost man in his synagogue – proud of his descent – conscious of his moral superiority to many of the Christians who scoffed at him, and fanatic enough, as a religionist, to believe that his vengeance had in it the element of a godlike justice …[42]

It is possible to see in this account the seeds of the shifting moods of Irving's subsequent creation, a man who can veer from being 'beside himself with passion' to 'self-possessed', from 'fawning' to 'stately'.[43] Equally, it reveals the Victorian fascination with the exotic 'other', but, more than this, a specific range of attitudes towards the Jew's exoticism, at once both admiring ('He was never undignified …') and patronising ('… and then he was picturesque.'). This complex set of sometimes contradictory attitudes towards Jews is not unlike that held by the producers of the earliest television documentaries about the Zulu or the Australian aborigine – and it is at the heart of the constantly shifting reinterpretations of Shylock through the last century and a half.

A particularly interesting detail of Irving's conversation with his friend Joseph Hatton is his description of Shakespeare's Jew as 'a type of the great, grand race'. It is easy to see how this romanticised perception could become the bedrock of a stage interpretation which would move the theatre historian A. B. Walkley to write in 1892:

It was the Jew idealised in the light of the modern Occidental reaction against the *Judenhetze*, a Jew already conscious of the

Spinozas, the Sidonias, the Disraelis, who were to issue from his loins.[44]

There was, of course, a quite different dimension to Irving's Jew. However much it reminded the audience of a wealthy Rothschild or a powerful Disraeli, it also aimed to evoke sympathy and understanding for an underdog, downtrodden and despised. If the portrayal fleetingly reflected prosperous and successful Jews, assimilated into the cultural and economic life of Victorian England, it also reminded us throughout of the abused and maltreated peoples from whom Shylock had sprung. This was undoubtedly a dimension which Irving held in the forefront of his mind. He called Shylock 'the type of a persecuted race',[45] a view consistent with opinions expressed in his book *The Drama* and with a performance which, as described by the critic J.C. Bulman, 'focused attention on questions of social morality ... – the rights accorded to aliens, the prejudices of those in power'.[46] And this is exactly the function that Shylock continues to serve today. Irving wrote:

> If you uphold the theatre honestly, liberally, frankly, and with discrimination, the stage will uphold in the future, as it has in the past, the literature, the manners, the morals, the fame, and the genius of our country.[47]

This is a salutary observation for anyone writing a theatre history of *The Merchant of Venice*. It confirms what Lichtenberg told us in the late 1700s: namely, that sensibilities about performing or watching Shakespeare's Jew were awoken long before the post-Holocaust era.

It would be a mistake, however, to assume, as some commentators have done, that Irving's historic performance of a semi-tragic and heroic Shylock was the model for all Shylocks over the next 50 years; or that the re-creation of Shakespeare's Jew as a sympathetic character would have a profound and lasting effect on audience sensibilities through the opening decades of the 20th century. Look, for example, at this comment by the critic of the London *Times* in 1919. Concluding a favourable review on the performance of the (Russian Jewish) actor Maurice Moscovitch, he writes: '... this Shylock is a terror. We do not excuse, but begin to understand, pogroms.'[48]

Comments like that – on a Shylock described as 'rather greasy, snuffling, with ... not a shred of dignity' – are not easy to swallow in the knowledge of what happened in Europe 20 years later; nor is this report of one of the performances of the celebrated actor-manager Sir Herbert Beerbohm Tree, in which the reviewer expresses satisfaction that

> ... 1,600 county council school children should rise as one and yell derision at the baffled Shylock. There was no sated indifference, no mild depreciating enjoyment among these guests ... and they screamed (it is the only word) with laughter at Gratiano's Jew-baiting. Indeed they were a delightful audience ...[49]

Similarly troubling is this observation by critic St John Ervine on Lewis Casson's Shylock in 1927. According to Hubert Griffith, Casson played the Jew in 'a nose that must have weighed nearly half a pound' and 'made him filthy and unkempt'.[50] This description does scarce justice to the reality, as evidenced in the *Daily Sketch*'s photographs which show a character who is little short of a monstrous grotesque. St John Ervine, describing Casson's Shylock as looking like 'an old clo'man from the Palestine Road in Manchester', goes on to say:

> Mr Ewer wrote a verse which runs thus: 'How odd of God to choose the Jews.' *That may be*, but such a choice cannot be made without enriching the chosen in some measure, and it is a prime defect of Mr Casson's performance that he does not for a single moment let us see that this humiliated man, Shylock, whose most

> sacred feelings are violated by that contemptible baggage, his
> daughter, is a member of a race which was once divinely-selected,
> *even if the selection was subsequently repented.*[51] [*My italics.*]

Looked at from our contemporary perspective, these anti-Semitic
comments raise troubling questions about audience attitudes and
response in performances of *The Merchant of Venice* during the early
decades of the 20th century.

Making moral judgements about performances and reviews from
a past age is a precarious activity, of course. Perhaps it is best simply
to take these critical responses as a reminder that no Shylocks have
been created in a social and political vacuum. In Germany in 1922,
for example (a year in which there were three productions of *The
Merchant of Venice* in London),[52] Hitler was writing that if he came to
power 'the annihilation of Jews will be my first and foremost task';[53]
and that was three years after the critic of *The Times* had announced
that watching Moscovitch's Shylock caused him to 'begin to understand', if not actually 'excuse', pogroms.

Act 3, scene 1: 'Let me say amen betimes, lest the devil cross my prayer, for here he comes in the likeness of a Jew …'

*A squat little man in black scurries into view, deeply agitated, fidgety –
on the edge, in fact. His daughter, his beloved Jessica, has been abducted
by, of all things, a Christian – worse, a friend of Antonio's, that same
Antonio to whom he, Shylock, had loaned three thousand ducats, asking
no interest in return. His black gabardine is disordered, his yarmulke a
tad off-centre, and we are inclined to laugh at his comic face with its
perennially plaintive expression.*

*He spots two of Antonio's friends, Salerio and Solanio (or is one of them
Salerino? – anyway, 'the Salads') and, playground bullies as they are, they*

bait him on his misfortunes. Determined to keep offering his jocular friendship to the Christians until it is absolutely certain that they will reject it, he plays down the force of his accusations:

'You knew', he says, pointing a finger as though to two naughty schoolboys caught scrumping, 'none so vell as you ...' (his accent stronger now) 'off my daughter's flight'.

Intent on not provoking these people, he even joins in with the Salads' laughter at his grief. But he can't keep up this forced jocularity for long and, when one of them grabs his balls ('Out upon it, old carrion, rebels it at these years?'), he squirms angrily away ...

This is Warren Mitchell, digging back into his own Jewish roots to give us a Shylock for the 1980 BBC Television Shakespeare who looks, moves and sounds 'alien'.

And you might think you would be safe in offering the public 'an ethnic Jew ... resolutely unassimilated, antagonistic to the proprieties of bourgeois Venetian behaviour'[54] if you could point out to any detractors that not only the actor, but the director (Jack Gold) and the producer (Jonathan Miller) were all Jews (or, in Miller's case, from a Jewish family). A team like that, you might feel, could not be accused of anti-Semitism when trying to portray Shylock as 'authentically Jewish'.

But you'd be wrong. The result of such a collaboration in this case was a performance which, for many, bordered on caricature and, especially in the United States, became the cause of some controversy. And a major problem was that 'Mitchell harked back not to the Elizabethan stage Jew ... but to the more recent stage "Yid" of music-hall reviews and vaudeville skits. This heritage made it hard to take Shylock's villainy seriously'[55] and easy to see him as merely conforming to the stale old stereotypes.

Act 3, scene 1: 'Let him look to his bond.'

The mistake Salerio and Solanio make is to ask him about Antonio: 'But tell us, do you hear whether Antonio have had any loss at sea or no?'

They must know what a provocatively insensitive question it is. He rounds on them furiously, cursing the Christian Antonio as 'A bankrupt, a prodigal, who dare scarce show his head on the Rialto, a beggar that was used to come' – he gestures mockingly – 'so smug upon the mart!'

Then, suddenly overcome with tiredness and misery, he leans on the rail of the bridge overlooking the canal. Studying him from behind, we are struck by his stooped, defeated posture and we observe the now shabby costume – he was once such a sharp dresser – and how the absence of his frock-coat reveals a creased shirt and black bank-clerk sleeve-protectors ...

We have become aware of a bell tolling ominously in the distance – a funeral knell? – and after three chimes, we sense Shylock's body stiffening, as though with a great shock ... For, as he slowly turns to face us, his features vividly express the appalled realisation that he has it in his power to make the Christian suffer ... Now comes the moment that will change Shylock's life ...

He stares right through us, eyes wide open and fixed on nothing. As the idea begins to take shape in his mind, his left hand moves up abstractedly to touch the lower lip of his slightly open mouth, clenches slightly and then slowly drops as he issues his terrifying warning: 'Let him look to his bond.'

It has simply never occurred to him before. But now, within seconds, it has become his sole reason for living. The Christians have stolen his daughter, Antonio was in on their plot, now Antonio can be punished. He comes down the steps like a drunk, almost jabbering in his mounting excitement —

*'He was wont to call me usurer. Let him look to his bond. He was wont
to lend out money for a Christian courtesy. Let him look to his bond!'*

That was Laurence Olivier in one of the great stage moments,
captured for television in 1973.[56] Olivier's Shylock was about as sympathetic as it could possibly be, and this moment of realisation was at
the heart of an interpretation which was at pains to point out that
Shylock turns bad only after the Christians have run off with his
beloved Jessica. As an interpretation it was hardly new – in fact it owed
much to that performance by the great Victorian actor (and first theatrical knight) Sir Henry Irving, given almost a hundred years earlier.
But it was a towering performance by Olivier, and thanks to its world-
wide television showing, it became the definitive Shylock of its
generation.

Jonathan Miller's *Merchant of Venice*, in which Olivier's Shylock
became a late-19th-century financier, had not been by any means the
first interpretation of this play to be set in a period other than
Shakespeare's own. When the Russian director Theodore Komisarjevsky planned his 1933 production (to be performed in the new
theatre at Stratford),[57] he portrayed the Christians as pampered
modern capitalists ignorant of the Depression, judging that his interpretation might be enhanced by such a dimension of topicality.

Komisarjevsky's decision is significant inasmuch as it demonstrates that productions of the play from the mid-1930s to the late
1940s had the option of topical reference if they chose to take it. That
no major production during that period did choose to take it – by
presenting unambiguous parallels between the treatment of Shylock
and the persecution of the Jews under Hitler – is one of the more
perplexing features of this challenging play's stage history.

It is a sad and puzzling fact that many of the major productions
of *The Merchant of Venice* during the 1930s and 40s could hardly have

been less topical in their presentation of the conflict between the Jews and the Christians had they tried. Gielgud, for example, directing the play at the Old Vic in the same year as Komisarjevsky's Stratford production, deliberately shifted the emphasis of the plot away from Shylock (played by Malcolm Keen), making Portia the centre of a play which was studiedly unrealistic in design.[58] Many later productions sound merely bland, such as that at the New Theatre in 1943:

> Here … is a treatment which in style gives the public what it has never ceased to want – a chance to enjoy the story as a story, with its fairy-tale romance …[59]

Others, such as Donald Wolfit's in 1938, seem in retrospect quite remarkable for the savagery of their interpretation at a time when they might have been expected to be wary of charges of – at the very least – insensitivity:

> … [Wolfit's] Shylock is then the kind of Jew whose humiliation an Elizabethan audience would probably have revelled in, the very Jew the bare plot seems to require, one who, as he leaves the court, spits in the face of Antonio …[60]

In many ways even more extraordinary, when we consider the political context from which they arose, are portrayals which emphasised Shylock's physical repulsiveness. Most striking in this respect are Mark Dignam's Shylock, in a 1935 production 'purged of its Irvingesque sentiment and Shakespearean humanity'[61] and Gielgud's, performed in the year preceding the outbreak of war. Both of these recall vividly those German propaganda posters which sought to represent Jews as skulking rats:

> [Dignam's] Shylock, a dirty, down-at-heel moneylender in a bowler hat several sizes too big for him, has no shred of dignity

left, and whether bewailing the loss of his ducats and his daughter or pleading the cause of a common humanity he is never more than a grotesque little man in a temper.[62]

[Gielgud's] … Shylock: puling, remorseless, toothless – utterly revolting in the remnants of a ginger wig …[63]

[Gielgud's] appearance throughout was extraordinary – gummy, blinking eyes, that suggested some nasty creature of the dark …[64]

The theatre's completely apolitical stance on Shylock during the 1940s is bewildering; especially so given the fact that theatre critics in the popular newspapers commonly alluded to Jewish persecution when reviewing the play. For example, the phrases 'Jew-baiters' and 'Jew-baiting' appeared frequently to describe the Christians in their role as tormentors of Shylock, typified by these three examples from *The Times* in different years: 'If [an Elizabethan] retained his taste for a little Jew-baiting he might have laughed uproariously at the despairing rage of the crafty alien usurer …' (26 July 1932); 'Jew-baiters these Christians might be …' (15 April 1936); and 'a Jew baited by the Venetian riff-raff …' (17 February 1944).

Moreover, review comments like the following make it perfectly clear that theatre critics could see the topicality of Shylock's persecution, even if the productions themselves were determined to ignore it:

FEMINISM AND JEW-BAITING
Modern Mr. Shakespeare
… Though set in medieval Venice it is full of modern interest. Feminism: the leading woman is a lawyer. Anti-Semitism: there are Jew-baiting street scenes … [65]

'The Merchant of Venice', which was produced by Mr Iden Payne, the Festival director, at Stratford-on-Avon Memorial Theatre, yesterday, is one of the most-played and most popular of the Shakespearean dramas.

That fact is somewhat remarkable in these days, when Jew-baiting has ceased to be the sport of gentlemen. ... One is forced to the conclusion that in the 'Merchant of Venice', though Shakespeare started his play as an anti-Semite, before he had finished it he found himself with his tongue in both cheeks.[66]

At a time when Jews are being driven to mass-suicide by unsurpassed brutalities, the spectacle of Shylock's baiting becomes almost unbearable.[67]

There can be few reviews from the period which so eloquently testify to the fact that critics were as alert to the play's topicality as producers and directors were blind to it.

Added to these theatre reviews was a whole series of prominent newspaper articles throughout the 1930s and 40s which drew the public's attention to the link between Shakespeare's play and the plight of the Jews in Germany. These articles were of three kinds. The first catalogued the Nazis' determination to establish and define their relationship to Britain's greatest dramatist; the second expressed the growing unease among the Jews in Britain concerning the study of *The Merchant of Venice* in schools; the third took the form of a series of forceful reminders in the newspapers, by journalists and correspondents alike, of the obvious link between Shylock's 'Hath not a Jew ...?' and the persecution of his people by the Nazis.

Throughout the 1930s, articles such as the following are commonly to be found in the British press:

Shakespeare 'Especially Dear' to Nazis – Berlin, Monday
'Nordic thought and Nordic character are stamped through and through the creations of Shakespeare, but, in addition, no one is more definitely Germanic.'

This is the conclusion of an article by Herr Thilo von Trothe, an official of the Foreign Dept of the Nazi Party, who refers to the poet's 'ancient, heroic, warlike view of life.'

Shakespeare, he says is 'especially dear to us of the present day who are experiencing the Nordic rebirth'.[68]

Wilhelm Shakespeare

Not for the first time, Germany has acclaimed Shakespeare as 'a true German'. He appears to be, if anything, rather truer than before.

Professor Hecht pointed out yesterday that 'the more heroic ideals' of Nazi Germany make it possible to view the poet's personality in quite a new light.

I would give a lot to see a production of 'The Merchant of Venice' in Berlin today.[69]*

In many respects the last sentence is the most interesting, one of many comments which show that, even if the theatre itself were not acknowledging the obvious links between the behaviour of the Nazis and Shylock's tormentors, journalists in the popular newspapers were. The German obsession with Shakespeare was, in fact, frequently reported upon.† In this report in the *Evening Standard*, the reader is

---

*Similar articles appeared in the *Daily Telegraph* (26 April 1934) and the *Morning Post* (27 April 1934), which reported Professor Hecht as having claimed that Shakespeare – the 'greatest poet of the Germanic race' – was 'In the realm of the theatre ... as German as the German classic dramatists themselves'.

†In February 1936, the *Manchester Guardian* commented that Dr Goebbels was to make a decision concerning the 'Proper Translation' of Shakespeare, the choice to be made between Schlegel's 18th-century version and a modern one by Hans Rothe (*Manchester Guardian*, 8 February 1936). The year before, the *Daily Express* had informed its readers that 21 theatres in Germany were currently staging Shakespeare's works and that no fewer than 46 productions of his plays were to be presented in the 1935–6 season (*Daily Express*, 23 September 1935).

obliged to consider the wider implications of the Nazi philosophy and its proponents' interest in Shakespeare:

Shakespeare As 'Germanic Poet' – Weimar, Wednesday

'If Shakespeare's plays are performed with success in Moscow and Harlem, New York's negro quarter,' declared Professor Werner Deetjen, president of the German Shakespeare Society, in his opening speech to this year's meeting of the society at Weimar, 'it is because they misunderstand this great Germanic poet.'

… Professor Guenther endeavoured to show how Shakespeare, in his attitude to the problem of choosing a companion in marriage, laid stress 'not on numerical fertility, but on the qualitative breeding of a finer race,' and compared him in this respect to Nietzsche, the German philosopher of the 'Superman'.[70]*

Moreover, as Nazi oppression becomes more widely reported, so the perspective of *The Merchant of Venice* is more commonly invoked:

Shakespeare Verboten

The latest restriction is that Jewish booksellers must not sell Shakespeare …

… If the Nazis want to be true to their quaint principles, they should compel Jews to sell copies of 'The Merchant of Venice' as an additional humiliation.[71]

On the same day, under a headline which read: 'Shakespeare not to be sold by Jews. New "Aryan" books restriction. Nazi campaign to force emigration', the *Daily Telegraph* reported:

---

* In the following year, the same newspaper carried a similar report, under the headline 'Weimar and the Fuehrer': '… I do not think that the Fuehrer himself has as yet referred to Shakespeare in his speeches. But his lieutenant, Dr Goebbels, has given the Bard the Nazi OK. Shakespeare, he once said, had more in him of the Teuton than of the modern Englishman.' (7 November 1938)

... The latest restriction concerns Jewish booksellers. Under an order which came into force at the beginning of this month, they may only sell books by Jewish authors and serve only Jewish customers, who must present written evidence of their racial origin.

This item was ominously linked to a report that Jews were now unable to leave the country unless they were emigrating.

While the Nazis were busy accommodating Shakespeare to their philosophies and reshaping him for their own particular ends, British Jews were similarly, but more painfully, coming to the conclusion that *The Merchant of Venice* did not and could not exist in a political and social vacuum. The absence of debate on the stage seems even more remarkable when we read an article such as the following:

SHYLOCK AS HERO
Jewish Complaint of Misinterpretation
Was Shylock a hero or a villain? The question, which has been canvassed for some years among literary critics, has now been brought forward by the Board of Deputies of British Jews as a matter which affects them wherever 'The Merchant of Venice' (or Mary Lamb's story of the play) is taught in schools.

It is urged by the Board that the 'unsympathetic' interpretation of the character creates a prejudice in the minds of schoolchildren against Jews ...[72]*

When seen in the context of the reports which were at this time

* The article went on: 'No objection is taken to the play, the greatness of which is recognised, but it is felt that, either the play should not be taught in schools, or that the character of Shylock should be "interpreted" by the teacher in such a way that the dignity and nobility of the Jew should not be obscured by the less pleasant traits of his character. It may be remembered that in the opinion of some critics, Shylock, by contrast with the other male characters, emerges as a heroic figure. No action is at present contemplated by the Board but the position is being carefully watched. If necessary, they will protest to the Board of Education.'

coming out of Germany, it is not difficult to appreciate the Board's anxiety. It is impossible to know how individual teachers were handling the play in schools; but what is certain is that the British newspaper-reading public was repeatedly made aware of the connection between Jewish persecution and Shylock's famous plea, especially in popular and patriotic publications such as the *Daily Express*:

The Jews

Hitler's treatment of the Jews calls to mind the following lines: 'Hath not a Jew eyes? Hath not a Jew hands, organs, dimensions, senses, affections, passions, fed with the same food, hurt with the same weapons, subject to the same diseases … as a Christian is? If you prick us, do we not bleed? If you tickle us, do we not laugh? If you poison us, do we not die? And if you wrong us, shall we not revenge?'

These words of Shakespeare are the only comments necessary on the Nazi persecutions.

Edinburgh – S. Marcus

Jews

This renewed attack on Jews in Germany, not because of any individual offence but in blind antagonism to a race, is merely bestial. 'I am a Jew. Hath not a Jew eyes …' [etc.] *The Merchant of Venice*.

Heil Hitler!

Hitler, studying Shakespeare, must have picked on this bit:

Hath not a Jew eyes? Hath not a Jew hands, organs, dimensions, senses, affections, passions, fed with the same food, hurt with the same weapons, subject to the same diseases … as a Christian is? If you prick us, do we not bleed? For Herr Loeffler, Nazi leader, announces that persons spreading the idea that Jewish blood is not permissible for transfusion are guilty of damaging the health of the people since it results in unnecessary restrictions when quick action is essential. The blood, of course, becomes Aryan on transfusion.[73]

The writer's grimly appropriate juxtaposition of '… do we not bleed?' with a report about transfusions is matched only by the journalist who chose to quote Portia's 'take thou thy pound of flesh' speech in an article on meat rationing.[74]

The link between *The Merchant of Venice* on the wartime British stage and Hitler's persecution of the Jews is like that of Conan Doyle's dog that did not bark in the night – significant because of its absence. And it has more than one ironic coda. The first is that, although, as we have seen, Shakespeare's plays were widely performed in the Third Reich, *The Merchant of Venice* was not; for, as Wilhelm Hortmann points out, there was actually a sharp drop in the number of performances: from an average of 20 or 30 productions a year to less than a third of that, reaching an all-time low of only three productions in 1939 – and not a single production of the play in Berlin during the whole Nazi period.[75] Why was this? Was the German theatre consciously exercising restraint, motivated by shame and revulsion at their government's policies? Or, conversely, were they concerned that even the most grotesquely loaded portrayal of Shylock would have to include the dangerously subversive 'If you prick us, do we not bleed'? Gerwin Strobl offers a grimmer explanation for the absence of *The Merchant* from the Nazi stage:

> Apart from being not nearly anti-Semitic enough – Marlowe's *Jew of Malta*, largely unknown in Germany, was suggested as a 'more powerful' alternative – there was the matter of Shylock's daughter marrying an Aryan youth. In deference to 'contemporary sensitivities', Jessica tended either to become an adopted (Aryan) child bound for bliss in Lorenzo's arms, or stayed Jewish (and celibate).[76]

It is easier to see why parts of the German population might have been opposed to performances of *The Merchant of Venice* immediately after the fall of the Third Reich. For example, while the Folk House in Stepney was celebrating the end of the war with a Yiddish production of the play,[77] it was being banned in Frankfurt

> … as a result of threats and protests from Jewish and Communist quarters, who claimed that 'Shylock cannot be portrayed on the stage without re-awakening anti-Semitism.'[78]

The Stepney production, by virtue of its Yiddishness, must have contained at least some implicit allusion to recent history. But, for the mainstream British theatre, it was as though nothing had happened, as witness this Stratford Shylock in 1947:

> The Jew of Mr John Ruddock is like some blandly smiling archimandrite showing a party of foreign visitors over his monastery … and when he ventures to ask if a Jew has not passions like other men, we can only suppose that he has not …[79]

And it was not as though there had been some tacit agreement to keep Shakespeare free from the taint of politicisation. In 1944, as we have seen, Olivier's film of *Henry V* had been prefaced by a dedication to 'the Commandos and Airborne Troops', and was, two years later, being shown in Berlin to 1,800 students and school-children as part of a political 're-education' programme. It seems strange that a version of *Henry V* could have been made as virtually an institutionalised part of the war effort, while productions of *The Merchant of Venice*, even after pictures of the concentration camps had appeared on cinema screens throughout the land, remained doggedly silent about the greatest atrocity in the history of the 20th century.

Grotesque and repellent Shylocks remained the norm throughout the 1950s. Of Robert Helpmann's Shylock, for example, the critics wrote:

The small, neat Helpmann features were completely submerged in a melancholy black-haired Hebraic make-up – tortured eyes, red, sensuous lips, and the noblest nose in all Jewry …

… this Helpmann Jew … is like a sad, bedraggled vulture – crook-back, hook-nosed, grotesque. Malice peers from sunken eyes, defiance yowls from twisted lips …[80]

And this an interpretation from an actor who was himself a Jew – the first to play the role on the Stratford stage, in fact. Michael Redgrave's interpretation was of a 'slobbering, hideous old Jew …', 'greasy, hissing, hiccoughing …',[81] a preview of which the actor had given to a visiting journalist the day before the first performance:

The players were not in costume, but in his dressing room Mr Redgrave put on his wig and beard and a cleverly constructed nose and let me have a glimpse of the Jew my colleagues will see tomorrow night …[82]

According to a selection of reviewers, Emlyn Williams's 'repulsive, Fagin-like Shylock' was 'a matted and slightly disgusting old figure', 'unwashed, leering, greasy', 'insect-like', 'a kind of revengeful, Hebraic gnome', a portrayal summarised by one headline as 'Squalid – But the Real Shylock'.[83]

A photograph in *The Observer* shows that Eric Porter's Shylock was given bags under the eyes and a long hooked nose,[84] while Emrys James depended for his repulsiveness less upon make-up than saliva. Described by one critic as '… barefoot, robed in old curtains, with a mouthful of spittle …',[85] James was 'a medieval Jewish stereotype in a large, baggy kaftan, with grey ringlets spilling from beneath his skull cap'.[86] The same reviewer went on:

This is a Jew straight out of the Penny Dreadful magazines, literally salivating at the thought of his pound of Christian flesh.

In accord with their attempt at physical repulsiveness, most of these actors elected to convey what they saw as the racial origins of the character by adopting an appropriately grotesque manner of speech and gesture. In this, they seem to have drawn upon the still familiar tradition of comic stage Jews. Of Helpmann's Shylock, the reviewers observed:

> Certain stock stagey tricks of Jewish speech and gesture crept in – the ponderous lisp, the extravagant shrug …

> … as played by Robert Helpmann, this was an unimpressive figure, with a rolling eye, a prodigal indulgence in formalised gesture, an extravagant make-up and a delivery which suggested the raconteur rather than the actor.[87]

Writing of Redgrave's delivery, the critic of the *Evesham Journal* offers the following attempt at a phonetic transcription: '"Ugh! what zees Christians are … I will buy wiz you …" etc.',[88] and somewhat surprisingly refers to this as the actor's 'skilfully accented voice'. Emlyn Williams and Emrys James are described respectively as 'talking something between a Welsh lilt and a Hebraic lisp' and perpetrating 'strange oscillations between stage Jew and Welsh preacher'. James is also guilty of 'plenty of "Oi – yoi – yoi" noises and low, throaty giggles', which mannerism, interestingly, is apparently enough to establish him in the eyes of the reviewer as 'a stage villain, in fact'.[89]

Almost all the portrayals from Helpmann to James were founded upon a system of well established signs which audiences could be relied upon to read without difficulty, and were predicated upon a logic which – however much the directors might have denied it – appeared to go like this: villains are repulsive in appearance; Jews lisp and shrug and have matted hair, hooded eyes, hooked noses and full lips; Jews are therefore villains. That this was a common train of thought is testified to by the critic who wrote about Emlyn Williams's interpretation:

> As portrayed by Mr Williams, Shylock was villainous and even repulsive in appearance … A cringing Jew … A whining cur …[90]

Here he inadvertently speaks for many of his colleagues when he damningly links his idea of 'a cringing Jew' with villainy and physical repulsiveness. This craven surrender to sloppy thinking and the distressing dependence upon stereotyping are – to say the least – surprising, given the time in which they prevailed.

One reviewer pertinently asked of Emlyn Williams's portrayal ('repulsive' … 'disgusting-looking' … 'squalid'): 'Why must Shylock so often look dirty and bedraggled?'[91] Not one critic noted that the same actor wore a prominent Star of David on his chest, which suggests that, even though the connections with recent history had been made by the designer, the performer's portrayal failed to convey them. In the case of Redgrave, the actor had even visited Holland prior to his performance, a country whose Jewish population had experienced terrible suffering only a few years before, and he was said to be 'basing his portrayal on some of the Jews he met in Amsterdam'.[92] How this personal contact encouraged him to portray a 'slobbering, hideous old Jew' is hard to imagine. So unpleasant was the portrayal, argued the critic of the *Daily Herald*, that 'he could never put the performance on the screen, for America would ban it'.[93]

OK for Britain, though. Five years before this, the American Legion of Decency had demanded that 40 minutes be cut from Olivier's film of *Hamlet*,[94] and in 1949 the New York Board of Education was threatened with legal action if it refused to ban *Oliver Twist* and *The Merchant of Venice* from its schools. Both were alleged by Joseph Goldstein, a former New York magistrate, to be anti-Semitic, inculcating 'bitter hatred and malice against American citizens of the

Jewish faith' and instilling in children 'an unwholesome prejudice and hatred against the Jews'.[95]

Yet the ability of British actors to dissociate the portrayal of Shylock from its wider contemporary context seems not only to have been accepted by critics, but even applauded. One reviewer, commenting on Helpmann's 'thoroughly satisfying villain' of a Shylock in 1948, congratulated the actor on succeeding in

> ... convincing a modern audience that this is what Shakespeare meant. No mean feat, for recent events in Europe and the many excellences of more sympathetic Shylocks have obscured the fact that Shakespeare's Jew is very far indeed from the dignified martyr that some actors would have him.[96]

It seems to me extraordinary that, at a time when the topicality of other plays was being recognised and translated into theatrical reality,* not one critic thought it relevant to point out that Helpmann was himself a Jew; and that he should be praised for allowing his interpretation of Shakespeare's Shylock to remain uninfluenced by contemporary history and by the enormity of 'recent events in Europe'.

Puzzled by this apparent dent in the reputation of British actors as 'the abstract and brief chronicles of the time', my explorations lead me to the offices of The King's Fund, off London's Bond Street, to meet Rabbi Julia Neuberger. She is unsurprised by the fact that the 1950s theatre did not make the link between Shylock and the

---

*Examples include the 1948 *Coriolanus* at the Old Vic ('Topical Shakespeare', *Sunday Express*, 4 April 1948) and the 1949 modern-dress *Julius Caesar* at the same theatre, of which the *Times* reviewer wrote: 'Recent hard experience disposes us to regard all things political with eager and anxious interest.' (20 September 1949) Much later (writing about the 1965 RSC production) a reviewer does refer to 'Shakespeare's Venetian *Herrenvolk*' (the reviewer's italics), but the use of this term does not seem to have been inspired by an interpretation which asked the audience to recall Nazi persecutions.

Holocaust, recollecting that her own mother, a refugee from Nazi Germany, didn't talk about the fact until 1995:

> 'I don't think that the real consciousness of horror actually per-colated for quite a long time … Those who survived came here and just got on with their lives. It took a lot of time for people to speak … I think you're expecting a 1990s/2000 reaction at a time when, in a sense, it was almost covered over. Even people who'd lived through it blanketed it …'[97]

But the contrast with Germany is again instructive; there, throughout the 1950s and 60s, there was a predominance of noble Shylocks in the Irving mould – 'expiation Shylocks', as they came to be called – who reflected national feelings of guilt and satisfied a deep need for making moral amends.[98]

One actor did not remain uninfluenced by the Holocaust, and did not play Shylock either. On 16 January 1960, an article by Orson Welles appeared in the *Morning Post*, carrying the headline: 'Why I won't play Shylock … at any rate not just now.' Welles's testament has a tendency to self-dramatisation and he admits his occasional pomp-osity; many would say that its major conclusions are also flawed. But it is worth our attention as it provides the contemporary perspective that actors from John Gielgud in 1938 through to Emrys James in 1971 – all with their villainous and physically repulsive Shylocks – appear not to have taken.

Welles introduces his article with the fact that he had expected to be playing his 'dream part' at that moment in London, but that the current 'global fever of anti-Semitism' had caused him to abandon the project. He goes on:

> Certainly our own particular plans for the theatre have no impor-tance whatsoever. But perhaps the reasons forcing me to change them do involve some issues worth talking about.

Suggesting that the box-office is not the only criterion by which we should judge the appropriateness of a particular play, Welles acknowledges that, in cancelling his production, he is hardly making a 'brave blow for freedom'; but he does believe that the media attention on his performance, successful or otherwise, would be damaging:

> In this case there would be pictures of me made up as Shylock – a picture of a ghetto Jew ... The picture of a Jew to be published just now is not Shylock. The Jewish story to be told just now is not the one about the pound of flesh. Not so long ago, 6,000,000 Jews were murdered. I think I know what Shakespeare would have felt about that story. I only wish he were alive to write it.

Welles's conclusions might be questioned. He could, for example, have elected to proceed with the production and play the part for sympathy, as Olivier was to do ten years later.* A cynic might also suggest that he is putting a moral gloss on an economic decision. But none of that invalidates his reasoning for not coming before the public as 'a ghetto Jew', and it throws into relief the concomitant puzzle of why so many of his fellow actors did.

Act 3, scene 3: 'I will have my bond!'

The figures have plainly all been walking in the same direction, but now Shylock turns back and his out-thrust arm halts the pleading Antonio in mid-step. The swathes of his sober black gabardine contrast vividly with the merchant's extravagant scarlet and nicely pleated white ruff.

'I'll have my bond', he shouts, 'I will not hear thee speak'.

---

* Welles did, in fact, make a film of *The Merchant of Venice* in 1969, a year before Olivier's stage performance; but the theft of two reels prevented its release. See Pamela Mason, 'Orson Welles and Filmed Shakespeare', in *The Cambridge Companion to Shakespeare on Film*, p. 184.

And, within a second, he will be gone into his house, leaving the hand-cuffed merchant to the gaoler waiting ominously in a deep and gloomy shadow which portends Antonio's grim fate. The Christian's overdressed companion Salerio stands, frustrated by his powerlessness, beneath an open upstairs window ... an unlocked casement which reminds us of Jessica's flight and Shylock's losses.

Why did the artist Richard Westall decide to paint over his original background before completing this painting in 1795 (Figure 9)?[99] Possibly because the first-version dramatic outlines of the Basilica San Marco, the Libreria Vecchia and the Campanile would have detracted from the drama of this encounter, and have risked overwhelming the figures, who are surely more effectively set in the street before Shylock's house. So that we can imagine that, within a second, he will have slammed the door in the Christian's face, leaving him in the hands of the shady gaoler. It is a powerful moment and the scene is perfectly set for the trial in the Doge's palace.

Act 4, scene 1: 'I pray you, give me leave to go from hence ...'

By the time he arrives at the Duke's court he has made a pact with God, and enters the room cold and committed.[100] *The scene which follows is painful to watch, morally harrowing. 'Shylock listens to Portia intently, for a good Jew ... wants to believe in due process; and you sense that he has always wanted to be spoken to, and reasoned with, like this, by Christians.'*[101]

Shylock seems almost visibly shaken and moved by this intense and persuasive Portia. Not only does she speak this religious man's language, but, for Shylock, it is as though his wife is sitting next to him, saying 'Be reasonable'. For an instant you feel that he is capable of change; but the moment passes; and, when the loyal and patient Tubal has finally had enough, and makes a dignified and disapproving exit, and Shylock cries:

'I have a daughter: Would that any of the stock of Barabas
Had been her husband rather than a Christian!'

— you know that it's too late.

Tidily, clinically, he ties an apron round his waist. It's a simple domestic action – he must have seen Leah do it ten thousand times, and he doesn't want his suit to be splashed and stained – but for Portia, watching him with a desperate intensity, it provides the answer … Of course. It's all about blood …

'Tarry, a little …'

Defeated, and in a moment of terrible denial, Shylock throws his yarmulke into the empty pan of the scales and quietly leaves. There is no physical collapse or harrowing off-stage scream, so no one can predict what fate awaits him. But he leaves the court thinking: 'It's my fault and God has taught me a lesson and if Leah had been here it would have been different …'. He knows too that he will now be what he, the outsider, worked so hard not to be: an outcast.

For those who remain, things will never be the same. Even Salerio quits the court, unable to accept what he has just witnessed; and no one present at the subsequent Belmont frolics can quite forget Shylock, when, accompanied by a rumble of thunder, Jessica sings the lament taught to her by her now broken father.

Watching the famous trial scene enacted in this way by Henry Goodman (with Derbhle Crotty as Portia)[102] is when you realise that Shylock's story is perhaps, after all, a tragedy; one in which we are confronted with the question, in Goodman's own words: 'What should we value in life?'

Having talked to Goodman only a few weeks into rehearsals, I decide to go back, now that the production is running, and ask him about the experience of taking the role of Shylock before the National Theatre audience. As one of a fairly select band of Jewish actors who have played the part (others include Robert Helpmann, Warren Mitchell, David Suchet, Antony Sher and Dustin Hoffman), Goodman says that he had for a long while resisted taking on 'this quintessentially Jewish role'. As a Jew, and the son of parents who wanted above all to 'fit in', Goodman understands alienation and feels that the great challenge for him in playing Shylock is to ensure that

> '... there's a real sense of a culture and a life off-stage ... I wanted to get the sense of a man who reads Hebrew all day long, who speaks Yiddish at home, for whom English is a second language ...'

I ask Goodman about Patrick Stewart's observations concerning 'playing the inconsistencies' in Shylock.[103] Stewart had approached the part

> ... With the belief that, if you played all the inconsistencies, when the final inconsistency slotted into place like a piece of a jigsaw puzzle, then you would no longer have an inconsistency but a complete and wonderfully colourful and complex whole ... Instead of getting all the inconsistencies, putting them in a pot, stirring them up, making a blend of them and playing the blend, from the beginning to the end ...[104]

Goodman replies: 'That's what I'm in the middle of ... If the audience can love him and hate him, understand him, then not understand him ... then you've got him.' Goodman – the greatest Shylock of modern times, in my opinion – unquestionably got him.

Set in the 1930s, the Trevor Nunn *Merchant* explicitly addressed anti-Semitism as a central issue – if not *the* central issue – of the play. But, even without period settings of this kind, almost every major production in recent years has re-opened the debate about whether the play is indeed anti-Semitic.

In 1984 the Royal Shakespeare Company staged *The Merchant of Venice* with Ian McDiarmid as Shylock.[105] William Frankel, recalling having studied the play in a class at school where he was the only Jew, asked whether Jews should have to go on suffering 'this old infamy'. As Frankel saw it, McDiarmid played the part

> ... as it might have been in Shakespeare's time – comic, villainous and avaricious, cruel and insolent in success, servile in defeat – everything, in fact, apart from the hooked nose and devil's costume.[106]

In so doing, he argued, McDiarmid had – however unwittingly – based his interpretation upon modern Jewish stereotypes.

Frankel felt strongly that McDiarmid's 'Jewish' portrayal challenged the reticence that Jews normally displayed when it came to arguing that Shakespeare's play was anti-Semitic. As his argument is particularly compelling when attached to careless interpretations such as McDiarmid's, it is worth quoting at length:

> Actors and directors operate in a world which is not entirely populated by the educated and sophisticated. Prejudice, bigotry, discrimination and even persecution have not disappeared. The reproduction, in this real world, of ancient stereotypes should take into account their potential for inciting or reinforcing racial or religious prejudice.
>
> I believe that Mr McDiarmid's Shylock can have that effect, a view which was fortified at Stratford by the approving reception some members of the audience gave to the most virulent passages in the play.
>
> ... Even actors and directors most dedicated to their art might possibly agree that other factors exist of no less consequence than artistic freedom of expression. I wonder whether Mr

McDiarmid did think about them. If he did, his Shylock suggests that the post-Holocaust inhibitions on public anti-Jewish presentations are fading.[107]

The interpretations which followed McDiarmid's suggest that Frankel's fears have thankfully not been realised, and that a high degree of sensitivity still exists when it comes to portraying Shylock on stage. But even sympathetic portrayals can prompt angry reactions.

David Thacker's 1993 production for the RSC[108] – ironically one that went out of its way to avoid giving offence, featuring one of the most sympathetic Shylocks imaginable in David Calder – incensed the playwright Arnold Wesker sufficiently for him to publish his feelings and subsequently enter into a newspaper debate with the director concerning the play in general and Thacker's production in particular. While making it very clear that he 'would defend the right of anyone anywhere to present this work',[109] Wesker declared:

… but nothing will make me admire it, nor has anyone persuaded me the holocaust is irrelevant to my responses.

Citing arguments which have by now become familiar – that 'Hath not a Jew …' is a reflection of a deeply offensive Christian arrogance 'which assumed the right to confer or withdraw humanity as it saw fit'; that Shakespeare did not have to make the cruel money-lender a Jew; and that at no point does any character suggest that there might be a distinction to be drawn between his being a Jew and his being a murderous villain – Wesker concluded that any production of the play – and perhaps especially the well-intentioned ones – can inflame audiences with the anti-Jewish sentiments inherent in the text. Thacker, in my opinion, got the worst of that particular debate.

Wesker once wrote: 'Shylock has entered the language. To be called it is to be insulted for being mean like a Jew.'[110] His creative response was to write a new play, *The Merchant*, in which Shylock Kolner, a bibliophilic 'loan-banker', faces the terrible dilemma of having to choose between his Jewish community and his old friend Antonio. Having no alternative but to sacrifice his friend, he destroys himself.

But there might actually be a more intractable problem with the portrayal of the Jew who demands his pound of flesh than the issue of whether or not the play is in fact anti-Semitic.

I am back with Rabbi Julia Neuberger. And I'm interested to know how a well-known and respected liberal Jew responds to Shylock these days, and whether she views the play as anti-Semitic or, at the very least, unfair. Her response is instructive and illuminating: 'I have certainly come away from productions of *The Merchant of Venice* feeling angry', she says. 'But I don't think the play is dangerous; I just think it's unpleasant … It's some years since I saw a production of it, and I shan't rush to see another …'

This reaction reminds me of David Nathan, the astute drama critic for the *Jewish Chronicle*, who believes that 'Is the play anti-Semitic?' is the wrong question to ask – the answer being 'Only as far as is strictly necessary'. He adds: 'Ask another question – "Is it offensive?" – and the answer is an unequivocal "yes".'[111]

He goes on:

> … it hardly matters whether the play is produced as an anti-Semitic or an anti-Christian tract. What emerges in either case is a Jew so rancid with hatred that his ringing declaration of a common humanity in blood is forgotten. The positions are reversed; the Jew has become the bigot who has dehumanised his object of hatred;* the bigot has become the Jew.

* This dehumanisation is particularly noticeable in 'sympathetic' interpretations which, in an attempt to represent Shylock as deeply pious, rather than vengeful, portray him in Act 3, scene 3 and Act 4, scene 1 as dedicated to the fulfilment of 'an oath in heaven'.

An implacable Jew, as immune to pleas of mercy, or appeals to reason or self-interest as any racist, sharpens his knife on the sole of his shoe, the better to cut into a pound of human flesh. He has no more compunction than an SS man would show in shooting down a rabbi, or a Ku-Klux-Klan member in looping a rope over a branch to lynch a black man ...

I have had enough of this damned play. There can be no question of banning it or of even campaigning for its less frequent exposure. But actors and directors should be left in no doubt that, to a large number of Jews, probably the majority, and not a few Christians, it is deeply offensive, no matter how it is done.

I have no easy answer to Nathan's argument. To say, as many apologists do,[112] that the play is frequently performed in Israel, misses the point: it may well be easier for a Jew to cope with the portrayal of Shylock when sitting in an audience of Jews, rather than isolated in the auditorium at Stratford upon Avon; and infinitely easier than standing exposed in a school classroom. I also believe that there is a higher good than artistic freedom. The only observation I can make is that, if Philip Voss is typical (it was from a review of his performance of Shylock that Nathan's comments were taken), then actors most certainly are aware of the offence that this play can cause, in Voss's case leading him to lengthy research into the history of Judaism and repeated discussions with the rabbi of a London synagogue. Describing the sensitivity required for playing the role as 'treading on egg-shells', he says:

'Well, the secretary to the rabbi, who'd obviously seen nearly every production of The Merchant of Venice going and can quote the ones she liked and the ones she didn't like – she said she would bring tomatoes and throw them at me if she didn't like it. But all I could say to her was that I hoped to present a rounded human being. I mean, he's got that speech, anyway: Shakespeare made him rounded ...'

Ultimately, we have to trust actors and directors to be aware of the potential for offence (as Voss was – and productions in the fifteen years after the liberation of Auschwitz decidedly were not) and use their skill to create interpretations which are sensitive without compromising artistic integrity.

All of which leads me to the conclusion that, to aver that Shylock 'lives' is to miss the point – he simply won't go away. We are reminded of that fact every time somebody is accused of wanting 'their pound of flesh'.

Shortly after the first performance of Arnold Wesker's *The Merchant*, Charles Marowitz published his own version of Shakespeare's play.[113] Its opening stage directions make a chilling setting for anyone proposing to put Shylock on the stage in the 21st century. After the sound of an explosion followed by pandemonium, slides illustrate the events described to the audience in a news reporter's voice-over:

> *Jerusalem, July 22nd, 1946. At 12.30 pm today a tremendous explosion ripped off an entire wing of the King David Hotel destroying seven floors and 25 rooms occupied by the Secretariat of the Palestine Government and the Defence Security office of the British Military Headquarters. There are 91 known dead ... Known Zionist terrorists are being rounded up throughout Jerusalem. Several have been shot in skirmishes with British patrols in the old part of the city.*

> (Lights up on dead body covered with khaki blanket: group of Jews huddled around, SHYLOCK, TUBAL, CHUS, JESSICA, etc.)

But it would be a mistake to associate Shylock only with anti-Semitism and sectarian conflict; and it might be appropriate to conclude with a more personal angle on this enduring character. It is a feature that many actors have based their interpretations upon, and one which Heinrich Heine identified when his narrator imagines himself visiting a synagogue in contemporary Venice on Yom Kippur, the Day of Atonement.[114] At first not able to identify Shakespeare's Jew among the congregation, he suddenly hears —

> … a voice in which tears flowed that were never wept from human eyes … It was a sobbing that might have moved a stone to pity … These were sounds of agony that could come only from a heart that held locked within it all the martyrdom which a tormented people had endured for eighteen centuries … And it seemed to me that I knew his voice well; I felt as though I had heard it long ago, when it lamented, with the same tone of despair: 'Jessica, my child!'

CHAPTER 5

Richard the Third

'A royal usurper, a princely hypocrite, a tyrant and a
murderer of the house of Plantagenet'

William Hazlitt

You will no doubt have heard about the camping shop which advertised its January sale with the slogan 'Now is the winter of our discount tents'. It's a pleasant gag, but what interests me about that story is the fact that the proprietor clearly expected his customers to get the joke. And that's because Richard's opening line is up there with 'Friends, Romans, countrymen …' and 'Romeo, Romeo …' in the league table of Shakespeare quotes with which the general public are more or less familiar.

Of course, as Al Pacino found, when he famously walked the streets of New York *Looking for Richard*,[1] familiarity with a quote does not ensure any great knowledge of the character who utters it. Yet there has always been something vividly recognisable about Shakespeare's Richard the Third …

Act 1, scene 1: '… not shaped for sportive tricks'

He limps and lurches forward until his head and shoulders fill the camera. His hair is lank, long and black, his mouth a cruel, thin gash. He pauses,

milking the moment, and then utters that famous line in the famous voice,
staccato, clipped, menacing ...

'Now is the winter ...'

The audience roars with appreciative laughter, for this is comedian
Eric Morecambe in a *Morecambe and Wise* show from the 1970s. And
it's interesting to speculate on what assumptions the comedian and his
script-writers had made when planning and rehearsing this moment.
For one thing they had counted on the audience recognising the
speech as Shakespeare and finding something inherently funny in Eric
doing the Bard. But, more than that, they had been confident that the
audience would identify a stereotypical Shakespeare 'delivery'; and
that a significant number would associate that voice, the wig and the
swaying limp with a particular exponent, Laurence Olivier, playing a
particular character, Richard the Third ...

Act 1, scene 1: 'Deformed, unfinished ...'

The palace doors open and then silently close behind us, immediately
quietening the sounds of festivity in the streets outside. Richard stands by
his ceremonial seat at the far end of a great chamber, and then approaches
us. He is dressed in dark burgundy and black, the hanging sleeves at first
masking, and then accentuating, his limp. By now he is only a yard away,
prepared to address us but pausing to ensure that he has our full attention.
Then he says it.

> *'Now is the winter of our discontent*
> *Made glorious summer by this sun of York*
> *And all the clouds that loured upon our house*
> *In the deep bosom of the ocean buried ...'*

He remains quite still. There is the subtlest of glances up on 'sun', down
on 'deep', but his most significant movement here is a thoughtful sideways

*look as he hears the 'lascivious pleasing' of the lute. For, he tells us, this is
not a sound that pleases him. He isn't 'shaped for sportive tricks', but*

> *'rudely stamped ...*
> *Deformed, unfinished, sent before my time*
> *Into this breathing world, scarce half made up,*
> *And that so lamely and unfashionable*
> *That dogs bark at me as I halt by them ...'*

Richard's mis-shapenness, so much a part of our image of him, is well
established, not only in the play which bears his name, but in the
Shakespeare trilogy which precedes it. And it is from part of that trilogy,
Henry VI Part 3, that Olivier borrows most of the remainder of his opening speech in the 1955 film of *Richard III*,[2] for the lines from the earlier
play permit him to descant on his deformity and leave us in no doubt
as to the effect it has had upon him. Explaining the root cause of his
malignity with disarming matter-of-factness, he looks us in the eye and
tells us quite simply: 'Why, love foreswore me in my mother's womb.'

It is a devastating explanation, but no less ugly than the assertion
which follows, that —

> ... for I should not deal in her soft laws,
> She did corrupt frail nature with some bribe
> To shrink mine arm up like a wither'd shrub,
> To make an envious mountain on my back ...
> To shape my legs of an unequal size,
> To disproportion me in every part,
> Like to a chaos, or an unlick'd bear-whelp
> That carries no impression like the dam.[3]

Throughout the performance history of this character, actors have
drawn on this description not only for their physical representation of
Richard, but also as a way into his psychology. We cannot know how

Richard was first performed (probably in 1593 on the stage of the Theatre, Shoreditch), but a politically prudent Elizabethan actor would have tuned his performance to the Tudor myth. This glorified Richard's conqueror (and Elizabeth's grandfather), Henry the Seventh, in seeing Richard's deformity as merely an outward representation of the inner corruption he was born with, a general badness which – understandably, they would say – caused, rather than was caused by, his mother's alienation. In recent times, though, with changing views of disability, and profoundly different concepts of psychology, one tendency has been to see Richard's cruelty and violence as an outcome of his deformity and the denial of mother love, rather than the other way round.

Olivier's inclusion of the lines from *Henry VI* might easily have led him to an expressly 'psychological' interpretation of the character, but in the event it didn't. Nonetheless, Olivier simply *was* Richard the Third for the whole post-war generation; and, for many people who don't get to see that much Shakespeare, probably still is. So famous was his interpretation by the late 1960s that Peter Sellers was able to get into the charts by singing the Beatles' 'It's Been A Hard Day's Night' in Olivier's Richard voice (incidentally drawing every ounce of innuendo out of an interpolated pause in the line 'You make me feel ... all right', and thereby brilliantly underlining the old adage that comedy is all about timing and incongruity).

Olivier, in fact, was in a long tradition of great actors who have made Richard their own, a lineage which started, in all probability, with Shakespeare's leading actor, Richard Burbage ...

Upon a time when Burbage played Richard III, there was a citizen grew so far in liking with him that before she went from the play she appointed him to come that night unto her by the name of Richard the Third. Shakespeare overhearing their conclusion went before, was entertained, and at his game ere Burbage came.

Then message being brought that Richard the Third was at the door, Shakespeare caused return to be made that William the Conqueror was before Richard the Third.

Thus John Manningham, an Inner Temple law student, writing in his diary on 13 March 1602.[4] Anecdotes like this are extremely revealing. For, while this is almost certainly apocryphal, it serves to tell us something about the public perception of Shakespeare, while at the same time suggesting that Burbage's portrayal of Richard was both popular and sexy. These are qualities notably shared by a more recent Richard, the American movie-star Al Pacino …

Act 1, scene 2: 'I'll have her, but I will not keep her long'

'Stay, you that bear the corse, and set it down.'

Richard's irreverent command halts the small cortège as it emerges from the darkness. The resistance from Lady Anne's companions is token only, and Richard begins his wooing. She is young and extremely pretty, and his emollient words sound sincere enough. But this is the man who killed her husband and her father-in-law, and she spits at him. At which, cut to —

EXT. A GARDEN
RICHARD turns to camera, confidingly.

RICHARD
I'll have her —

As soon as he begins to plead her beauty as the motive for killing her husband, she is lost, fascinated by his boldness and sexuality, as he tells her:

Your beauty was the cause of that effect —
Your beauty that did haunt me in my sleep
To undertake the death of all the world,
So I might live one hour in your sweet bosom …

At which, cut to —

    EXT. A GARDEN
    RICHARD smiles.

The rest is easy. Of course she refuses to stab when he gives her his dagger and bares his chest, predictably she offers no resistance when he places a ring upon her finger, and naturally they embrace passionately before a temporary parting ... Cut to —

    EXT. A GARDEN
    RICHARD to camera
    Ha!

More Juliet than Lady Anne, she whispers in his ear: '... since you teach me how to flatter you, / Imagine I have said farewell already ...'

    RICHARD V.O. as Anne departs.
    Was ever woman in this humour wooed?

    Cut to:
    EXT. A GARDEN
    RICHARD to camera
    Was ever woman in this humour won?
    I'll have her—

He begins to laugh, louder and louder, as he recedes from camera ...

    — but I will not keep her long!

There was much derision when Al Pacino, best known for a film career as a succession of gangsters (most famously Michael Corleone in *The Godfather*), announced that his directorial debut would be a film of Shakespeare's *Richard III*:

Al Pacino playing Richard III? It sounds like a Spitting Image sketch, a follow-up to The Godfather: 'A horse! A horse! What's dis – you only gave me da head!'[5]

And there is a fair bit of street style in Pacino's Richard, as when, declaring his plan to marry Anne, he glances to camera and says: 'What though I killed her husband and her father?', and the line 'is accompanied by that most practised and instinctive of movements, the New York shrug'.[6]

But the full outcome, a documentary about the process of researching and rehearsing Shakespeare's play, has had many admirers and few serious detractors. *Guardian* critic Jonathan Romney happily summed up Pacino's achievement as having filmed, not the play *Richard III* itself, but 'a rehearsal-in-progress' in which he asked 'assorted actors, academics and variously nutty members of his entourage to explain it to him'. And some of these 'explanations' owe more to inspired intuition than to a considered understanding of Shakespeare's play. But the scenes in which Pacino actually rehearses and performs to camera are enough to suggest that, in different circumstances, the Hollywood star would have made a compelling Richard. Not least because, while not overtly presenting himself as a Mafia-style tyrant, his portrayal could draw on our previously established screen image of him as exactly that. In fact there was a certain inevitability in the way critics felt obliged to refer to Pacino's iconographic status as a Mob hard-man, especially when linking it to his demotic quick-fire delivery of the soliloquies.

But it's the bits in between the filmed rehearsals which are most interesting, as Pacino walks the streets of New York and Stratford-upon-Avon, asking passers-by what Shakespeare means to them today. As the *Guardian* critic observes: '… he's well aware how ridiculous he looks, stalking around in his baseball cap and milking the traditional Olivier crouch for all it's worth …'. But there are some memorable moments, as when one New Yorker sidles up to Pacino – who's in dark suit, shades and reversed baseball cap – and the two converse in hushed conspiratorial Italian (rather like, if I can draw on the obvious image, a Mafia hitman reporting to his boss); or when a departing sidewalker jocularly shouts 'To be or not to be, that is the question!', and we are reminded that Shakespeare's most familiar lines take on unexpectedly new meanings in new contexts – in this case, our aware-ness and Pacino's that the planned film of *Richard III* might, or might not, be scrapped before it ever hits the screens.

I'm not sure that I'd go as far as writer H.R. Coursen, in describ-ing the framing structure of *Looking for Richard* as '[reaching] back to the *Odyssey* and the Grail and *Don Quixote* and [coming] forward through *Gatsby* and the Joads and Jack Kerouac ...'.[7] For me that's a bit over the top, and risks placing the film in unwarrantedly exalted company. But *Looking for Richard* is nonetheless an absorbing picture of what happens when a group of people try to make a Shakespeare film and actually question why they're doing it, how relevant it is, and what it all means. At the risk of sounding unforgivably patronising, I'd say that *Looking for Richard* has an innocent charm. And if I had to find classical archetypes myself, I'd look to Voltaire's *Candide*, given that the child-like Pacino asks some devastatingly innocent questions from a position of profound inexperience of Shakespeare. Observing the actor's 'almost religious quest',[8] we find ourselves asking: *Why perform* Richard III *today? Why do Shakespeare at all? Does a typical audience understand even a fraction of the language?* – fundamental questions that academics, the National Curriculum for schools and the Shakespeare industry as a whole too often choose not to address. As Chris Lawson observes:

> The inter-relationship between aspects such as actors, characters and locations, or the play as a text, as a piece of performance and

as an event mediated through film, raises questions concerning the place of Shakespeare as a continuing force in American and British society.[9]

Serious questions apart, *Looking for Richard* is also extremely funny, as when, visiting Shakespeare's birthplace, Pacino excuses his apparent lack of response by claiming that he'd had an epiphany but just didn't show it. What that episode graphically demonstrates is that heritage Shakespeare isn't going to get him very far; but, with its doublet-and-hose rehearsals, faux-medieval cloister settings, and awed pilgrimages to the Globe and Stratford-upon-Avon, *Looking for Richard* confirms what a pervasive grip 'Bard as cultural icon' still has.

Act 4, scene 2: Sound a sennet. Enter Richard as King, in pomp …

87 INT. ARENA – NIGHT

The arena is packed with thousands of RICHARD'S SUPPORTERS, male and female, young and old, civilian and blackshirts. On the platform, DRUMMERS AND TRUMPETERS are lined behind the CITY GENTLEMEN, all in place. The last to enter are the ARCHBISHOP and LORD STANLEY, looking somewhat appalled at the vast crowd.

On BUCKINGHAM'S entrance onstage, the place erupts. He approaches the podium, which is bristling with microphones.

  BUCKINGHAM
  Long live King Richard!

There is a gasp of delight at this unexpected announcement. The trumpets sound the percussive martial music which RICHARD played to himself in his office.

The mighty arc-lights swing across the heads of the crowd, signifying that the Lord Protector has arrived in the auditorium. As RICHARD slowly marches onstage, from up centre, the entire audience rises and cheers and waves. A CHILD breaks ranks and throws RICHARD a posy of flowers. Film cameras whirr. Flaming torches are lit.

EVERYONE

Amen! Amen! Amen! Amen! Amen!

As RICHARD reaches the podium, the orgiastic climax surpasses itself.

RICHARD acknowledges his subjects with a dazzling smile and as he raises his good arm in greeting, behind him his new flag unfurls – red, white and black. RICHARD is happy for the last time in his life.[10]

When Ian McKellen decided to commit his successful stage performance[11] of Richard to film, he and co-director Richard Loncraine decided to set the story in the 1930s. This was McKellen's reasoning:

> The historical events of the play had occurred just a couple of generations before the first audience saw them dramatised. The comparable period for us would be the 1930s ... appropriately a decade of tyranny throughout Europe, the most recent time when a dictatorship like Richard III's might have overtaken the United Kingdom, as it had done Germany, Italy, Spain and the empire of the Soviet Union.[12]

In following Richard Eyre's original stage conception, Loncraine and McKellen were opting, in fact, for a 'period analogue' setting – one which sets the play in an identifiable period, usually between Shakespeare's own and the present day, and draws analogies between the chosen era and the events of the original story. Period analogue has been a popular approach in recent years, and notably for Shakespeare on film. Kenneth Branagh chose to set both his *Much Ado About Nothing* and *Hamlet* in the 19th century, and his *Love's Labour's Lost* at the outset of the Second World War; Michael Hoffman's *A*

Midsummer Night's Dream is also 19th-century, as is Trevor Nunn's film of *Twelfth Night*; while Nunn's filmed RNT *Merchant of Venice* was set, like the McKellen–Loncraine *Richard III*, in the 1930s (but in middle Europe, rather than Britain). Recent RSC productions have seen *The Merry Wives of Windsor* set in the post-war austerity years, and *Coriolanus* placed in samurai-period Japan (the two played in repertory).[13]

Period analogue gives the director the chance to remove the story from the kind of doublet-and-hose straitjacket (if I can be forgiven both a mixed metaphor and a cliché) that so constricted Pacino. More importantly, it enables the director to highlight those particular features of the world of the play on which they wish to focus, by drawing parallels with a historical context with which the audience will be familiar. Setting *Twelfth Night* in the Victorian or Edwardian period, for example, permits the audience to recognise immediately certain social distinctions between Malvolio and Olivia (what status did an Elizabethan 'steward' have, after all?), and also allows the director to 'place' difficult-to-define characters such as Feste (what was a 'fool', exactly?) and Maria (confusingly referred to in the Folio both as 'My niece's chamber maid' and 'Gentlewoman'). In Trevor Nunn's 1995 film, for instance, Nigel Hawthorne's Malvolio is quite clearly the butler of a grand Victorian country house, with all the below-stairs power and above-stairs restrictions that our understanding of the role implies. He generates terror among the kitchen-maids and has power and influence enough to make things very sticky indeed for Maria (here in noticeably inferior position as the housekeeper). But, in everything from his dress to his accent (his over-conscious version of Received Pronunciation contrasts starkly with Olivia's and Sir Andrew's easy vowels), he is placed irredeemably on the wrong side of the green-baize door.

Period analogue in this way allows the director to offer the audience a historical and social context which is likely to be much more familiar and specific than an Elizabethan or Jacobean one, thereby giving us a light on who the characters are, where they are placed in society, and why they behave in the ways they do.

There are, of course, disadvantages too. For one thing, the correspondences are necessarily approximate at best, and sometimes distracting. An Edwardian butler is not the same thing as a 16th-century steward. Identifying Maria as a housekeeper 'fixes' a character whose social status in Shakespeare's play is intriguingly ambiguous. And there is no 19th-century equivalent of the Shakespearean fool. For another, representing Antonio and Bassanio (in *The Merchant of Venice*) as a pair of 21st-century closet gays is to give them a relationship that Shakespeare's audience would simply not have recognised. I'm not saying that Antonio and Bassanio should never be portrayed as homo- or bi-sexual; merely making the rather obvious point that Elizabethan and Victorian and modern concepts of sexuality are all profoundly different.

A period analogue interpretation is therefore bound to get some things wrong. But then – and this is a point of fundamental importance for our attitude to performing Shakespeare today – so is any interpretation, and for the simple reason that we are not Elizabethans or Jacobeans and don't have their mind-sets. To misquote Shylock – we don't buy like them, sell like them, talk like them (and so following …), nor do we eat what they ate, drink what they drank or pray as they prayed … We are different people. And no amount of interpreting can make us come anywhere near responding to Shakespeare's characters and their actions exactly as his own audience did (assuming for the moment that it is feasible to describe such a multifarious collection of individuals as '*an* audience' – then or now). That's why the shortcomings of period analogue don't matter to me very much at all. Whatever we do with Shakespeare will, by definition, be an adaptation. Rather a period adaptation which gives the audience new insights into the story, than an attempt at Elizabethan 'authenticity' which doesn't.

The McKellen–Loncraine film displayed both the strengths and the shortcomings of a period analogue *Richard III*. To take a major failing first, one of the problems in presenting Richard as a 1930s fascist tyrant is that Richard almost inevitably *becomes* Hitler – especially if he is dressed in an SS-style uniform and backed by red and black banners which evoke the Nuremberg rallies. And we then start to bring to our interpretation of the story all the things we know about the Nazi tyrant, his rise to power and behaviour in office, fragments of knowledge which have nothing to do with medieval or Tudor England, and actually get in the way of our understanding of the Richard that McKellen and Loncraine have attempted to create.[14]

On the plus side, the period analogue setting for this film made it very easy for the audience to think itself into the period of British history when Sir Oswald Mosley peddled his particular brand of fascism, and thereby to envisage a political context in which a ruthless and plausible politician like Richard could well have come to power. There were also imaginative and illuminating parallels between the Yorkist story and the events of the 1930s, my favourite being the portrayal of the Queen and her Woodville family as a bunch of parvenu Americans (Robert Downey Jr in especially gauche form as the Queen's playboy brother), which evoked the whole Wallis Simpson episode and the constitutional crisis it precipitated. Seeing King Edward's consort as a Mrs Simpson surrounded by flashy upstarts helped us to understand that at least part of the Yorkist establishment's objection to the marriage might have been founded in snobbery and social resentment. And this emerged with entertaining clarity in the opening 'Victory Ball' sequence, where we watched the censorious and deeply disapproving looks of the formally attired and be-medalled

English upper classes, as Annette Bening's sexy young Queen indecorously squealed her delight at the arrival from the States of her casually lounge-suited brother. You felt that, quite apart from political considerations, the Woodvilles simply weren't quite the thing ...

Act 4, scene 2: 'Come hither, Catesby. Rumour it abroad / That Anne my wife is very grievous sick ...'

Now that he is King, Richard no longer needs the Warwick alliance, and his wife is dispensable ...

This is Antony Sher (a brilliant Richard for the RSC in 1984) describing in his journal an early rehearsal under director Bill Alexander, with Anne played by Penny Downie:

> Bill's idea of having Lady Anne sitting there, white and semi-poisoned [while Richard tells Catesby to spread the rumour that she is 'sick and like to die'] is going to work marvellously. Shakespeare doesn't have her in the scene, but it will be a strong image – this silent, sick presence at Richard's side. Penny sits with eyes opened, but sightless. 'Valiumed out of her mind,' as she describes it. She also talks about a practice in Australian aboriginal witchcraft – 'pointing the bone' at someone to make them die (the power of suggestion). She says that Lady Anne has inadvertently done this to herself: in her first speech one of her curses against Richard was directed at his future wife.[15]*

Anne's removal will enable Richard to marry his niece, Edward the Fourth's daughter Elizabeth; and that just leaves two small obstacles, her royal brothers ...

---

* The speech referred to is in 1.2.26–8 when, addressing the corpse of Henry VI, Anne curses: 'If ever he have wife, let her be made / More miserable by the death of him / Than I am made by my young lord and thee!'

Like Macbeth, Richard frets that 'To be thus is nothing; But to be safely thus!'. Also like Macbeth, the source of his insecurity is a rival (in this case, a pair of rivals) with a legitimate claim and popular support. They have to be dispatched; and who better to arrange the removal than a 'discontented gentleman': 'James Tyrrel, and your most obedient subject …'

Act 4, scene 3: 'The tyrannous and bloody act …'

As the pre-Raphaelite painter John Everett Millais pictured the story …

They are on their way to the chamber in which they will die, but seem to have turned back at the last moment, putting off the ascent of those stone steps behind them, which curve up and behind the heavy black wall of the Tower of London. Both boys have beautiful blond hair, curling to their shoulders, set off by the contrasting darkness of their velvet suits and framing their delicate, feminine faces. Edward, the older child, protectively grasps his brother Richard's hand and looks back the way they have come. Richard glances off to the side, his other hand lifted to touch his brother's shoulder, as though alerting him to some half-perceived danger. They look small in the centre of the picture, framed ominously by the massive stones which will soon enclose their corpses …[16]

This is how Millais pictured them, and he knew his public.

Public opinion has usually been ready to forgive most medieval and Tudor monarchs the occasional political assassination or tactical execution; and it is sometimes difficult to get terribly upset at the deaths of Clarence ('false … fleeting, perjured Clarence',[17] a turncoat who had fought on both sides in the Wars of the Roses) or Hastings (foolishly taking over Edward the Fourth's mistress, Jane Shore). But nobody is ever going to let Richard off the hook for the murder of the young Edward and his little brother the Duke of York. They are among the select band of historical victims for whom we have a memorable collective title – 'The Princes in the Tower' – but whom most members of the public would struggle to identify by name or family connection. (One, in fact, was no longer a prince: he was the uncrowned King, Edward the Fifth.) What makes the crime so heinous is the simple fact that they are innocent, defenceless children; but Shakespeare intensifies our abhorrence of the deed, first by introducing them to us, and second by describing their deaths, rather than depicting them.

The McKellen–Loncraine film memorably sets the children's arrival in London at Victoria Station; and there is a shudderingly horrifying moment when little York leaps playfully onto Richard's humped shoulders and Richard's face momentarily morphs into the fanged snarl of a provoked boar. The effect is odd, though; for there's a part of us that feels for Richard in this moment of physical discomfort and personal humiliation, and can understand his violent reflex response. Nonetheless it is impossible not to be affected by our knowledge of what is to become of the children as they are ushered into waiting cars and driven off to the Tower, deemed 'most fit / For [their] best health and recreation'.

The account of their deaths (in 4.3) is an extraordinary piece of theatre. Like the report of the reunion between the kings in *The Winter's Tale* (5.2), or the assassination of Duncan in *Macbeth* (2.2) – both potentially great stage moments – Shakespeare elects to have the children's murder reported rather than acted out. In fact, the speech in which their killing is described is a report of a report; for we hear Tyrrel, the man employed by Richard to eliminate his nephews, quoting Dighton and Forrest, the sub-contractors who actually did the job. Tyrrel himself is by now sufficiently moved to call the murders 'ruthless butchery', and describes how Dighton and Forrest

> Albeit they were fleshed villains, bloody dogs,
> Melting with tenderness and mild compassion,
> Wept like to children in their death's sad story.

In a description that has influenced pictorial representations through the ages, appealing especially to the Victorians, Tyrrel goes on:

> 'O, thus,' quoth Dighton, 'lay the gentle babes.'
> 'Thus, thus,' quoth Forrest, 'girdling one another
> Within their alabaster innocent arms.
> Their lips were four red roses on a stalk,
> Which in their summer beauty kissed each other ...'[18]

While there are those who consider those lines to be a description of quite repellent sentimentality (and I have to confess to being among them), the scene remains an intriguing piece of stagecraft. And it seems likely that Shakespeare tells the story in this way because our responses to the children's deaths need to be guided more strictly than they would be if we were simply left to see the murders taking place. We have to know that, if a ruthless villain such as Tyrrel can describe the act as 'The most arch deed of piteous massacre / That ever yet this land was guilty of', then it must be bad indeed. And in one important respect the key words are 'this land', because we need to set this piece of brutality in the context of English history; specifically in the reign of a bloody tyrant who was to be replaced by Shakespeare's Queen's heroic and virtuous grandfather. This, says the scene, is the kind of man Richard was – even 'fleshed villains' wept at his cruel and pitiless murders. He had to be replaced. It is an argument for 'régime change' which has become disturbingly familiar.

But did the 'real' historical Richard have the Princes killed? Was he actually a hunchback? Was England universally glad to see the end of him? According to which historians you ask, the answers seem to

be: possibly, but there's no evidence (and he was by no means excep-
tionally bloody as medieval and Renaissance monarchs go); perhaps,
though the description was just as likely to have been Tudor propaganda; and probably not, given the apparently genuine mourning that
his death engendered, especially in the north (following the Battle of
Bosworth in which Richard was killed, the people of York wrote: 'This
day was our good King Richard piteously slain and murdered; to the
great heaviness of this city').[19] In fact, Richard is probably one of the
best examples in Shakespeare's history plays of 'our bending author'[20]
bending history in order to make a better story, or tread a safer, pro-
Tudor political path. So how far was Shakespeare responsible for
creating one of English history's most notorious bogey-men?

As E.A.J. Honigmann tells us in his Penguin edition of the play:

> In the chronicles of Edward Hall (1548) and Raphael Holinshed
> (1577, 1587) Shakespeare had the good fortune to find a portrait
> of his hero that was already a finished work of art. The chronicles
> provided a general assessment of character, and presented sugges-
> tive psychological details in a narrative that switches every so
> often into direct speech and all the tensions of drama.[21]

And these chronicles themselves seem to have been heavily indebted
to the vivid and psychologically absorbing life of Richard written by
Sir Thomas More.[22]

More was only eight when Richard died, and therefore could not
claim to have witnessed the life he described at first hand. As a child
he had been page in the household of Cardinal Morton (right-hand
man of Henry the Seventh, Richard's overthrower) and he later served
as Chancellor to the second Tudor monarch, Henry the Eighth. More,
in other words, formed his picture of Richard on the basis of information provided by Tudor spin-doctors, a faction in whose interest it
was to present 'the last of the Plantagenets' as a murderous tyrant.

And it is More's Richard, reconstituted in the chronicles of Hall and Holinshed, on which Shakespeare bases his dramatic creation.

Should we blame Shakespeare for so uncritically regurgitating the Tudor party line on Richard? I don't think so. For one thing, we shouldn't be surprised if he actually admired Henry the Seventh. And even if he didn't, given the political circumstances under which he was writing, Shakespeare could hardly have done other than to recreate and embellish the monster Richard already described in his sources. Talking on BBC Radio 4 about the context to another of Shakespeare's history plays, *Henry V*, written only a few years after *Richard III*,* Michael Dobson said:

> 'Shakespeare was writing the equivalent of *The West Wing*. In 1599 the government banned the publication of history without express permission of the Privy Council, they were so worried about the application of the past to the present.'[23]

This was not an era in which playwrights enjoyed the artistic licence to write whatever 'history' they wanted in the expectation that actors could act it with impunity. And anyway, Shakespeare was a dramatist, not a historian. Deformed tyrants make better plays than averagely decent monarchs who clumsily get themselves deposed.

But one major by-product of Shakespeare's success in his creation is that Richard has become a by-word for tyranny and for the Machiavellian arts that ruthless monarchs notoriously practise. John Milton, for example, in *Eikonoclastes* (1649), a closely-argued riposte to the pro-Charles I tract *Eikon Basilike: The Portraiture of His Sacred Majesty in His Solitudes and Sufferings*, specifically cites moments from Shakespeare's play when he attacks Charles's supposed piety. Declaring that 'the deepest policy of a tyrant hath been ever to counterfeit religion', he goes on:

**Richard III was probably written in 1592–3, *Henry V* almost certainly in 1599.

I shall not instance an abstruse author, wherein the King might be less conversant, but one whom we well know was the closet companion of these solitudes, William Shakespeare;* who introduces the person of Richard the Third, speaking in as high a strain of piety, and mortification, as is uttered in any passage in this book [i.e. in *Eikon Basilike*]; and sometimes to the same sense and purpose ...

For Milton, as for others after him, Richard is quoted as the type of the 'deep dissembler, not of his affections only, but of his religion'.

A few centuries later, the prologue Announcer in Bertolt Brecht's allegory of Nazism, *The Resistible Rise of Arturo Ui* (1941), asks: 'Who can fail to think of Richard the Third?' And as the play unfolds, echoes of Shakespeare's tyrant abound as we witness a comic version of Richard's wooing of Lady Anne over a coffin, and a moment when the ghost of a murdered rival appears to Ui, just as Richard's victims had arisen before the Battle of Bosworth Field. For Milton in the 17th century to Brecht in the 20th, Shakespeare's Richard the Third had become, and was to remain, the type of the dissembling, murderous tyrant.

The rehabilitation of Richard as an able and effective ruler whose reputation was systematically destroyed by the dynasty that replaced him has been famously promulgated, not just by professional historians, but in works of fiction as diverse as Josephine Tey's *The Daughter of Time* and Rosemary Hawley Jarman's *We Speak No Treason*.[24] In Tey's unusual contribution to the detective story genre (it was successfully published in the Penguin Crime series), Alan Grant, a policeman confined to a hospital bed after breaking his leg, decides to relieve his boredom by investigating the murder of the Princes in the Tower. Led by an intuitive reaction to a postcard of Richard's

---

* Milton here uses Charles's love of Shakespeare as a weapon against him: for Puritans like Milton, theatre-going was a sign of depravity.

portrait that he is looking at a kindly, somewhat 'over-conscientious' man, 'responsible in his authority', his researches lead him to the conclusion that 'Crouchback' – 'The monster of nursery stories', 'The destroyer of innocence', 'A synonym for villainy' – had far less reason to want the Princes dead than did his successor – the man Grant fingers for the felony – Henry the Seventh. As Tey readily admits (when her detective discovers the fact for himself at the end), this theory which places the guilt on Henry is not a new one. But her reworking of a historians' debate as a piece of crime fiction is wonderfully original and great fun to read.

Also taking the rehabilitationist line, *We Speak No Treason* is a historical romance in which four narrators recall their dealings with Richard. These invented characters – the Maiden, the Fool, the Man of Keen Sight (an archer) and the Nun – contribute to a picture of the man as he might, in the author's opinion, have appeared to his contemporaries: a flawed hero who could inspire great love and loyalty.

Act 5, scene 5: 'Let me sit heavy on thy soul tomorrow! … / despair therefore, and die!'

It is the eve of battle. Having retired to his tent by Bosworth Field, Richard tells Ratcliffe to return at mid of night to arm him. Left alone, with the knowledge that at daybreak he will have to defend his crown against the pretender Henry, Richard sleeps … And then the ghosts come …

Henry the Sixth and his son, both of whom Richard murdered when securing the crown for his Yorkist brother, Edward; Richard's other brother, Clarence, drowned in a butt of Malmsey on Richard's orders; the executed Woodville faction, Rivers, Grey and Vaughan; the hapless Hastings, killed because he drew back from supporting Richard's claim to the throne; the Princes, murdered in the Tower; Anne, Richard's 'disappeared' wife; and finally Buckingham …

'The first ... that helped thee to the crown;
The last ... that felt thy tyranny ...'

Staring out in terror, his face a combination of horror and amazement,
Richard leans back and sideways on his couch, side-lit against the darkly
sumptuous hangings of his camp tent, his right hand raised, fingers splayed,
as though vainly attempting to push these avenging furies away ...

Or, as one Victorian enthusiast was later to describe the scene:

> The lamp, diffusing a dim, religious light through the tent, the
> crucifix placed at his head, the crown, the unsheathed sword at
> his hand, and the armour lying on the ground, are judicious and
> appropriate accompaniments ... So great is his agitation, that
> every nerve and muscle is in action, and even the ring is forced
> from his finger ...[25]

William Hogarth's painting of the celebrated 18th-century actor
David Garrick as Richard (Figure 12) is among the best-known of all
Shakespearean portraits. It depicts Garrick in the role which made
him famous when he first performed it at Goodman's Fields on 19
October 1741, and, in its heroic simplicity, perfectly evokes the theatric-
ality of the moment when the murderer is confronted by the ghosts of
his victims. For art historian William L. Pressly, Hogarth's depiction
is 'More than a portrait: it becomes a work illustrating the national
past that raises Garrick to the role of a tragic villain.'[26]

It is hard to know how accurate a portrayal of Garrick's actual performance Hogarth's is, given that it is clearly based on well-established
pictorial conventions which determined the representation of emotion through stylised gesture and facial expression. But there is plenty
of evidence to suggest that Garrick's acting was daringly innovative in
its rejection of stale conventions and in his ground-breaking attempt
to base what he did on a conception of individual character rather

than merely a sense of a previously established dramatic type. This doesn't mean that he would appear to us today as a 'modern' actor in the style of an Ian McKellen or a Judi Dench (his start at the apparitions in Act 5 has been cited as an example of his 'moments of extravagant artifice').[27] But he would certainly be distinguishable from the Shakespearean actors who at that time held sway – people like James Quinn and Colley Cibber – not least for the very personal touches with which he illuminated each of the roles he undertook. In the words of one contemporary, Garrick's biographer Thomas Davies:

> Mr Garrick's easy and familiar, yet forcible style in speaking and acting, at first threw his critics into some hesitation ... They had been long accustomed to an elevation of the voice, with a sudden mechanical depression in its tones, calculated to excite admiration and entrap applause. To the just modulation of the words, and concurring expression of the features from the general workings of nature, they had been strangers for some time ... Mr Garrick shone forth like a theatrical Newton; he threw new light on elocution and action; he banished ranting, bombast and grimace; and restored nature, ease, simplicity, and genuine humour.[20]

No one can doubt that Garrick drove Shakespearean acting into new dimensions with his individual interpretations and originality of method. But we are as mistaken in seeing Garrick as a lone trail-blazer as we are in picturing Shakespeare as an isolated genius cocooned in a garret; because much of the credit for Garrick's achievement has to be given to the theatre commentators who had for many years been arguing for changes in theatrical style.

And there is one particular influence on the development of acting in the 18th century who, to my mind, rarely receives the acknowledgement he deserves. I am talking about Garrick's great contemporary on the London theatre scene, Charles Macklin.

Macklin, a crazy unpredictable Irishman, had spectacularly made his name as a vengeful and malicious Shylock, as we have seen, fully eight months before Garrick's debut as Richard the Third. When Macklin opened as Shylock on 14 February 1741, it was the first time that audiences had been obliged to take the character seriously; and this was due in no small measure to Macklin's acting style, a naturalistic approach that he enthusiastically passed on to aspiring youngsters. In the words of his contemporary, the theatre historian John Hill:

> [Macklin] would bid his pupil first to speak the passage as he would in common life, if he had occasion to speak the same words, and then give them more force, but preserving the same accent, to deliver them on stage.[29]

Macklin trained other actors from 1742 (he ran a School of Oratory from 1753), and advised young people new to the stage

> to know the passion and humour of each character so correctly, so intimately, and (if you will allow me the expression) to feel it so enthusiastically as to be able to describe it as a philosopher.[30]

The term 'philosopher' is used here in the 18th-century sense of 'scientist'; and it was the fruits of Macklin's scientific approach to the craft of acting – researching a role and performing it with a degree of naturalism – which must have impressed Garrick when he observed the older actor's Shylock. For, only a year later in 1742, we find Macklin training Garrick in the ambitious role of King Lear.

During the period of Garrick's management of Drury Lane Theatre (1746–76), *Richard III* was performed 100 times, Covent Garden staged it for a further 113 performances,[31] and Hogarth's picture of Richard terrified by ghosts went on to become the most frequently engraved and most widely disseminated image of the 18th century.[32] It hung on respectable walls throughout the land, and

Staffordshire potteries capitalised on its familiarity to produce colourful figurines depicting Richard beneath a bell-shaped tent, raising his hand (though more, as it appeared, in salutation than terror). As an image it had become, in all but the most literal sense of the word, iconic.

Act 5, scene 4: 'A horse! A horse! My kingdom for a horse!'

As Tyrell fires the machine-gun recklessly at the approaching tank, Ratcliffe strives in vain to reverse the jeep, but, struck by a bullet, he slumps back. With no thought for sentimentality, Richard cynically elbows him out of the door and takes over the steering himself; but in vain – the back wheel is jammed in a rut and screams as it turns uselessly in the battlefield dirt. Cursing the jeep's failure, Richard cries:

> *'A horse! A horse! My kingdom for a horse!'*

— while, twitching in the dirt, blood seeping from his mouth, the loyal Ratcliffe gasps for 'Rescue!'

It is now that Tyrell, in a misguided act of loyalty, tries to help his king from the crippled vehicle, calling on him to escape while he can. The enraged Richard, mad with frustration at his impotence and in no mood to listen to defeatists, turns in outrage and shoots his henchman between the eyes ...

McKellen's interpretation of Richard's famous cry – with its sub-text of 'To hell with these modern contraptions! Give me the good old-fashioned cavalry any day!' – was quite different from Antony Sher's when he played the King for the RSC in 1984. For Sher's Richard, the loss of his horse left him completely immobilised, such was the nature of the crippling disability with which he was afflicted. Sher describes in his brilliantly illuminating journal *Year of the King* the process by which he came to define for himself the nature and extent of the disability that Richard describes. Early in rehearsals he visits the RSC wardrobe mistress, who presents him with a grisly display of the prosthetic deformities that have graced the Stratford stage in former productions:

> 'This is Ian Holm's foot, this Ian Richardson's and here's Alan Howard's.' They are boots built up to look like club feet. Howard's is the most spectacular with studs and the chain used to drag the foot along. 'Now over here,' she says, leading us across the room as if in a department store, 'I dug out some of the humps we've used. Just to give you an idea of what you might want. This is Alan Howard's again and here is Anton Lesser's.' These are vests with the humps built into them. 'They're both side humps but we've also done two lovely big central humps for the Gobbos [in *The Merchant of Venice*] this season ...'[33]

In the event, a new hump is created, which arrives only days before the play is due to open:

> With my heart in my mouth, I hurry over to see my back.
> It's much softer than I imagined, lying on the floor like a big pink blancmange, a slice of blubber, a side of Elephant Man ...[34]

But it wasn't the hump alone that was to characterise Sher's disablement; for it was set off by a pair of sinister crutches, huge black arachnid-legs which flew him across the stage in giant leaps, and which he used as extension limbs to fight off attackers, beat lackeys and, in one famous moment, lift Lady Anne's skirt and probe between her legs. With his hump and long-sleeved black costume (see Figure 14), he had indeed become the 'bottled spider' of Queen Margaret's most vitriolic curse.[35]

While Richard has long been associated with his deformity, it is a fairly recent phenomenon that performances evoke other men who have been famously disabled. No doubt prompted by our changing attitudes to disability, Kenneth Branagh's Richard[36] was so conceptualised in metal leg-supports as to remind Mark Lawson, on BBC Radio 4's *Front Row*, of Franklin D. Roosevelt in his wheelchair and John F. Kennedy with his back-brace.[37] Given that neither of these men is, for most of us, an out-and-out hate figure, Lawson's comparison testifies to the way in which Richard's physical shape is rather more likely these days to evoke sympathy in an audience than repulsion.

While we are on friendlier resonances, it's also the case that in two particular realms outside the theatre, Richard has for some time been a bit of a joke. For final-year undergraduates, 'a Richard' is a *third*-class degree (not as clever as 'a Desmond' for a *two-two*, but as widely used); while cockney rhyming slang has for years embraced the phrase 'Richard the Third' to denote a variety of different referents. A 'Richard the Third' in rhyming slang is most commonly a 'bird'. So that we find 19th-century audiences, for example, giving some second-rate performer 'the Richard'; cockneys feeding the Richards in Trafalgar Square; and a young man meeting his Richard for a drink after work. Though rare, an oath-taker in court might give his 'Richard' (his word); while, more commonly, pedestrians walking along dog-frequented pavements would step warily to avoid the Richards left steaming in their path ...[38] While there is no way of proving this, it is difficult to believe that Richard the Third could have attained such colloquial familiarity through the history books alone. To become part of the cockney lexicon, we surely have to thank Shakespeare's dramatic creation, and its visual reinforcement in the popular consciousness by portrayals as vivid and individual as Garrick's, Hogarth's and Olivier's.

Rosemary Hawley Jarman said that she published her novel *We Speak No Treason* 'because I feel so strongly for Richard's innocence'. It is difficult to assess how the Richard the Third mythography would read today, were it not for Shakespeare's play. Possibly the Tudor spin-doctors would have done their job just as effectively without the play-wright's contribution. But it seems likely that, however many times the case against Richard is declared by historians to be 'unproven', however often we are told that he was in reality a decent man and a reforming monarch, the image in our minds will always be that of the hunchbacked monster who killed the Princes in the Tower. The bloody tyrant whose final, desperate words echo down the ages —

'A horse! A horse! My kingdom for a horse!'

Chapter 6

Lady Macbeth

'The magnitude of her resolution almost covers the magnitude of her guilt'

William Hazlitt

She has long black hair, dark, somewhat masculine eyebrows, a powerful nose and severe mouth. When she looks across at her soldier husband, it is with high-voltage flashes of exasperation at his stupidity, frustration at his weakness, anger at his hesitations. They are playing for very high stakes indeed and her husband is threatening to throw it all away.

No, not Lady Macbeth. I'm describing Diana Ingram, wife of Major Charles Ingram who is struggling to answer a question that will land him a million pounds on television's *Who Wants to Be a Millionaire?*:

'A number one followed by a hundred zeros is known by what name? Is it (a) a google; (b) a megatron; (c) a gigabit; (d) a nanomole?'

Ingram ought to have no problem with this. Not that he knows the answer – he doesn't – but because, sitting among the group of would-be contestants is one Tecwen Whittock. And every time Ingram mentions the correct answer as he runs through the possibilities, Whittock strategically coughs ...

In April 2003, a jury at Southwark Crown Court found Ingram, his wife, and Whittock all guilty of attempting to defraud the show. Interestingly, nobody in the trial had suggested that the major was spurred on, reluctant to do the deed, by his ambitious and ruthless wife. Yet, within seconds, it seemed, of the pronouncement of sentence, the press had dubbed Diana Ingram 'a Lady Macbeth'. And we all knew exactly what they meant.

It is curious that, of all the things Lady Macbeth might have become famous for in the four centuries since her first appearance – blood-soaked palms, sleep-walking, self-destruction – the one that has captured the media's imagination most vividly is the notion that she plays the determined, manipulative wife behind the ambitious yet weak man. These days, any politician's wife who dares to deviate for a moment from her allotted doormat status, and whose career background, wit and professional skills ought to recommend her as a potentially valuable helpmeet, will sooner or later be labelled 'the Lady Macbeth of ...' (Downing Street, the White House, Fleet Street ... fill in as required), her alleged influence suspected as being both sinister and dangerously unaccountable. Take this, for example, from *The Times*, in an article about the German Finance Minister Oskar Lafontaine and his novelist wife, Christa Müller. Headlined 'Banker's bogeyman gets a few tips from his Lady Macbeth', it goes on:

> ... If Frau Müller only wrote books, all would be well. But the 42 year-old Social Democrat has also emerged as a gifted television performer and has earned the label of 'Oskar's Hillary'. A senior Green politician refers to her privately as the Lady Macbeth of the Government.[1]

This is a classic Lady Macbeth reference. Christa Müller would have avoided any kind of slur had she stuck to modestly publishing genteel poems, as Norma Major did when she was consort of the British premier John Major. But Christa's success as a novelist and – heaven forbid! –

her television celebrity immediately put her into the clever-wife-pulling-strings-in-the-background bracket, and she stands condemned alongside that most notorious Lady Macbeth *de nos jours*, Hillary Clinton.

Hillary, of course, was perfect Scottish Queen material. As the first First Lady in years to be recognised for her brain rather than her couture, Hillary never stood a chance of avoiding the Lady Macbeth sobriquet, and references started to abound almost as soon as her husband acceded to the Presidency in 1993:

Hillary Clinton denies 'Lady Macbeth' role
By Stephen Robinson in Washington

Mrs Hillary Clinton has dismissed suggestions that she wields too much power over her husband's troubled presidency or that she vets his choices for senior White House jobs …

She appears to have maintained a sense of humour during a difficult few months in the White House.

Her interviewer referred to some commentators likening her to Lady Macbeth.

'You don't walk around the White House saying, "Out, damned spot?"'

'Only when I'm trying to wash something,' Mrs Clinton replied.[2]

In that report, the Lady Macbeth allegations are softened a little by the television interviewer's joke and the First Lady's retort; but the tone is colder and harsher in the article from *The Times* which appeared on the same day:

Hillary Clinton rejects Lady Macbeth image
By Martin Fletcher

Hillary Clinton, America's unorthodox First Lady, was quick to deny that she is a latter-day Lady Macbeth when she made a rare television appearance last night.

Asked about comparisons between her and Shakespeare's ruthlessly ambitious wife of a weaker husband, she retorted that the problem was that it was not true. She specifically rejected suggestions that she was the driving force behind many of President Clinton's nominations for government office ...[3]

Here, the loaded epithet 'unorthodox' is combined with a definition of what 'a Lady Macbeth' is (a 'ruthlessly ambitious wife of a weaker husband'), and by her much lamer reply to the allegation ('the problem was that it was not true'), to make this an altogether nastier slur. Equally unfriendly is *New York Times* columnist Maureen Drudge's description of Hillary as 'Lady Macbeth in a black, preppy headband',[4] which contrives to be both an attack on her behaviour and a social/sartorial put-down.

Given the similarities between the Clintons and Britain's First Couple, the Blairs, it was always going to be only a matter of time before Cherie got the Lady Macbeth treatment previously meted out to Hillary when Tony Blair became Prime Minister in 1997. This time, though, the allusion seems to have originated, not in the press, but in the office of Tony Blair's long-standing rival next door, Chancellor of the Exchequer Gordon Brown:

> According to a well-placed political journalist, Cherie Blair is known informally by Gordon Brown's advisers as Lady Macbeth ...[5]

Before long, columnist Melanie Phillips, claiming to be 'reveal[ing] the political agenda of the PM's better half', had nicknamed Cherie 'Lady MacBlair';[6] and then the Tory politicians waded in after she had had the temerity to express support in a daily newspaper for Labour's flagship Human Rights Act. For this misdemeanour Conservative shadow Home Office Minister John Bercow accused her of being 'an unaccountable cross between First Lady and Lady Macbeth' – alleging, somewhat improbably, that she had broken a long-standing convention that the spouse of a Prime Minister does not engage in party politicking; of 'trying to direct policy from the throne'; and of behaving like a British version of Hillary Clinton.[7]

The Guardian's 'Pass Notes" witty take on this parliamentary episode both exposes the absurdity of Bercow's 'somewhat dubious comparison between Cherie Blair and the murderous Lady M', and confirms how deeply-rooted in the educated reader's psyche the dramatic character and her story have become. Characterising Shakespeare's Queen as an

> Ice-hearted and ultimately insane manipulator bent on realising her maniacal ambitions through her craven and desperate husband. And now, it seems, a crucial role model in the New Labour Project, too …

'Pass Notes' wryly assists readers with a summary of the *Macbeth* plot, in which

> … a well-bred Scot abandons all his principles in a bid to fulfil a political destiny decreed by a mysterious 'focus group', and ends up by bitterly regretting it.[8]

To compare Hillary Clinton or Cherie Blair with a character who goads her husband into bloody regicide is plainly silly. But, if there was one woman in recent times who did deserve such an analogy, then it was Mirjana Markovic, wife of Serbian leader Slobodan Milosevic. Nicknamed 'the Lady Macbeth of Serbia', 'the Red Witch', 'Rasputin' and 'Serbia's Elena Ceaucescu', Mirjana seemed to be more widely hated than her husband by Serbs who saw her as the real power in this malignant relationship:

The Balkans' own Lady Macbeth

... When she married Slobodan Milosevic she decided he was the new Tito. Insiders believe it was her paranoia that propelled her husband's regime to its worst excesses ...[9]

Sometimes, according to the stories in Belgrade, her irritation with his reluctance to act reached Lady Macbeth-like proportions ('Thou art too full o' the milk of human kindness / To catch the nearest way'). She urged him to make his bid for power in the late 1980s ...; she, by all accounts, demanded that some of those who attacked him or stood in his way should be murdered ...

Now Macbeth is carrying the can for the things his Lady urged him to do ...[10]*

Less seriously, a trawl through the press cuttings reveals a wife who complained to the divorce court judge that her husband had compared her to Lady Macbeth (his Honour observing in his summing-up that 'She found that comparison humiliating, particularly as she is Scottish, born and bred'); while a report on colourful MP Ann Widdecombe's final appearance at the dispatch box is headlined 'Lady Macbeth's last harrumph'. But Lady Macbeths are everywhere. She is considered an apt comparison for John McEnroe's mother ('If I had the chance, I would drill the ball down his throat', she tells interviewers about little Johnny's childhood tennis practice with mom); for 'blond, sulky ice-maiden' gymnast Svetlana Khorkina ('the Lady Macbeth of the uneven bars'); and for Brazilian footballer Ronaldo's

---

* In similar vein, when, after years of relative anonymity, the Irish courtesan Elisa Lynch suddenly becomes the subject of a novel and two biographies, she is predictably dubbed 'The Lady Macbeth of Paraguay'. (Again, not without reason. Lover of the Paraguayan dictator's son Francisco Solano Lopez, Elisa presided over the deaths of a million of the republic's citizens in the fifteen years leading up to her flight in 1870 – following the murders of both Lopez and their son.)

girlfriend Susannah Werner, accused of having kept her lover out of the World Cup Final after kicking him in the groin. And then we have novelist J. G. Ballard, who, when asked by the *Times* 'Bibliofile' 'With which character would you have an affair?', replies: 'Lady Macbeth. I've always admired strong-willed women and an affair with Lady Macbeth would be short but invigorating.'[11]

By the turn of the century, the Lady Macbeth allusion had become the preserve of the strong woman behind the flawed man, notably in the persons of Christine Hamilton and Mary Archer. These are women who have stood by their men, British politicians Neil and Jeffrey, through corruption, court and criminal proceedings (leading to prison in one case) and who, according to novelist Jeanette Winterson, have become a by-word for two things: 'the way they control their men and the way they control the media'. Winterson goes on: 'Or do I mean the Medea? Both women have been compared to Lady Macbeth, but Medea is a closer role model ...',[12] pointing out that, like Lady Macbeth, Euripides' heroine is a character who exercises a curious pull on the national psyche (understandably – when Jason gets married, Medea kills his bride and then their own two children). In an interesting article about the Hamiltons and Archers headlined 'Lady Macbeth is innocent', journalist Amanda Craig observed:

> More and more political marriages seem to conform to the Macbeth pattern, with the wife marked down as the instigator and chief villain ...
>
> Even Cherie Blair and Posh Spice get tainted with the Lady Macbeth image ...

Examining the basic premise on which the comparison is based, Craig asked:

Why do we persist in seeing every other politician's wife not as the dismally confined and tight-lipped creature she usually is but as a Lady Macbeth figure, full of wicked wiles?

It is beyond question that Christine Hamilton, like Mary Archer, Cherie Blair and Hillary Clinton, is brighter than her husband – and more likely to be the driver of the chariot. Yet these are, in all but the Hamiltons' case, women with successful careers of their own …

Why don't we admire women in the public eye who show themselves to be bloody, bold and resolute – albeit married to blithering idiots?[13]

While we're on the subject of blithering idiots, it will come as no surprise that there is no male equivalent to the Lady Macbeth figure: no term for a ruthless and manipulative husband behind a prominent wife. Denis Thatcher, millionaire consort of Britain's first woman Prime Minister, was never branded 'the Macbeth/Iago/Richard the Third … of Number Ten' (in fact, he was something of a joke – the classic blithering idiot of *Private Eye*'s 'Dear Bill' letters); nor is Prince Philip 'the Macbeth of Buckingham Palace', however unpopular he might otherwise be. Milosevic can be called 'a Macbeth' – but only as a consequence of his wife already having become known as 'the Lady Macbeth of Serbia'. It's accepted that a powerful man behind a powerful woman is either nothing to write home about or faintly ridiculous; the reverse – the Lady Macbeth syndrome – is still deemed a cause for anxiety.

Which brings us back to Diana Ingram, wife of the cheating major, and an article which appeared in the *Guardian* newspaper three days after a television audience of seventeen million had watched a programme which showed key moments of the episode in question, plus interviews with the programme-makers, a voice specialist (to analyse the coughing) and fellow-contestants. Picking up Lady Macbeth's injunction to 'look like the innocent flower / But be the serpent under't ...',[14] the article was headed:

The serpent under't

The major's wife has been called a Lady Macbeth. Is that fair, asks John Mullan.

It opened:

> The label seems irresistible. Before I read yesterday that Diana Ingram was denying that she was 'a Lady Macbeth' I had heard friends likening her to just this character. It is not just journalistic shorthand. It is a female character type so powerful that the cheating major's wife feels she must publicly dissociate herself from it.[15]

Referring to Mirjana Markovic, Hillary Clinton, Cherie Blair and Christine Hamilton (and also Princess Michael of Kent, whom I'd forgotten about), Mullan says:

> The Bard's influence reaches widely in this matter. Recently the Spanish paper *El Pais* called national security adviser Condoleezza Rice the Lady Macbeth of President Bush's cabinet ...
>
> Those who use the Lady Macbeth label undoubtedly borrow from Shakespeare's brilliant and terrible characterisation a disturbing idea about female ruthlessness. In the play, the villainess herself supposes that an evil woman has more kindness to overcome than an evil man. 'Unsex me here', she implores the spirits of night. To achieve her 'fell purpose', she must renounce all 'compunctious visitings of nature'. She must cancel all natural feelings. 'Bring forth men-children only', says her spouse, in appalled admiration. Though the man might do the deed, the bad woman is a darker and therefore more intriguing being.

Both Mullan and Sarah Sands ('Why Lady Macbeths get a bad press', quoted earlier) reflect a profound unease about the application of the 'Lady Macbeth' label. It is a discomfort that I share, not only because it helps perpetuate a distortion of the character who appears in Shakespeare's play; but because it implies a deep-rooted misogyny, the male fear of the powerful woman.

All this labelling, in fact, tells us more about the users and their prevailing attitudes to women with talent and influence than it does about Shakespeare's Lady Macbeth. Except for the fact that once again, when journalists and politicians are reaching for a by-word, it's a Shakespeare character who most conveniently leaps to mind.

Act 1, scene 5: 'Come, you spirits / That tend on mortal thoughts, unsex me here / And fill me from the crown to the toe top-full / Of direst cruelty …'

Framed by a gothic archway through which we see a louring, storm-laden sky, the whiteness of her garments stands out against the surrounding gloom. Her right arm is stretched powerfully forward, fist clenched; her left hand, pressed to her breast, clutches the letter from her husband, the letter in which he has informed her of the weird sisters' promise of kingship. Frowning slightly, her face, framed by an unruly mane of long, black hair, is turned towards the heavens. It is the face of an amazonian heroine of indomitable spirit …

Lady Macbeth – here described as she appears in a painting from 1800 by Richard Westall – derives primarily from one of Shakespeare's favourite sources, the monumental *Chronicles* of Raphael Holinshed. First published in 1577, and expanded ten years later, Holinshed's *Historie of Scotland* contains two accounts in which we meet likely originals for the character. The first, a narrative detailing the murder of King Duff, features an otherwise trusty nobleman called Donwald, whose wife persuades him to kill the King, showing him 'the meanes whereby he might soonest accomplish it'.[16] In the second, concerning the rise and fall of Macbeth, the thane's wife 'lay sore upon him to attempt' the killing of the King, being 'verie ambitious, burning in unquenchable desire to bear the name of a queene'.[17] Working with such fruitful material as Holinshed provides, Shakespeare creates a character who, within the 70 lines of her first appearance, builds the foundations for her status as one of the great iconic figures of world drama.

This first scene (1.5) is evocatively captured in Westall's composition. Widely circulated in the 1800s in the form of an engraving by J. Parker, the picture was actually a representation of the actress Sarah Siddons, justifiably one of the most celebrated Lady Macbeths in the history of the role. Siddons reputedly overshadowed the Macbeth of her brother, John Philip Kemble, himself one of the 18th century's great actors. One famous contemporary, the essayist William Hazlitt, commented:

> The enthusiasm she excited had something idolatrous about it; she was regarded less with admiration than with wonder, as if a being of a superior order had dropped from a higher sphere to awe the world with the majesty of her appearance. She raised tragedy to the skies, or brought it down from thence. It was something above nature, We can conceive of nothing grander ... Power was seated on her brow, passion emanated from her breast as from a shrine; she was tragedy personified.[18]

Another contemporary, the lawyer George Joseph Bell, saw in Siddons's depiction of the character a 'turbulent and inhuman strength of spirit', and wrote that:

> ... when you see Mrs Siddons play this part you scarcely believe that any acting could make her part subordinate ... She turns

Macbeth to her purpose, makes him her mere instrument, guides, directs, and inspires the whole plot. Like Macbeth's evil genius she hurries him on in the mad career of ambition and cruelty from which nature would have shrunk;[19]

— while the dramatist Sheridan Knowles exclaimed of her sleep-walking scene, 'I smelt blood! I swear that I smelt blood!'[20]

As Georgiana Ziegler observes in her illuminating essay on 19th-century pictorial representations of the character, the effect of paintings like this, as well as of Siddons's performance and Hazlitt's comments, was 'to allegorize the character of Lady Macbeth and make her larger than life'.[21]

Act 1, scene 6: 'See, see, our honoured hostess …'

Inverness … Tired, sweating and filthy from their ride, many still caked with blood from the previous day's battle, King Duncan's soldiers collapse on the ground before the gates of Macbeth's castle.

Actress Sinead Cusack picks up the description:

> 'All those rough soldiers were lying around, and then this woman swept through them in a green dress and shawl. To those men she was like a vision, a drink of water in the desert. I felt very strongly that the scene had to be beautiful, and she had to look welcoming, to highlight the horror of what she was doing – and all those men had to react to her.'

This is Sinead Cusack's own description of her cool, sexually charged entrance in 1.6, as she emerged from her castle to welcome the trusting King Duncan.[22]

A hundred years earlier, a similarly powerful entrance had been made by another great actress, Ellen Terry. And we know this because of a painting by John Singer Sargent which depicts Terry at the beginning of 1.6, as she strides elegantly and confidently from beneath the castle gates, through a crowd of ladies-in-waiting and sword-brandishing soldiers who have parted as though in awe at the advent of some beautiful Teutonic goddess. The painting is of a performance in 1888, when Terry played opposite Henry Irving's Macbeth. Looking at it now (see Figure 17), we can appreciate the 19th-century *Times* reviewer's enthusiasm for this 'raw-boned daughter of the north'.[23] Responding warmly to her 'matted red hair, hanging in long tresses, and her ruddy cheeks', he went on:

> ... she wears an appropriate dress of garish green stuff embroidered with gold. There is nothing of the martial or adventurous spirit in her composition to bring her into harmony with her barbarous surroundings ...

The scenography of the 1888 *Macbeth* – set design, costumes, props – was conceived by Irving himself and was characterised by impressive costumes set against sombre and chilly torch-lit interiors. As an attempt at an authentic representation of the 11th century, it was a spectacular example of what the same *Times* critic termed 'archaeological correctness' (with, I suspect, a sneering tone similar to that which accompanies an allegation of 'political correctness' today). Because this reviewer was representing a line of criticism which was to have far-reaching consequences for Shakespeare performance in the decades spanning the turn of the 20th century, I quote his argument here in full:

> Archaeological correctness has, of course, been studied in this revival, and we are assured that the British Museum and all known authorities on archaeology have been laid under contribution for correct patterns of the costumes, weapons and furniture of the eleventh century. Shakespeare wrote *Macbeth* in the language of

the sixteenth century, and in the most important point of all, therefore, every performance of the play at the Lyceum or elsewhere must be grossly inaccurate as the personages of the story are concerned. The real Macbeth of the eleventh century would certainly have had some difficulty in expressing himself in Shakespeare's English, nor can we suppose him to have been in the habit of speaking blank verse. These matters, however, are overlooked by the archaeologists, who devote their best efforts to the cut of the clothes and the arrangement and number of the buttons worn by the different characters.

The scorn implied by the heavily ironic tone is one which persists in many quarters today for productions which attempt to impose a notion of 'historical authenticity' on a play which is itself a historical mish-mash. After all, *Macbeth* is a story in which (a) 11th-century Scots and Norwegians inflict varying degrees of medieval barbarism on one another; while (b) apparently responding to the social and political mores of Jacobean England; and (c) all the while framing their utterances in iambic pentameter. It's a glorious cocktail, but you wouldn't want to base a history lesson on it.

In fact, looking at this mix of periods, societies and literary styles, it is tempting to reach for the term 'anachronism'. Yet this seems to me to be a singularly unhelpful way of referring to the medieval–Jacobean mix in *Macbeth* (or, while we're about it, the chiming clocks in *Julius Caesar*, billiards in Cleopatra's Egypt and Gloucester's spectacles in *King Lear*). I prefer to think of each of these as a *polychronism* – a positive ingredient which, rather than jarring us out of the moment, has the effect of creating a bridge between the world of the story (classical Rome, Ptolemaic Egypt, pre-Christian Britain) and the world of Shakespeare. A bridge which, in turn, links the playwright's world to our own.

Anachronisms are mistakes – unless, of course, they are conscious and deliberate. And, while I'm fully alert to the risks of claiming to know (or care) what Shakespeare 'intended', it does seem to me that a man with his breadth of reading might well have known that Cassius couldn't have said 'The clock hath stricken three', but penned the line in the knowledge that the audience would be hearing it spoken by the play's Cassius rather than history's Cassius. In other words, by a character who came across to the audience as only *part* Roman conspirator – the other part being Elizabethan aristocrat.

The effect of this duality would have been enhanced if the conscious use of anachronism (which I will call *polychronicity*) carried over to eclectic costuming. Gabriel Egan is among those who believe that it did:

> Historical costuming was not important, and plays set in the ancient world were performed in Elizabethan dress with small additions to represent distant times and places: a curved sword to connote the Middle East, a sash to connote the Roman toga.[24]

While Egan's assumption seems to me to be intuitively right, it isn't based on much concrete evidence. The only extant contemporary illustration of a Shakespearean performance is the Longleat manuscript. This is a pen-and-ink drawing dated 1595, attributed to the author and artist Henry Peacham, which appears to portray a scene from *Titus Andronicus*. The costumes are clearly eclectic: some make gestures towards classical Roman garb; others (worn by figures who seem to be soldiers) are day-to-day Elizabethan.[25] If the Peacham drawing is in any way reliable, it shows that Shakespeare was clearly quite happy to have his Romans performed in 'modern dress'.

So, if we accept that Shakespeare himself seems not to have been bothered by these historical inconsistencies – or rather, is likely to have embraced them as part of his dramatic method – then it seems illogical to consider plays like *Macbeth* to be 'realistic' in any sense that would justify 'archaeologically accurate' scenography.

In adopting this critical line, I am building on arguments put forward in the early 20th century by William Poel, an actor and director who made it his mission to reform Shakespeare performance and return it to something approaching its pristine uncluttered simplicity. Poel was motivated at once by both a fanatical interest in the Elizabethan theatre and a deep loathing of Victorian stage methods – lavish, overblown sets, ponderous scene-changes necessitating cuts to the text, hordes of 'extras', *faux*-historicity. He decided that the way forward was to perform Shakespeare's plays in their original contemporary costumes on stages which would have been familiar to the King's Men.

After an Elizabethan-dress *Hamlet* at St George's Hall, London in 1881, Poel's ambitions were given a boost by the publication in 1888 of a sketch of the Swan playhouse by a visiting Dutch scholar, Johannes de Witt, dated around 1596. The de Witt drawing (actually a copy of the Dutchman's original by his friend Aernout van Buchel) remains the only surviving illustration of the interior of an amphitheatre playhouse from Shakespeare's time. It shows a stage projecting into a central courtyard, with an open gallery on the first floor of the tiring-house behind. The stage is partly covered by a small roof, supported by columns. Needless to say, the drawing has given rise to much heated debate, the most sceptical analysts asking how much credence can be placed upon a copy of a single sketch by a foreigner who had seen the structure only once. (Try drawing the interior of a building you visited for the first and only time recently, and then go back and compare your recollections with reality ...)

But de Witt's drawing motivated Poel to explore stage practice in Shakespeare's time; and his Elizabethan Stage Society, founded in 1895, went on to stage a number of ground-breaking productions through to the 1920s. His achievement is aptly summed up by Dennis Kennedy:

> Though his productions were usually marred by idiosyncratic notions of vocal tone and delivery, and though his understanding of Elizabethan acting was seriously flawed, he had great influence on the general twentieth-century project of invigorating Shakespeare by simple and open staging.[26]

'Historical' Shakespeare – toga-ed *Julius Caesar*s set in a Rome that we recognise from a thousand TV documentaries, doublet-ed *Romeo*s in locations that look like tourist-Renaissance Italy, be-furred *King Lear*s howling on pagan heaths – has not completely gone away, of course. In fact it had a real fillip with the spate of Shakespeare films precipitated by Olivier's *Henry V* in 1944. In this, the star actor's pudding-basin haircut is modelled on medieval images of the historical Henry, and heavily-armoured French knights are winched into their saddles by elaborate lifting mechanisms (on the grounds that the weight of their ironmongery would have prohibited traditional methods of mounting their chargers). Olivier also added shots of rain falling in puddles, and the English archers driving stakes into the ground to fend off the enemy at Agincourt – both historically verifiable, but neither mentioned in Shakespeare's script. These last features, incidentally, were picked up and elaborated upon by Kenneth Branagh when he filmed his version nearly half a century later.

But there is a difference between Victorian archaeological correctness and what we see in these *Henry V*s; or, for example, in Oliver Parker's 1995 *Othello* (with its sumptuously dressed tableaux in the Doge's palace) or the 1968 Zeffirelli *Romeo and Juliet* (with its Oscar-winning costumes and shimmering-hot Renaissance streets). In all of these, what's important is that the audience have the *impression* of authenticity. While the films' designers may well trawl through

Florentine art for ideas, their aim is to create a filmically acceptable version of what we *expect* the Scottish Middle Ages or Italian Renaissance to look like, given that the reality (were such a thing conjurable) would be either dull or confusing.

Polanski's *Macbeth* is a good example of this more recent form of historical correctness in that it offered its television-educated 1971 audience the picture of a semi-civilised and physically harsh Middle Ages that they had come to expect. Featuring windswept, barren hills and genuine castle exteriors, the Macbeths' world, in which the thane and his wife wash off Duncan's blood in water from a courtyard well, looks primitive, cold and filthy. It all seems authentic enough, and it doesn't matter that the hills are actually Welsh, rather than Scottish, or the castles Northumbrian … nor that the heraldry and the armour are largely invented. It is as historically correct as the audience of its time requires. And that seems to have been the policy of all the prominent post-war Shakespeare films which have opted for a historical – rather than a modern or period analogue – setting,[27] a collection of movies which, in addition to those mentioned above, also embraces Joseph L. Mankiewicz's 1953 *Julius Caesar*, Olivier's 1955 *Richard III*, Orson Welles's 1966 *Chimes at Midnight* (his version of the *Henry IV* plays) and Zeffirelli's 1990 *Hamlet*.

A brief look at each of those films is enough to show that, while they are all 'historical' in their approach, they are often so in ways which say more about the era in which they were filmed than about the period they purport to represent. Make-up, hairstyles and pronunciation betray some of the superficial traits of each film's decade. And the treatment of themes and incidents says more about contemporary social and political concerns than about those of Shakespeare's own time or the era in which the story takes place. Compare Olivier's Second World War *Henry V* and Branagh's post-Falklands version, and you'll see what I mean. And a film *should* reflect the year in which it was made, if Shakespeare is to carry on as it always has, saying something new and urgent to each succeeding generation.

Act 1, scene 7: 'When you durst do it, then you were a man ...'

PA UBU: Pschitt!

MA UBU: Ooh! What a nasty word. Pa Ubu, you're a dirty old man.

PA UBU: Watch out I don't bash yer nut in, Ma Ubu!

MA UBU: It's not me you should want to do in, Old Ubu. Oh, no! There's someone else for the high jump.

PA UBU: By my green candle, I'm not with you.

MA UBU: How come, Old Ubu? You mean you're content with your lot?

PA UBU: By my green candle, pschitt, Madam. Yes, by God, I'm perfectly satisfied. Who wouldn't be? Captain of the Dragoons, aide de camp to King Wenceslas, decorated with the order of the Red Eagle of Poland, and ex-King of Aragon. You can't go higher than that!

MA UBU: So what! After having been King of Aragon, you're content to ride in reviews at the head of fifty bumpkins armed with billhooks when you could get your loaf measured for the crown of Poland?

PA UBU: Huh? I don't understand a word you're saying, Mother.

MA UBU: How stupid can you get!

PA UBU: By my green candle, King Wenceslas is still alive, isn't he? And, even if he does kick the bucket, hasn't he masses of children?

MA UBU: Why shouldn't you finish off the whole bunch and put yourself in their place?

PA UBU: Ha! Madam, now you have gone too far, and you shall very shortly be beaten up good and proper.

MA UBU: You poor slob, if I get beaten up who'll patch the seat of your pants?

PA UBU: So what! Haven't I a bum like everyone else?

MA UBU: If I were you, I'd try to get that bum sitting on a throne. You could become enormously rich, eat as many bangers as you liked, and roll through the streets in a fine carriage.

PA UBU: If I were king, I'd get them to make me a great bonnet like the one I used to wear in Aragon, which these lousy Spaniards had the nerve to pinch off me.

MA UBU: And you could get yourself an umbrella and a guards officer's greatcoat that would come down to your feet.

PA UBU: It is more than I can resist! Pschittabugger and buggera-pschitt, if I ever come across him alone on a dark night, he's for it.

MA UBU: Well done, Pa Ubu, now you're talking like a man ...[28]

This version of Lady Macbeth's famous taunting scene is from *Ubu Roi*, a satirical take on Shakespeare by the French dramatist Alfred Jarry, first performed in Paris in 1896. Jarry's burlesque does not feature Shakespeare's characters, but, as you can tell from the opening scene above, when Père Ubu is incited by his wife to assassinate the Polish King and usurp the throne, the *Macbeth* parallels are obvious.

There are even some textual echoes. Expressing reservations about the murder, for example, Père Ubu says: 'King Wenceslas is still alive, isn't he?' And we might recall Macbeth's incredulous response to the witches' prophecy that he shall be Thane of Cawdor: 'The Thane of Cawdor lives / A prosperous gentleman ...' (1.3.71–2)

Similarly, Ubu's wife converts Lady Macbeth's taunt, 'When you durst do it, then you were a man' (1.7.49) into positive reinforcement when she praises her husband's masculinity: 'now you're talking like a man'. And, in Ma Ubu's incitement, 'And you could get yourself an umbrella and a guards officer's greatcoat that would come down to your feet', we might even be reminded of Angus's

> Now does he feel his title
> Hang loose about him like a giant's robe
> Upon a dwarfish thief. (5.2.20–2)

But, despite these examples, *Ubu Roi* is only loosely connected to Macbeth; it is not a caricature of its text or plot, in the way of the 19th-century English burlesques.

For that kind of imitation, we have to turn to spin-offs like Barbara Garson's *Macbird!* This was an American political burlesque which gained its title when the author, speaking at an anti-Vietnam war rally in 1965, perpetrated a piece of splendidly serendipitous Freudian slippery, accidentally referring to President Lyndon B. Johnson's wife Ladybird as 'Lady Macbird'. Garson's play advertises its anti-war credentials the moment the lights go up on a trio of protesters chanting 'When shall we three meet again / In riot, strike, or stopping train?', but maintains a sense of fun right through to Lady Macbird's appearance (in cold-cream and curlers) and her sleep-walking scene complete with Airwick spray.

Non-comic spin-offs have included two movies in which Shakespeare's characters are re-invented as gangsters: *Joe Macbeth* (1955) and *Men of Respect* (1991).[29] Tony Howard has pointed out that different Shakespeare plays 'have different adapting strategies', and that, of all the plays, '*Macbeth* has been adapted most directly, indeed almost naively'.[30] This is certainly borne out by the two gangland *Macbeths*.

Made in Britain with mostly US actors (the exception being Sid James as Joe's pal, Banky) from a screenplay by Philip Yordan, *Joe Macbeth* is first and foremost a gangster movie, only incidentally an adaptation of Shakespeare's play. Briefly: Joe has a rival eliminated, for which he is rewarded by the capo, Duca, who gives him a ring for his new bride, Lily. All is well until a tarot reading by flower-seller Rosie predicts that Joe, already Duca's 'number one boy', will become 'Lord of the Castle' and, in time, 'King of the City'. Within minutes of the fortune-telling, Duca has arrived to offer Joe the keys to a lavish lakeside mansion (the 'castle') and Rosie's prophecies begin to take on the ring of truth. Ruth Roman's Lily is a worthy spin-off from Lady Macbeth. To bring out the nature of her sexual hold over Joe, the screenplay makes them newly-weds; and her persuasive techniques – telling Joe that they will never be any more than Duca's 'stooges playing big-shots' – have the true Lady Macbeth ring about them.

In many ways a remake of its 1955 predecessor, *Men of Respect* featured John Turturro and Katherine Borowitz as the murdering couple, young and attractive in the Polanski mould. But the film stumbled in attempting to incorporate too many Shakespeare parallels. To give you an idea of how lumpen and cliché-laden William Reilly's screenplay was: the equivalent of Macbeth's 'Tomorrow and tomorrow …' speech came out as 'Shit happens'. Unsurprisingly, the film enjoyed neither critical nor box-office success.

Also set in 'a debauched gangster underworld, with the witches as drug-dealing, cocktail-mixing croupiers',[31] was a more recent stage spin-off, *Journey to Macbeth*. Involving witches on stilts and giant puppets from the Caribbean and Romania, plus a soundtrack of 'thumping Balkan rock, soul and ambient trance', this promenade re-jigging at the 1999 Edinburgh Festival starred Australian pop-singer Dannii Minogue. Staged by the alfresco company Theatrum Botanicum, who tour the world's botanical gardens, the production described itself as 'a hard-hitting, high-octane-fuelled bloodbath'. Director Toby Gough (who the previous year had cast Dannii's sister Kylie in a Caribbean version of *The Tempest* in Barbados), said: 'I'm more on the side of clowning and carnival rather than classical theatre. But beneath that,

I'm taking the audience on a serious spiritual journey, and looking at images of heaven and hell.'

For many, the greatest *Macbeth* spin-off (in fact, possibly the greatest Shakespeare movie-transformation ever made) is the Japanese director Akira Kurosawa's *Kumonosu Djo* (*The Castle of the Spider's Web*), known in English as *Throne of Blood*.[32] While not attempting to echo Shakespeare's language, Kurosawa's film follows the dramatic structure of its original very closely, with 15th-century samurai Japan providing a brilliantly effective context for Shakespeare's story of ambition and warrior ethics. In Kurosawa's film, Washizu (the Macbeth figure) encounters an ancient female spirit – a single entity replacing Shakespeare's three sisters – as he rides through the labyrinthine Cobweb Forest with his friend Miki (Banquo). Washizu receives prophecies that he will rule North Mansion and then Cobweb Castle – but is told that the castle will ultimately be taken over by Miki's son.

In a fruitful interpretation, the Lady Macbeth figure, Asaji, is cinematically linked to the 'weird sister' in the forest – both have the traditional white-painted oval faces and expressionless voices of Noh theatre. And this visual and aural connection becomes so strong that we begin to believe that the two might be in league. Asaji's toneless-ness well suits her ruthless determination and we can easily see why her husband submits to her urgings that they should kill Tsuzuki (Duncan) while they have him under their roof.

Where Shakespeare's Macbeth is a victim of his own weakness and ambition, Washizu's downfall is brought about by a constraining feudal order – an order represented metaphorically as the tangled webs of the forest. In that respect, *Throne of Blood* evokes something of Hamlet's metaphor, 'Denmark's a prison'. Like all Kurosawa's movies, it is

… characterised by the profound, frequently hard-edged humanity encountered in Shakespeare. [His films] were always designed, he once said, to confront audiences with the same fundamental theme: 'Why – I ask – is it that human beings … can't live with each other with more good will?'[33]

Though he was separated from *Macbeth* by four centuries and half a globe of cultural difference, it should not surprise us that, in order to give expression to this question, Kurosawa should so famously turn to Shakespeare.

Act 1, scene 7: 'I have given suck …'

He is wavering – 'We will proceed no further in this business' – and, to stiffen his resolve, she reminds him of his manhood, and her femininity:

> *'I have given suck, and know*
> *How tender 'tis to love the babe that milks me;*
> *I would while it was smiling in my face*
> *Have plucked my nipple from his boneless gums*
> *And dashed the brains out, had I so sworn as you*
> *Have done to this.'*

These lines have been a great puzzle to actresses and academics alike. Recalling preparations for her 1983 interpretation, Sinead Cusack asks:

> Lady Macbeth says 'I have given suck …'. So where is that baby? What happened to their child? I'm not certain who asked the question first, or whether we all had the idea simultaneously, but as we explored it in rehearsal, we decided that the Macbeths had had a child and that the child had died. The line can be interpreted differently but that's the interpretation we chose, and as the idea grew it seemed to have a beautiful logic …[34]

Investigating the same question herself when she came to rehearse the role some twenty years later, Harriet Walter was to write:

> One director I spoke to reckoned that Lady Macbeth is barren and that 'I have given suck' is a neurotic fantasy that Macbeth allows her. In Kurosawa's film *Throne of Blood* (1957) Lady Macbeth is pregnant and loses the child at the banquet. Every production has to find a solution. Scholars' concerns lie else-where. One footnote I read dismissed the question of Lady Macbeth's child or children as 'unprofitable'. That editor did not have to play the part.[35]

Nor, of course, did L. C. Knights, when in 1933 he wrote the now famous essay 'How Many Children Had Lady Macbeth?'.[36] Knights's polemic was an attempt to discredit the kind of extra-textual specula-tions made by critics such as A. C. Bradley, whose *Shakespearean Tragedy* (a discussion of *Othello*, *Hamlet*, *King Lear* and *Macbeth*) has nonetheless been described as 'probably the most influential book of Shakespeare criticism ever published'.[37] Knights's objection was that critics and performers such as Bradley and the actress Ellen Terry con ceived of Shakespeare's creations as flesh and blood 'characters', and that this was based on a misunderstanding of the nature of Shakes-peare's art. Knights mocked Ellen Terry for daring to speculate on whether Portia had herself thought up the 'drop of blood' clause which saves Antonio in *The Merchant of Venice*,[38] declaring:

> We are faced with this conclusion: the only profitable approach to Shakespeare is a consideration of his plays as dramatic poems, of his language as dramatic poetry, of his use of language to obtain a total complex emotional response. Yet the bulk of Shakespeare criticism is concerned with his characters, his heroines, his love of nature or his 'philosophy' – with everything in short, except the

words on the page, which it is the main business of the critic to examine.[39]

It will come as no surprise that I have little sympathy with a critical approach which sees the greatest *plays* in the language as 'dramatic poems'. Poetic dramas, unquestionably; dramatic poems, no.

I was in the Shakespeare Institute library the other day and overheard a user scoffing at a fellow student for having a copy of Bradley open on their desk. Disappointingly, the reader offered an embarrassed excuse instead of the spirited defence that Bradley deserves. Such a defence might offer this as evidence:

> [Lady Macbeth's] will, it is clear, was exerted to overpower not only her husband's resistance but some resistance in herself. Imagine Goneril uttering the famous words,
>
>> Had he not resembled
>> My father as he slept, I had done't.
>
> They are spoken, I think, without any sentiment – impatiently, as though she regretted her weakness; but it was there. And in reality, quite apart from this recollection of her father, she could never have done the murder if her husband had failed. She had to nerve herself with wine to give her 'boldness' enough to go through her minor part. That appalling invocation to the spirits of evil, to unsex her and fill her from the crown to the toe topfull of direst cruelty, tells the same tale of determination to crush the inward protest.[40]

Bradley's criticism is simple, direct and – in stark contrast to much modern Shakespeare criticism – comprehensible to 'the great variety of readers' interested in Shakespeare. Moreover, it makes complete sense to anybody who takes the view that Lady Macbeth, Goneril,

Cleopatra and the rest exist to be acted; and that any approach which insists upon defining them as nothing more than linguistic constructs is seriously missing the point.

I actually *do* want to know how many children Lady Macbeth had; and I anticipate a different answer from each of the actresses I ask. Not only that, but the act of facing the question can help to prevent the distortion of Lady Macbeth into the heartless monster many people conceive her to be. For Harriet Walter, it was working on the hypothesis that the Macbeths had had a son who had died, that forced her to confront afresh the import of those terrible lines 'I have given suck …':

> But how, I protested, could a woman who knows 'How tender 'tis to love the babe that milks me', and has seen that baby die, even contemplate the thought of dashing an infant's brains out? I had fallen into the trap of seeing this violent image as proof of Lady Macbeth's heartlessness. But once I started to act the scene and feel the desperate energy of it, I understood that the opposite was the case. Lady Macbeth is thinking up the supreme, most horrendous sacrifice imaginable to her in order to shame her husband into keeping his pledge. She never has to match deeds to her words, but to dare to speak such pain-laden words is in itself impressive, and Macbeth realises what it costs her.[41]

Act 2, scene 2: 'Why did you bring these daggers from the place?'

Macbeth has done the deed. Duncan lies dead, his silver skin laced with his golden blood, and his two grooms lie with him. One had cried 'God bless us' in his sleep and 'Amen' the other, as though they had seen the murderer with his hangman's hands, and Macbeth, a voice crying in his head 'Sleep no more! Macbeth does murder sleep …', now returns with blood on his hands that not all of Neptune's great ocean will ever quite wash off …

Hands that still hold, red and incriminating, the blood-stained weapons.

'Why did you bring these daggers from the place?' she demands, appalled at his stupidity.

> *'They must lie there. Go, carry them and smear*
> *The sleepy grooms with blood …'*

He reels back and stares in insane horror at the daggers, their bloody blades lifted towards his wife, who, one finger to her lips and a look of terrifying ferocity, stretches her hand to receive them …

For it is she who will return them to the place, promising:

> *'… if he do bleed,*
> *I'll gild the faces of the grooms withal,*
> *For it must seem their guilt.'*

Henry Fuseli's watercolour illustration of this moment (see Figure 15)[42] depicts David Garrick and Mrs Pritchard (actually Hannah Pritchard, but the familiarity seems both disrespectful and anachronistic) as a mid-18th-century couple. They are placed before a set of folding screens, he in wig and knee-breeches, she in a framed skirt so wide that even negotiating the wings to make a smooth entrance must itself have been a problem.

Garrick's performance of Macbeth – it opened at Drury Lane in January 1744 – cemented his reputation as a star in an artistic community that could already boast Samuel Johnson and Joshua Reynolds. But so significant was Mrs Pritchard's contribution to the success of this performance after she had joined the company (and went on to play Lady Macbeth for twenty years), that Garrick effectively gave up playing Macbeth when she retired. Her later acting years, we are told, were troubled by 'increasing obesity',[43] but this did not stop her selecting Lady Macbeth for her farewell to the stage in 1768.

Her cold determination in the part is perfectly captured here by Henry Fuseli, an English Romantic artist of Swiss origin. Born Johann Heinrich Füssli in 1741, Fuseli is one of the most famous illustrators of scenes from Shakespeare: 'a genius like a mountain torrent, a worshipper of Shakespeare, and now, Shakespeare's painter',[44] in the words of the 18th-century German essayist and Bardolater, Johann Herder. With an original approach to human physiognomy, and a predilection for the horrifying, the grotesque and the fantastic, Fuseli's idiosyncratic depictions (many of which reflect his admiration for the work of his friend William Blake) were to have a powerful appeal to the expressionists and surrealists of later centuries.

Fuseli is closely associated with the Shakespeare Gallery, an ambitious project to depict scenes from Shakespeare's plays, administered by the engraver, print publisher (and, in 1790, Lord Mayor of London) John Boydell.[45] Situated in a huge building in Pall Mall, Boydell's gallery opened in June 1789, its aim being to encourage the growth of 'a great national school of history painting'. From a modest 34 canvases in its first year to 167 by its close, the Shakespeare Gallery grew in popularity, and Boydell was quick to exploit its success, establishing a thriving business selling engravings of the paintings. But his hopes to leave the collection to the nation were thwarted by heavy financial losses sustained during the French wars when the European market for prints was cut off, and it was sold by auction in 1805.

The Shakespeare Gallery is therefore important not merely for the work that it helped to engender – distinguished contributors included Joshua Reynolds and George Romney – but also because it represented one of the first successful attempts to commodify and commercialise Shakespeare. Boydell realised that scenes from the plays, mass produced and affordably priced, would have a wide popular appeal. He is the patron saint of every mug, tea-towel and decorated tie on sale in the RST foyer.

Objecting to Boydell's commercialism, Fuseli severed his connection. But by the time of the gallery's demise his reputation as 'Shakespeare's painter' was secure. Holding Shakespeare to be 'the supreme master of passions and the ruler of our hearts', Fuseli's aim was to capture the great scenes in Shakespeare's plays, and to depict the instant at which the charge of emotion electrifies the atmosphere, moments at which we experience 'spontaneous ebullitions of nature'.[46] Garrick's (for its time) comparatively naturalistic acting, and his method of concentrating on the main characters for maximum intensity of impression, were ideal for a painter who loved to focus on instants of highest tension, and who believed that

> The middle moment, the moment of suspense, the crisis, is the moment of importance, big with the past and pregnant with the future.[47]

Jonathan Bate has memorably described Fuseli's paintings as 'declarations of the power of feeling in Shakespeare's plays'. Considering the way in which his portrayals start out as illustrations of Garrick and Mrs Pritchard as Macbeth and Lady Macbeth, but in later versions become idealised, almost platonic, visions of the characters themselves, Bate writes:

> In high Romantic manner, Fuseli goes beyond stage representation and seeks to take Shakespeare directly into the imagination, translating character into icon.[48]

Act 3, scene 4: 'When all's done / You look but on a stool ...'

'Here is a place reserved, sir.
Where?
Here, my good lord ...'

Macbeth starts, on the instant quite unmanned ('– in folly', she will later add). He has seen what Lennox and the other thanes cannot – the blood-bolted Banquo sitting at the table in the place reserved for himself ...

Does his wife know what he sees? Quickly she rises, her black evening dress, long gloves and gold earrings contrasting with the rough brick walls of the Roundhouse, calms their guests – 'My lord is often thus' – and drags him away.

'Are you a man?' she hisses, trying to persuade him that whatever he sees is one with the air-drawn dagger that – he claimed – led him to kill Duncan, shaming him that, when all's done, he looks but on a stool ...

It is the last time she will be in control, of him or of herself ...

This was Harriet Walter's Lady Macbeth for the RSC in 2000 (see pages 201, 203), in an eclectically costumed – though mainly modern – interpretation which vividly brought out the fragility of the character's precarious hold on sanity. This production was later filmed for Channel 4 Television; but, though effective on the small screen, it lacked the power of the stage performance in Stratford's Swan Theatre.[49]

I have to admit to being no great fan of TV Shakespeare. For me, it too often closes down and restricts, where the cinema has the potential to expand and explore. But two of the best post-war *Macbeth*s have been happily filmed for television: this one – worth recording for Walter's flaky Lady Macbeth and Antony Sher's wholly credible soldier-turned-tyrant; and the 1976 RSC version directed by Trevor Nunn at The Other Place, Stratford, which featured Ian McKellen and Judi Dench.[50] In a production which Jack Gold (who directed the BBC *Macbeth*) 'could not watch', finding it simply too oppressive,[51] Judi Dench's plea with the spirits that tend on mortal thoughts – 'Unsex me here!' – remains one of the supremely chilling Shakespeare moments, the character almost recoiling at her own evil.

The best known movie incarnations of the character are Jeanette Nolan in the 1948 Orson Welles film, and Francesca Annis, directed by Roman Polanski in 1971. Jeanette Nolan's first appearance in Welles's interpretation is described by Pamela Mason:

> When we first see her she is lying on a bed, but any easy assumptions about sexuality are challenged by the visual tension between the barbarism of the fur bed-covering and the forties' style, front-laced, high-necked dress with its zip-fastener and shoulder pads.[52]

I don't know if it's because she's a character who cries to be unsexed and then challenges her husband's manhood, but it's interesting how often accounts of stage and screen Lady Macbeths dwell on the actress's appearance and sexuality in this way: in another account, Nolan's Queen is described as having 'a touch of the dominatrix about her, with a Bride of Frankenstein hairdo and shrill voice'.[53]

Francesca Annis's pretty and disturbingly child-like Lady Macbeth for Roman Polanski in 1971 could hardly have been more different …

Act 5, scene 1: 'Yet here's a spot.'

In the semi-darkness, all we see of her at first is a timid eye peeping through a hole in the door.

'When was it she last walked?' whispers the doctor. And the nurse summarises her charge's recent nocturnal habits: rising from her bed, throwing a nightgown upon her, unlocking her closet, taking forth paper, folding

it, writing upon it, reading it, afterwards sealing it, and again returning to bed – 'yet all this while in a most fast sleep'.

Then she enters, completely naked, and re-enacts the movements just described, walking agitatedly across the room to sit at a writing desk illuminated by a single candle. She begins to twitch her hands …

'What is it she does now?' asks the doctor.

'It is an accustomed action with her to seem thus washing her hands', the fearful nurse explains. 'I have known her continue in this a quarter of an hour.'

But their whispered colloquy is interrupted by a tremulous voice – 'Yet here's a spot …'

Concerned that she was too young for the role (at 25) when Roman Polanski offered it to her, Francesca Annis formed half of an attractive, and for a time sympathetic, young couple in the successful 1971 film (Macbeth was the 28-year-old Jon Finch). Their tragedy was that, secure in royal favour, they had absolutely no need to kill the inoffensive and patriarchal Duncan. With its nude sleep-walking scene and hallucinogenic visit to the witches' lair, this was very much a *Macbeth* of its time, its explicit violence creating uneasy echoes of the death of Polanski's pregnant wife Sharon Tate in August 1969 at the hands of three members of Charles Manson's 'Family' cult.

The video of Polanski's *Macbeth* is now in every school English department stock-cupboard. How typically Shakespeare: that a play's evil and violence are able at one moment to evoke topical horrors from which we would prefer to shield our children – the Manson murder – and at another, be recruited as a central pillar of the school curriculum. In the face of those who would enlist him as part of the national heritage business, Shakespeare remains as much Sharon Tate as Tate Gallery.

And that leads me to an interesting *Macbeth* painting. In his study of art and literature in Britain, Richard D. Altick describes an 1864 painting by Charles Hunt, titled 'My *Macbeth*'.[54] In this composition, Hunt depicts himself, his wife and his son standing in their Victorian living-room, proudly contemplating an oil-painting of the banquet scene. The painting they are admiring is, in fact, one which Hunt had exhibited at the Royal Academy the year before (but which is now lost). The interesting thing is that the picture-within-the-picture is actually a schoolboy performance of *Macbeth*. What Hunt has done is to portray a Victorian family group who have admitted into their drawing-room a painting of children performing Shakespeare.

And this makes Hunt's composition the polar opposite of Fuseli's nightmarishly gothic images of Shakespeare's tragedy. Fuseli's illustrations tap into dangerous, unruly and potentially subversive emotions. Hunt's is a safe, neutered representation, which brings Shakespeare into the Victorian middle-class household and co-opts it, tamed and serviceable, as part of the British education system.

Which, of course, is where it remains. By the turn of the 21st century, successive governments of all political stripes had made the study of a Shakespeare play compulsory for every fourteen-year-old in mainstream state education in England and Wales. In the late 1990s, schools had to choose from *Romeo and Juliet*, *Julius Caesar* or *A Midsummer Night's Dream*; by the early 2000s, the choice was between *Twelfth Night*, *Henry V* and *Macbeth*. Two years after their obligatory injection, these same students (now sixteen) are required to

> ... demonstrate their understanding of, and engagement with, at least one [further] play by Shakespeare; [and show] awareness of social and historical influences, cultural contexts and literary traditions which shaped Shakespeare's writing and/or which have influenced subsequent interpretations of his work.[55]

It's a far cry from – and infinitely more rigorous than – the old 'O' Level exam, in which students could get a grade A (and I know because, to my shame, I used to drill them in it) merely by giving 'an account of the scene in which …'. These days, they undertake tasks which require them to write, for example:

> … an analysis of the dramatic qualities of one or more scenes, related to performance issues and/or alternative interpretations and related to the text as a whole, showing how these may be influenced by social or historical factors, or by different cultural contexts;

or character studies

> involving a response to dramatic features of the text and showing understanding of the author's language … [and] an understanding of literary and theatrical contexts.

It's challenging, it focuses on the right things – performance, interpretation, context, multiplicity of meanings – and it requires detailed study. I only wish it had the effect of turning young people on to Shakespeare. Sadly, the pressure placed on them by teachers who are themselves under intolerable pressure – from parents, league tables, unfriendly media, OFSTED (the government's inspection system) – means that students are too often primed and prepared to jump through the assessment hoops (I know that's a cliché, but it's apt) and that teachers teach to the exam. It absolutely is *not* the teachers' fault. But, as a result of this dismally reductive process, too many students still leave school heartily relieved that they won't ever have to suffer Shakespeare again.

Act 5, scene 1: 'What, will these hands ne'er be clean?'

It is the scene the audience have been waiting for – the 'Gran Scena del Sonnambulismo'. Throughout the opera, the stage has been bare except for mighty trees towering over every scene. A gantry provides a gibbet; earlier, underlit trap-doors have suggested the witches' cauldron and Duncan's bed-chamber; the only additional staging has been an industrial-chic bar that descended to make the table for Macbeth's dinner and a cat-walk for Banquo's ghost, and a blood-stained blade that formed a wall of the castle ...[56]

Now the lighter wind instruments are silenced, leaving only clarinet and cor anglais, but the scene is conceived on a grand scale; and as she washes her hands, the agitation is expressed through rapid gesture on muted strings, accompanied on stage by the fearful exchanges between the watching Doctor and Gentlewoman ...

> *'How came she by that light?'*
>
> *'Why, it stood by her ...'*
>
> *'Her eyes are open.'*
>
> *'Ay, but their senses are shut ...'*

The sleep-walker looks down at her hands and sempre sotto voce cries: 'Una macchia ...!' – 'Yet here's a spot ...'

This is the Kirov Opera Company's Olga Sergeeva as Lady Macbeth in Giuseppe Verdi's operatic version of Shakespeare's play performed in 2001. Gary Schmidgell, who describes the effect of Lady Macbeth's music in this scene as of 'one endless, uninterrupted, *unrepeating* melody', is one of many musicologists to suggest that it was only with his tenth opera, *Macbeth* (composed in 1847 and revised eighteen years later), that Verdi began to view his works as *opere ad intenzioni* – operas formed according to dramatic, rather than musical, convention:

> With *Macbeth*, in other words, he began to cease thinking of operas as aural necklaces of cavatinas, duets, ensembles, and

choruses strung one after another. In pursuit of these more pristinely theatrical intentions, Verdi ... opened his *Macbeth* project with his librettist, Francesco Maria Piave, with the exhortation, 'Brevity and sublimity' ...[57]

Verdi's first foray into Shakespeare (he was later to produce his two operatic masterpieces *Otello* and *Falstaff*) was in some respects a risky venture, given that the story had no love interest. But the four-act opera, a condensation of Shakespeare's play, was an instant success on its Florence première, with Marianna Barbieri-Nini as an imposing Lady Macbeth. To this day, in the words of one recent reviewer, its 'mixture of cheerful grand guignol, tormented sexuality and power politics, linked to Verdi's lyrical prodigality, exerts a unique fascination'.[58] And central to its continued success is the figure of the Queen. Music critic Nick Kimberley believes that Verdi's opera should be called *Lady Macbeth*, so strongly do her moods define the musical colouring.[59]

One opera which does feature, if not Lady Macbeth herself, then a Lady Macbeth figure, is Dmitry Shostakovich's *Lady Macbeth of the Mtsensk District*. Composed between 1930 and 1932,* it is the tale of a bored middle-class woman in a provincial town whose dull life leads her first to take a lover, and then to murder her father-in-law and husband. The opera was an immediate success with critics and public on its 1934 Leningrad première, and quickly clocked up nearly 200 performances. Then, in January 1936, Joseph Stalin decided to attend a staging in the Bolshoi Theatre, Moscow. Two days later, Soviet readers opened their *Pravda* to find the leader headed 'Muddle instead of music'. It was a savage attack on the opera for its 'distortion', and 'petty-bourgeois sensationalism'. Written at Stalin's instigation – and

---

* The four-act opera had a libretto by Shostakovich himself and A. Preys, based on a short story by N. Leskov, written in 1846.

possibly even penned by the man himself – the leader declared the music (recently described as containing 'vertiginous swings between brittle satire, dissonant expressionism and luscious romanticism')[60] to be 'fidgety', 'screaming', 'neurotic' and 'obscene'. *Lady Macbeth of the Mtsensk District* simply did not comply with Stalin's view of 'people's art'. Not only was it a thinly veiled comment on the state of post-revolutionary Soviet Russia; it openly depicted sex, and portrayed the murdering Katerina sympathetically. There were to be no more performances in Stalin's lifetime.[61]

Lady Macbeth has made a powerful impression on later artists working in a wide diversity of media. Returning to the sleep-walking scene, consider this extract from Dickens's *Dombey and Son*. Here the ruined Dombey, now living in desolate solitude, suffering 'strong mental agitation and disturbance', is haunted by the guilty memory of his dead son and estranged daughter:

A spectral, haggard, wasted likeness of himself brooded and brooded over the empty fireplace. Now it lifted up its head, examining the lines and hollows in its face; now hung it down again, and brooded afresh. Now it rose and walked about; now passed into the next room, and came back with something from the dressing-table in its breast. Now it was looking at the bottom of the door, and thinking.

— Hush! What?

It was thinking that if blood were to trickle that way, and to leak out into the hall, it must be a long time going so far. It would move so stealthily and slowly, creeping on, with here a lazy little pool, and there a start, and then another little pool, that a desperately wounded man could only be discovered through its means, either dead or dying. When it had thought of this a long while, it got up again, and walked to and fro with its hand in its breast. He glanced at it occasionally, very curious to watch its motions, and he marked how wicked and murderous that hand looked.

Now it was thinking again! What was it thinking?

Whether they would tread in the blood when it crept so far, and carry it about the house among those many prints of feet, or even out into the street.[62]

There are reflections of *Hamlet* here, of course, in the melancholy brooding – and a specific verbal echo ('It lifted up its head ...').[63] But the major inspiration is clearly Lady Macbeth, with Dombey, tormented by guilt, coming 'out of his solitude when it was the dead of night, and with a candle in his hand' and, obsessed by the thought of tell-tale blood, beginning to fear that 'all this intricacy in his brain would drive him mad'.

Act 5, scene 1: 'More needs she the divine than the physician ...'

Still seated at her writing-desk, she is approached by the doctor, who tentatively, and without much hope, passes his hand before her sightless eyes. 'Yet here's a spot', she mutters desperately. And the doctor diligently makes a written note of her words.

That particular doctor was Richard Pearson's soft-spoken yet ultimately self-seeking professional in the Polanski film, his actions here based on lines that the director cut:

> Hark! She speaks. I will set down what comes from her, to satisfy my remembrance the more strongly.[64]

Though absent from the 1971 film, that speech was certainly heard by Dr Simon Forman, quack, astrologer and play-goer, when he attended a performance of *Macbeth* on Saturday 20 April 1611.

Recording his impressions of the play, Forman wrote:

> Observe also how Macbeth's queen did rise in the night in her sleep, and walked, and talked and confessed all, and the Doctor noted her words.

Forman is of great interest to students of Shakespeare because he kept notes on some of the performances he had seen and collected them together in *The Bocke of Plaies and Notes Thereof per Forman S. – for Common Pollicie*. This book comprised summaries of, and comments on, three Shakespeare plays staged at the Globe during the last spring before Forman's death in September 1611: *Macbeth*, *Cymbeline* and *The Winter's Tale* (plus a play about Richard the Second not by Shakespeare). The book – or all that remains of it – is something of a treasure, given that the comments on Shakespeare's plays are from someone who actually saw them performed by the King's Men in Shakespeare's lifetime. And Forman's eye-witness accounts, though selective and in many ways unreliable – they were written as a source of moral lessons, not as theatre history – throw up some intriguing questions. What are we to make, for example, of the fact that he twice calls the Weird Sisters 'nymphs'? That they were played in 1611 as attractive young women, rather than hags?

Forman's accounts of the three Shakespeare plays are delightfully idiosyncratic. He omits key events (such as the return of Hermione in *The Winter's Tale*), gets things wrong (he has Cloten in Cymbeline banished for loving Imogen; and Macbeth made Prince of Northumberland), and adds details presumably gleaned elsewhere. One example is his comment that Macbeth and Banquo encountered the witches *on horseback* – an impression possibly formed from having seen the woodcut in Holinshed's *Chronicles*.[65] Not only that, but his observations 'for Common Pollicie' (i.e. helpful moral and social pointers for daily life) home in on features which are hardly central to the play. At the end of his section on *The Winter's Tale*, for example, where we might expect him to warn us against irrational jealousy, or precipitous action, or lack of faith, his injunction is to 'be ware of trusting feigned beggars or fawning fellows'. Maybe Forman had been cozened more than once himself; whatever the reason, Autolycus had clearly made a greater impression on him than Hermione.

But my favourite idiosyncrasy is in the account of *Macbeth* above, which Forman concludes with the detail 'and the Doctor noted her words'. It's easy to imagine him, alone among the Globe crowd, identifying with this observant, note-taking fellow-professional rather than the tormented Lady Macbeth, especially when the character later ruefully and materialistically observes:

> Were I from Dunsinane away and clear,
> Profit again should hardly draw me here.[66]

Forman is not the only contemporary eye-witness to a Shakespeare play. In February 1602, the law student John Manningham (who we encountered in Chapter 5) attended a performance of *Twelfth Night* at the Inner Temple, went home and jotted down the following:

> At our feast wee had a play called Twelve Night or What You Will, much like the Commedy of Errores ... A good practise in it to make the Steward beleeve his Lady Widdowe was in love with him, by counterfeyting a letter as from his Lady in generall termes, telling him what she liked best in him, and prescribing his gesture in smiling, his apparaile, &c., and then when he came to practise making him beleeve they tooke him to be mad.[67]

Nothing about Viola, nothing about Orsino. For Manningham, 'Twelve Night' was notable for Malvolio and the deceptions practised upon him, just as *The Winter's Tale* for Forman was important for its lessons about 'fawning fellows' and the sleep-walking scene in

Macbeth memorable at least in part for the note-taking doctor.

Forman's accounts, like Manningham's, have an interest and importance which transcend Shakespearean scholarship. Because we can compare them with the texts that have come down to us, they show us that eye-witness reports, written only a short time after the event, can err in fact and be idiosyncratic in emphasis, a salutary lesson for historians and theologians alike. They also demonstrate that, however authoritatively some people might try to tell us what is 'important' about a Shakespeare play, we will derive our own significances. And these might well lead us to conclude that the humble note-taking doctor is as worthy of comment as the fiend-like Queen.

CHAPTER 7

Hamlet

'It is we *who are Hamlet'*

William Hazlitt

GUIL: It really boils down to symptoms. Pregnant replies, mystic allusions, mistaken identities, arguing his father is his mother, that sort of thing; intimations of suicide, forgoing of exercise, loss of mirth, hints of claustrophobia not to say delusions of imprisonment; invocations of camels, chameleons, capons, whales, weasels, hawks, handsaws – riddles, quibbles and evasions; amnesia, paranoia, myopia; day-dreaming, hallucinations; stabbing his elders, abusing his parents, insulting his lover, and appearing hatless in public – knock-kneed, droop-stockinged and sighing like a love-sick schoolboy, which at his age is coming on a bit strong.

ROS: And talking to himself.

GUIL: And talking to himself ...[1]

It's hard to say much about the impact of Shakespeare's most famous character without reaching for the words 'iconic' and 'iconographic'. Hamlet has become both a collection of ideas and a set of images.

Delay. Procrastination. Introspection ... Iconically, that's what 'Hamlet' means. Icon*ographically*, 'Hamlet' is a young man in black, holding a skull and gazing at it, deep in thought.

Both the concepts and the images are so powerfully embedded in our cultural consciousness that a newspaper article about new research linking procrastination with depression and attention deficit disorder[2] will be illustrated not by a photograph of the behavioural psychologist who has published her findings, but by a still of Olivier as the brooding Dane in his 1948 film,[3] a character who, as the caption explains, 'clearly put off important decisions'; while former Spice Girl Geri Halliwell, asked about a spell of professional inactivity, can choose to explain it by reflecting: 'I had Hamlet's disease of introspection. I was always looking for the integrity behind it.'[4]

There is always something more than faintly disparaging about being called a Hamlet, especially if your job requires you to be a decision-maker. This is William Rees-Mogg, in an article on Conservative politician Michael Portillo, headed 'Hamlet, lazibones and the grandma's friend':

> The British do not naturally admire intellectuals, and associate high intelligence, which Portillo obviously possesses, with untrustworthiness and indecision. They do not want a Hamlet in Downing Street ...[5]

Portillo was at that time being touted as a possible Tory leader and future Prime Minister, and the 'Hamlet' tag is clearly damning. And the same goes for a very different political figure, Labour's John Prescott, when correspondent John Cole writes:

> At school John Prescott played Grumpy in 'The Seven Dwarfs'. Some Labour colleagues think he has never grown out of the part. Yet during our long, boring run-up to the general election, Prescott is understudying Hamlet: racked by doubts that colour his zeal.[6]

It is clear that other people whose jobs actually require them to think a lot – scientists, say, or writers – don't usually get called 'Hamlets'. The term is reserved for people we expect to be action-types – a category which in Britain seems to include politicians as much as characters like the athletic hero of Sven Lindqvist's *Bench Press*, here described by reviewer Mark Simpson:

> Sven does a lot of talking to himself in this book: he's the Hamlet of the weights room, wrestling not just with barbells on his bench, but with visions of his dead father, ethical dilemmas and mixed metaphors, taking up big arms against a sea of troubles …[7]

That last cutting, with its 'arms against a sea of troubles', is also a reminder of the seemingly endless capacity that Hamlet quotations have for re-invention, especially in the hands of journalists. Their favourite, of course, is 'To be, or not to be', surely the most famous literary quotation in the English language, some version of which is trotted out every time somebody in the public eye is faced with a dilemma. And it has such currency that it is rarely quoted in its original form. Media writers are so confident that their audience will get the allusion, that we find (from a wide selection):

- 'To shake or not to shake' – whether the England cricket captain will shake President Mugabe's hand if the team plays in Zimbabwe (they didn't);
- 'To shred or not to shred? That is the modern dilemma' – whether, as a young graduate in the company, you unethically shred 'the minutes of yesterday's meeting with that dodgy guy from the Middle East …';
- 'To share or not to share?' – Premier Tony Blair torn between retaining or devolving power; and
- a piece on the advisability of purchasing share options, predictably headed 'To buy or not to buy?'.[8]

Hamlet and his expressions – 'there's the rub', 'shreds and patches', 'hoist with his own petard', 'to the manner born', 'be cruel only to be kind' – are as much a part of our language as anything from the Bible.* They are as celebrated as the character's brooding melancholy, his madness (is he or isn't he crazy? – to commit or not to commit?) and his alleged procrastination.

One quality not normally associated with Hamlet, though, is stoical acceptance in the face of a malign fate …

Background sound effects of a busy railway station … The scene: the interior of a photo-booth. From the booth camera's eye-view, we are look-ing at a man (actually Scots comedian Gregor Fisher) meticulously comb-ing a long, lank strand of hair across his bald head, then fumbling in his pocket for a coin, which he inserts in a slot beneath our field of vision. Technicalities accomplished, he sits back and assumes a debonair smile for the camera …

Nothing happens. Undaunted, he re-fixes the smile and waits. Then bends to check the machine …

At which point the camera flashes.

He replaces the hair and poses once more. Once more, nothing happens and he stoops to check – and the camera flashes for a second time.

---

* It has become a commonplace of books on the English language to list the many expressions we have derived from Shakespeare. But, as David Thatcher has pointed out, we are rather too ready to credit Shakespeare with the creation of expressions which in fact pre-dated their appearance in his plays. According to Thatcher, phrases which *are* first recorded in *Hamlet* include, in addition to those quoted above: 'sick at heart', 'the glass of fashion', 'heart of hearts', 'man and boy', 'patch of ground', 'the primrose path' (also in *Macbeth*), 'mortal coil', 'give us pause', 'protest too much', 'cudgel thy brains', 'a tow'ring passion' and 'germane to the matter'. (See David Thatcher, 'Shakespeare as Phrasemaker: Attributions and Misattributions', *The Shakespeare Newsletter*, Winter 2002/2003, pp. 95–6, 98.)

On the third occasion, the flash hits him just after the moment when his adjustable seat has decided to re-adjust itself and he has plummeted a foot downwards.

All we can see now is the top of his bald head.

Then a wisp of smoke appears and the station noises are replaced by the sound of a match striking and Bach's Air on a G-String ...

The scenario, the music and the smoke have by this time become so famous that we do not need the product name for this advertisement to have its full effect. In a series of TV commercials that stretched from 1964 until 2003, Hamlet, 'the mild cigar', promoted itself as the ideal consolation in moments of adversity. It was an unusual pitch, but extraordinarily successful, the mood of consoled stoicism evoking, if somewhat indirectly, the brand name's association with Shakespeare's most conspicuously philosophical character. As its advertising director Paul Welland said: 'Always the best campaign idea in advertising is very simple ... [and] you can ... borrow from any area, whether it's films, theatre or real life ...'[9] It's not easy to say exactly what this popular cigar borrowed from Shakespeare's character beyond a vague cultural cachet acquired through the name; but, whatever it was, it worked.

Borrowing the iconography rather than just the name, one Carling Black Label advertisement from 1986 began with the most famously iconographic moment in the whole of Shakespeare: Hamlet gazing at the skull ...

'Alas', he gloomily intones, 'poor Yorick ...'

And clumsily drops the skull.

But the moment is not totally ruined. Catching it skilfully on his foot, he deftly tosses it up and embarks upon a game of 'keepie-uppie', juggling it from toe to shoulder to head, encouraged by the enthusiastically vocal approval of the theatre audience.

On cue, a second actor enters. 'My noble lord Hamlet –', he begins. But the address is quickly abandoned in favour of 'Over 'ere, son – on me 'ead', and the ball-play now involves two players in a sequence which ends only when Hamlet punts the skull accurately if painfully into the balls of an evening-suited audience member in one of the boxes.

Like some ventriloquistic Shakespearean Epilogue, the skull (in 'Johnny Gielgud' voice) gives us the expected punch-line: 'I bet he drinks Carling Black Label.'

Derek Longhurst has pointed out how this kind of appropriation works on its mainly male working-class or lower-middle-class target audience by 'disrupting and supplanting "alien" cultural practices with a comic *spectacle* of the performance of expert skills in a "familiar" cultural activity …', observing that:

> … [the] images construct a polarity between a middle class culture of constraint and inhibition overturned by the freedom, power and vitality of popular culture – and of the products consumed, supposedly, by its most distinctively skilful proponents.[10]

The same kind of thing happened with an advertisement from 1997, in which King Lear overlooks two of his daughters in favour of the third, who is attractively stocked with Coca Cola; and in a 1994 Typhoo Tea commercial, where the 'Englishness' of the product is conveyed by a voice-over of Gaunt's 'This royal throne of kings … this England' speech from *Richard II*.[11] In each case, the advertisers ingratiate themselves with their target group by purporting to elevate the ordinariness of a popular high street product – cheap lager, a soft drink, household tea – over an élitist high culture represented by

Shakespeare. Here's one in the nuts for you snobs, it seems to say. Perversely, of course, it serves only to acknowledge and reinforce the 'Bard's' perceived cultural supremacy by the very act of setting it up to be lampooned.

These advertisements, for Hamlet cigars and Carling Black Label lager, are acknowledging that *Hamlet* the play, metonymically, *is* Shakespeare; and that Hamlet the character stands for *Hamlet* the play. (We could take that a stage further and say that the skull iconographically stands for Hamlet, but that wouldn't get us anywhere.) The point I am trying to make is that, however towering a Lear might be, we don't find ourselves talking about something being 'like *Lear* without the King'; or 'like *Romeo* without the lovers'. And yet any situation with a key ingredient missing is '*Hamlet* without the Prince' … It can be the Lazio–Inter Milan game with Ronaldo absent with his chronic knee problem; script-writers Reeves and Mortimer missing from television's *It's Ulrika!*; or the fact that the National Changeover Plan (amazingly) said nothing about monetary policy or the exchange rate! And then, expanding upon the Shakespearean theme, a headline can proclaim: 'An education photo opportunity with no Blair is not so much Hamlet without the Prince as Macbeth minus all the Scots.'[12]

Act 1, scene 2: 'I shall in all my best obey you, madam'

Hamlet sits slumped on a chair, a sulky presence in the context of the court's extravagant celebrations, his mother standing behind him, her hands caressing his shoulders. And he shows no reaction when Claudius names him as next in line and declares his paternal affection. Only when his uncle-stepfather expresses his opposition to Hamlet's return to university, and his mother moves round to face him, placing her hand on his cheek, does he react. Responding to her request that she should not lose her prayers in asking him to stay at court, he lowers his eyelids (glancing down at her body as she stoops over him? – it's hard to tell) and replies: 'I shall in all my best obey you, madam.'

Claudius is pleased: 'Why', he proclaims, "tis a loving and a fair reply'.

And Gertrude, still caressing her son's face, bends and kisses him on the lips, slowly and tenderly … and then kisses him again, only stopping at Claudius's somewhat peremptory command: 'Madam, come.'

As the court exit to prolonged fanfares, Hamlet remains motionless, and Vaughan Williams's gloomy cellos accompany a slow closing in of the camera …

Casting a Gertrude who is actually thirteen years younger than Hamlet, as was the case in this 1948 film with Eileen Herlie and Laurence Olivier,[13] or with only a few years between them (Glenn Close and Mel Gibson in 1990), is one of the easiest ways of suggesting to an audience that Hamlet and his mother entertain incestuous longings. And the point can be dramatically reinforced by including a moment in which the mother kisses the son passionately on the lips, as happens in both these movie versions. This ambiguous mother–son relationship has become as famous as Hamlet's proclaimed procrastination and his debatable madness; for many people it is what 'Freudian' means.

Sigmund Freud was very keen on Shakespeare. We are told that he began reading the plays when he was eight, and his collected works are liberally illustrated by references to characters such as Macbeth, Lady Macbeth and Richard the Third,[14] as well as to the patterns in plays such as *The Merchant of Venice* and *King Lear*.[15] Most famous, though, are Freud's psychoanalytic interpretations of *Hamlet*, notably his suggestion that the Prince's delay and inability to act can be explained by the workings of an Oedipus complex.

Initially exploring the enduring power of another great tragedy, Sophocles' *Oedipus Rex*, Freud came to the conclusion that:

[Oedipus'] destiny moves us only because it might have been ours – because the oracle laid the same curse upon us before our birth as upon him. It is the fate of all of us, perhaps, to direct our first sexual impulse towards our mother and our first hatred and our first murderous wish against our father. Our dreams convince us that that is so.[16]

Drawing a link between *Oedipus Rex* and *Hamlet* ('which has its roots in the same soil'), Freud went on:

Strangely enough, the overwhelming effect produced by the more modern tragedy has turned out to be compatible with the fact that people have remained completely in the dark as to the hero's character. The play is built on Hamlet's hesitations over fulfilling the task of revenge that is assigned to him; but its text offers no reasons or motives for these hesitations and an immense variety of attempts at interpreting them have failed to produce a result ...

Summarising one or two of these attempts (including Goethe's view that Hamlet's power of action is paralysed by an over-developed intellect), Freud asked:

What is it, then that inhibits him from fulfilling the task set him by his father's ghost? The answer, once again, is that it is the peculiar nature of the task. Hamlet is able to do anything – except take vengeance on the man who did away with his father and took that father's place with his mother, the man who shows him the repressed wishes of his childhood realised ... The distaste for sexuality expressed by Hamlet in his conversation with Ophelia fits in very well with this ...

So confident was Freud in his unique capacity to have explained Hamlet's problem that he was able to claim:

... the conflict in *Hamlet* is so effectively concealed that it was left to me to unearth it.[17]

He later wrote:

> I have followed the literature of psychoanalysis closely, and I accept its claim that it was not until the material of the tragedy had been traced back by psychoanalysis to the Oedipus theme that the mystery of its effect was at last explained. But before this was done, what a mass of differing and contradictory interpretative attempts, what a variety of opinions about the hero's character and the dramatist's intentions![18]

In 'explaining' the 'mystery' of Hamlet, what the psychoanalyst had 'unearthed' was that Hamlet's procrastination was all to do with guilt:

> We know that it is [Hamlet's] sense of guilt that is paralysing him; but, in a manner entirely in keeping with neurotic processes, the sense of guilt is displaced on to the perception of his inadequacy for fulfilling his task.[19]

This was a major claim, but there was more to come. Not content with having solved the problem of Hamlet's conflict in this way, Freud took the whole thing a stage further by asserting:

> For it can of course only be the poet's own mind which confronts us in Hamlet. I observe in a book on Shakespeare by Georg Brandes (1896) a statement that *Hamlet* was written immediately after the death of Shakespeare's father (in 1601), that is, under the immediate impact of his bereavement and, as we may well assume, while his childhood feelings about his father had been freshly revived.[20]

The problem with this last deduction, of course, is that recent scholarship assigns *Hamlet* to a year or so *before* John Shakespeare's death: 1600–01.*[21] This doesn't of itself invalidate Freud's claim that the play confronts us with 'the poet's own mind' and specific 'childhood feelings'; but it does demonstrate that the basis for his claim was probably fallacious. In fact, Freud had to revise this assertion himself, when he later decided that Shakespeare hadn't written the plays at all – at which point the psychoanalyst had to re-allocate the dead father to the Earl of Oxford.[22]

Trying to link a writer's fictitious creations with real events in his or her life is always a perilous business. But it is especially so with Shakespeare, a figure about whose personal biography we know a limited amount and whose characters represent a bewildering diversity of world views. But it may well be the province of psychoanalysis to do this, and, if it is, as a layman, I certainly don't propose to challenge Freud on psychoanalytic grounds. More problematic for me, though, and for a host of readers before me, are the premises on which Freud builds his Oedipal theory for Hamlet, and the conclusions they enable him to draw. Because here the psychoanalyst is moving into the territory of the literary critic, ground on which I feel more qualified to challenge him.

Let me focus on one foundation-stone of Freud's interpretation: 'We know', he states, 'that it is [Hamlet's] sense of guilt that is paralysing him'. The problem is, we can't *know* anything of the kind; and there are very good reasons for thinking that he might be being paralysed by all sorts of other things, if indeed he is being paralysed at all. To take one alternative view ...

My own favourite interpretation is that Hamlet's problem has

---

*The play was entered in the Stationers' Register in July 1602, but external and internal evidence place the play around the turn of the 17th century.

very little to do with sex and a great deal to do with death.* Allow me to explain. Time after time, we see Shakespeare taking a popular genre and doing something revolutionary with it; or picking on a common set of assumptions and challenging them. He takes the patriotic history play and turns it into an interrogation of war, its justifications and modes of conduct (*Henry V*); or he lures people into the playhouse with the expectation of watching another usurious Jew get his come-uppance (following Marlowe's Barabas), and confronts them with Shylock's 'If you prick us, do we not bleed …?' (*The Merchant of Venice*). And he takes the popular revenge play and turns it into *Hamlet*.

In the most successful revenge play of the early Elizabethan era, Thomas Kyd's *The Spanish Tragedy* (1592), a ghost appears and demands that his death be avenged. This is a common device to get the plot going, and works tremendously well in Kyd's play, the hero Hieronymo prompted to set about his work with relish after the murder of his son. But what does Shakespeare do with this same ghost device? Or rather, what is the effect of the Ghost's appearance on the hero-avenger? Instead of being spurred on to instant implementation of revenge, Hamlet thinks about it. Why? Freud says it's all to do with Hamlet's Oedipus complex. I believe it's all to do with the business of seeing the ghost of your dead father.

When he played Hamlet in 1989, Daniel Day-Lewis famously cracked up because he started seeing his own dead father on stage. It is inconceivable that this could have happened had he being playing Kyd's Hieronymo. No actor playing Hieronymo 'sees' his dead son. Why? Because Hamlet is in a 'real' situation in crucial ways that Hieronymo isn't. And, I believe, the *Hamlet* ghost is real in ways that

---

* In a later phase of his writing, of course, Freud was to link 'Eros' and the death instinct. See *Beyond the Pleasure Principle* (1920) and *The Ego and the Id* (1923) (Penguin Freud Library, vol. 11).

the ghost who opens *The Spanish Tragedy* isn't. Shakespeare's play doesn't have a ghost in it merely to set the plot in motion. The appearance of the shade of the dead king is asking us to think: What would happen if you were actually faced by the ghost of your dead father? What effect would it have on you?

And we see some of the possible answers to this question as we follow Hamlet's story: he obsessively questions what the ghost he has seen actually *is* ('the spirit I have seen may be a devil …'); pondering suicide, he questions what he might face after death in 'the undiscovered country from whose bourn / No traveller returns'; 'thinking too precisely on th'event', he is incapable of planned action (I discount his spur-of-the-moment thrust through the arras). Until … until what? Well, until his own life is threatened and the possibility of death becomes a reality; when, inspired by Fortinbras and determined that 'from this time forward' his thoughts should be 'bloody or be nothing worth', he sends Rosencrantz and Guildenstern to their deaths without a single qualm ('They are not near my conscience'). And then what is it that finally settles his mind about death? It is when he is faced with Yorick's skull (and it's no coincidence that, of all the comic characters Shakespeare might have chosen to illuminate Act 5, he gives us a grave-digger). And he realises that, however beautiful or painted a living human being might be, 'to this favour she must come'. That is why he is able to face a patently sinister duel with a wronged rival, set up by a notorious villain, with the words:

> There is special providence in the fall of a sparrow. If it be now, 'tis not to come. If it be not to come, it will be now. If it be not now, yet it will come. The readiness is all. Since no man knows of aught he leaves, what is't to leave betimes? Let be.[23]

And finally, it is significant that, of all the things Shakespeare might choose to give Hamlet as his dying words, he opts for 'the rest is silence', surely the Prince's serene conclusion to all his speculations about what happens when we die.

I have indulged myself, explaining my own pet theory about Hamlet and his problems, not because I believe it to be worth any more than a thousand others, but to explain *why* it happens to satisfy me, in the same way that Freud's satisfied him. I am a rationalist (atheist, if you will), and it pleases me to think of Shakespeare's play as endorsing the rationalist philosophy by which I lead my life. As a psychoanalyst, it satisfied Freud to see a key theory borne out in the two most famous creations of two of the world's most famous writers, Sophocles and Shakespeare. As Kenneth Muir very neatly put it over 50 years ago:

> It is only when we recollect that Coleridge's Hamlet was very like Coleridge, Murry's was very like Murry, Schopenhauer's like Schopenhauer, C. S. Lewis's prince weighed down by the burden of original sin what we might expect from the author of *The Screw-tape Letters*, that we are apt to wonder whether it is an accident that the disciple of Freud [critic Ernest Jones] should diagnose an Oedipus complex and that the propagandist for the Orestes complex [Frederick Wertham] should find one in Hamlet.*[24]

Muir might also have added that Nietzsche's Hamlet was very like Nietzsche. In his first major publication, *The Birth of Tragedy* (1872), the young philosopher celebrated 'Dionysiac man' who could see into the heart of existence. Given his concomitant belief that, when we return from the ecstatic state to everyday reality, we are filled with

---

* Jones was the best-known literary critic to espouse and develop Freud's theory of Hamlet's Oedipus complex (in *The Problem of Hamlet and the Oedipus Complex* (1911) and *Hamlet and Oedipus* (1949)); Wertham's *Dark Legend* (1946) argues that Hamlet suffers from an Orestes complex – an attachment to, and hostility towards, the mother image leading to a general hatred of women.

loathing for the world, it is no surprise that Nietzsche's Hamlet should be thoroughly Dionysiac:

> ... Dionysiac man might be said to resemble Hamlet: both have looked deeply into the true nature of things, they have *understood* and are now loath to act. They realise that no action of theirs can work any change in the eternal condition of things, and they regard the imputation as ludicrous or debasing that they should set right the time which is out of joint ... What, both in the case of Hamlet and of Dionysiac man, overbalances any motive leading to action, is not reflection but understanding, the apprehension of truth and its terror.[25]

Each of us finds or creates his or her own Hamlet, one who reflects our core beliefs.

But the reverse happens too. Isn't it equally true that writers like Sophocles and Shakespeare actually shape the way we think (and that their ability to do that is part of our definition of 'genius')? Could Freud have come up with the Oedipus complex without Sophocles' Oedipus? Could it have been confirmed in his mind without Hamlet? It's hard to say. But, allowing for my limited grasp of psychoanalysis, and trusting to my understandings of Shakespeare, I'm attracted by the argument that:

> Shakespeare precedes psychoanalysis epistemologically, just as he does historically: that is, the modes of narrative, rhetoric, imagery and characterisation that Freud ... [encounters] in Shakespearean drama help to shape the development of psychoanalytic notions about dreamwork, the operations of the unconscious, and the nature of the self.[26]

Or, as Norman N. Holland, himself a prominent post-Freudian critic, says:

> Perhaps ... it is not so much that Freud brought the Oedipus complex to *Hamlet* as that *Hamlet* brought the Oedipus complex to Freud.[27]

It would be inappropriate for me to try to criticise Freud's view of *Hamlet* from a psychoanalytic viewpoint – I'd be out of my depth. Looking at it from the Shakespeare angle, however, I would have to say that Freud's claim to have 'unearthed' Hamlet's conflict is foolishly hubristic, and his attempts to link the character with the author (an author who is first Shakespeare, then Edward de Vere) misguided. I also think that treating a Shakespeare play as a puzzle to be solved does little to illuminate it.

But it's equally true that we can't un-invent Freud, and he has had a powerful influence on some impressive interpretations. Chief among these has to be Olivier's 1948 film, which ignored the political dimensions of the story to focus on the troubled relationship between Hamlet and his mother. Olivier had by that time long been influenced by Ernest Jones's psychoanalytic interpretation of the play, and cast the 27-year-old Eileen Herlie as Gertrude. Thirteen years his junior, Herlie could have passed for Hamlet's daughter, and it was easy to see why, with the glamorous Herlie as his mother and eighteen-year-old Jean Simmonds as his girlfriend, the poor chap might have such a confused relationship with the opposite sex.

Taking the Ophelia–Gertrude confusion a step further, director Celestino Coronado cast Helen Mirren as both characters in his disturbing 1976 film version, in which Hamlet's troubled and divided nature was graphically represented by having him played by twins, Anthony and David Meyer. Performing the soliloquies as duologues, frequently naked, at times abusing, at times caressing both Gertrude and Ophelia, these Hamlets were explicitly incestuous and outrageously Oedipal, and would have left Freud little to 'unearth'.

More popularly, the 'Freudian' interpretation of Shakespeare has been delightfully parodied in *Shakespeare in Love*, when Will consults 'Dr Moth, apothecary, alchemist, astrologer, seer, interpreter of dreams, and priest of psyche':

WILL
I have lost my gift.
(not finding this easy)
It's as if my quill is broken. As if the organ of the imagination has dried up. As if the proud tower of my genius has collapsed.

DR MOTH
Interesting.

WILL
Nothing comes.

DR MOTH
Most interesting.

WILL
(interrupting)
It is like trying to pick a lock with a wet herring.

DR MOTH
(shrewdly)
Tell me, are you lately humbled in the act of love?[28]

With the exception of the Zeffirelli film in 1990 (see below), Freudian *Hamlet*s have become rather passé. But I doubt that the bearded psychoanalyst will ever quite go away. And each generation of actors that embarks upon this extraordinary play will find him scribbling in his notebook in the corner of the rehearsal room, impossible to ignore.

Act 1, scene 2: '… this too too sullied flesh'

Gertrude skips down the castle steps to bid an affectionate farewell to her new husband as he prepares to set off on a day's hunting – or possibly join him for a ride. Looking down from a tower window, Hamlet observes her public frolicking. He is disgusted, devastated … And, for the first time in our acquaintance with him, he contemplates self-slaughter, fervently wishing that his too too solid (or is it 'sullied'?) flesh might melt …

When word first started getting around that Franco Zeffirelli had approached Mad Max to play Hamlet, a lot of people assumed it must be a joke. But the effect of casting *Lethal Weapon*'s Mel Gibson opposite *Fatal Attraction* star Glenn Close[29] was to create an action-picture *Hamlet* which earned respectable box-office receipts, some grudgingly favourable reviews from at least a section of the critics, and an encouraging response from younger audiences.[30] And, while this version cuts the script down to about 40 per cent of Shakespeare's, truncates the longer speeches, and interrupts dialogue and soliloquy with action shots, it is arguably closer in spirit to the way the King's Men's Richard Burbage played it than any of the more introspective versions that have graced our stages in the past century.

And how do we know how Burbage played it? Well, we don't. But there are some possible indications in a fascinating book by the man who served as 'book keeper and prompter' of the Lincoln's Inn Fields Theatre from 1662 to 1706, John Downes. In his stage history, *Roscius Anglicanus* (1708), Downes delineates an unbroken tradition linking the actors of his own time, the Restoration, to those of Shakespeare's. In particular he states that Sir William Davenant, his theatre's licensee, had seen Joseph Taylor play Hamlet. Taylor (c. 1586–1652) was the actor brought in to be the leading player of the King's Men after Richard Burbage's death, and had, according to Davenant, been instructed in how to play his new roles by Shakespeare himself.

Downes avers that Davenant had himself schooled Thomas Betterton (the greatest Restoration actor) in how to play Hamlet, and indeed had 'taught Mr Betterton in every particle of it',[31] thereby perpetuating the Burbage tradition. Burbage is instructed by Shakespeare, who talks to Taylor, who is seen by Davenant, who schools Betterton.

The problem with that is that Taylor could not, in fact, have been trained in the role by Shakespeare: he joined the King's Men only in 1619, on Burbage's death, and this was three years after Shakespeare had died in Stratford. However, given the way acting companies worked at that time, it seems likely that Taylor would have been expected to perform his inherited roles much as Burbage had done. Whether Shakespeare had had any hand in Burbage's performance remains a matter for conjecture. On the one hand, Shakespeare was an extremely busy writer and businessman with possibly little time for the daily practicalities of staging a play. On the other hand, he too was an actor, and might well have found time to discuss a character like Hamlet with the player performing him, especially when that actor was as interesting and as gifted as Richard Burbage. And the King's Men would plausibly have ensured that Burbage's replacement Taylor performed the role much as his predecessor had done. So Thomas Betterton's fast-paced and vivacious Hamlet, first performed in 1663, could very well have been modelled on Burbage's, which, we assume, would at the very least have met with Shakespeare's acceptance, if not approval.*

Thomas Betterton, aided and abetted by Sir William Davenant, started a tradition for savagely cutting *Hamlet* which persists to this day. When David Garrick approached the role in 1772, he wrote that he was planning to do

---

* There are interesting insights into rehearsal processes in Tiffany Stern, *Rehearsal from Shakespeare to Sheridan* (Oxford University Press, 2000).

... the most imprudent thing I ever did in my life ... I have dared to alter *Hamlet*, I have thrown away the gravediggers, and all the fifth act ...[32]

And his altered version, though he refused to publish it, was a great success (especially the moment when, on encountering the Ghost, his hair stood on end).

An even leaner and fitter *Hamlet* hit the stage in John Philip Kemble's interpretation. Kemble acted the part from 1783 to 1817, and it was by all accounts a fast-moving, action-packed run-through in the Zeffirelli mould, high in energy but short on introspection, pacy but not deep. Not everybody liked it, and the 19th-century critic William Hazlitt's reaction to it is instructive. He wrote:

> We do not like to see our author's [i.e. Shakespeare's] plays acted, and least of all, *HAMLET*. There is no play that suffers so much in being transferred to the stage.[33]

Having already had a go at Freud in this chapter, I am reluctant to take on the great William Hazlitt. But I do have to say that this is an attitude to Shakespeare that I find bewildering, especially in a writer whose passion for the theatre pervades his work. You might have noticed that throughout this book I have tended to refer to Shakespeare's *scripts*, rather than *texts*, for the simple reason that I regard them as written material for actors to act – quite unlike poems or novels, which are to be digested in the quiet of the armchair. Scripts – and Shakespeare's are no different in this regard from those produced for *EastEnders* or *The Sopranos* – are only one stage in a creative process. Reading a script and not wanting to see it acted is, for me, like reading a recipe for apple pie and being reluctant to cook the dish because the reality can never match the platonic pie that exists in our imaginations. I simply can't conceive of having a book with Hamlet's words in, and not having Jacobi's Hamlet, Olivier's, Burton's, David Warner's, Mark Rylance's, Branagh's, and, yes, Mel Gibson's, to make the character come alive in an infinite variety of existences way beyond the capacity of my poor imagination to conjure up. I remember seeing Branagh look at Yorick's skull on the stage at Stratford and say '... I knew him Horatio' so naturally that it was as though I had never heard the line before. I can't analyse what he did or how he did it. But I do know that my experience of this remarkable role would be seriously impoverished without that moment; and that nothing I could possibly do in merely reading the play could ever make up for having missed Branagh act it.

Act 2, scene 2: 'I am but mad north-north-west …'

Rosencrantz and Guildenstern trailing in his wake, Hamlet strides out onto a gallery overlooking the great hall. He has seen through these former school-friends and knows that they have been sent for to spy on him. Hence his gabbling and off-hand conversation. But, before deserting them for the more congenial company of the travelling players, he slips them a piece of information, let them make of it what they will —

'But my uncle-father and aunt-mother are deceived', he confides.

'In what, my dear lord?', asks Guildenstern, hoping for some illumination, but by now sceptical of receiving any.

'I am but mad north-north-west', replies the Prince. 'When the wind is southerly, I know a hawk from a handsaw …'

Kenneth Branagh here, and throughout his interpretation,[34] portrays a Hamlet whose madness is never any more than pretence. With not the faintest trace of genuine derangement, nor even a remotely Oedipal sub-text, Branagh's Hamlet is angry, mean and dangerous, enunciating crisply, hitting every consonant, resolutely sane to the end.

The tradition of completely sane Hamlets can be traced back to the 19th-century actor Barry Sullivan. Sullivan, of Irish parentage, first played the character in 1852 and was greatly admired by George Bernard Shaw who opined that, compared to his rivals, Sullivan was 'Hyperion to a satyr'. The American Edwin Booth played a similarly sane Prince, first in the 1860s, and as a farewell appearance in 1891, just two years before his death. In Britain, Johnston Forbes-Robertson developed Booth's intelligent and bitter concept of the role into something more graceful and melancholy when he came to it rather late in his career (he was 44) in 1897. For many people, Forbes-Robertson's Hamlet, a Renaissance courtier trapped in a barbaric Teutonic court, was the definitive performance of its day. Encouraged by acclaim and undaunted by advancing years, Robertson committed his legendary interpretation to silent film in 1913 at the age of 60.[35]

The most influential Hamlets in the early 20th century were those of Barry Jackson and John Gielgud. Jackson, who founded the Birmingham Repertory Theatre in 1913, produced the first notable modern-dress *Hamlet* in 1925 (the year in which he was knighted). Directed by A. J. Ayliff, the production was quickly termed 'Hamlet in plus-fours' by a public unused to seeing Shakespeare in anything other than Shakespearean costume.

John Gielgud was unquestionably the most celebrated Hamlet of his generation. Coming to the role first in 1930 at the age of 26, he went on to play Hamlet over 500 times in the ensuing sixteen years. Gielgud was among the youngest actors to have played the role in a major theatre. Recalling his Old Vic debut (in an Elizabethan-dress, uncut version which ran for four and a half hours), he wrote with typical modesty:

… many people said that my original performance in 1930 was the best, because I had no idea I was going to be good.[36]

Describing Gielgud's impact in the role (allowing for the changes in interpretation between 1930 and 1946), Richard Findlater writes:

By some people the first Hamlet is remembered for his sweetness, sadness, princeliness and elegance; by others for his neuroticism, aloofness, hysteria, self-lacerating sensitivity, with a tendency to lose control of top notes and go shrill in moments of crisis.[37]

In his contemporary review of the 1930 performance, the great theatre critic James Agate was able to declare Gielgud's Hamlet to be 'as good as any reasonable person could desire'.[38] Agate went on:

One says reasonable, because the part makes demands that are unreasonable. It demands every grace of body, mind, and heart, and the power of expressing intellectual and spiritual ugliness. Hamlet, the noble heart, the sweet prince, and all the rest of it, must make us feel that Horatio, bidding flights of angels sing him to his rest, came near to saying the wrong thing. There was so much that is murky churned up in that tormented brain that the demons might have been asked to lend a hand, respectfully, at a distance. Hamlet must make us cry one minute and shudder the next …

This seems to be a wisely observed, if necessarily incomplete, definition of the role's demands, and Gielgud's interpretation went a long way to fulfilling Agate's expectations:

This Hamlet is noble in conception. It has been thought out in the study and is lived upon the stage, with the result that you feel these things are happening to Hamlet for the first time, and that he is here and now creating words to express new-felt emotion …

James Agate was one of those critics whose reviews enable milestone performances to live on. And here he has surely identified a key quality of great Shakespearean acting: the ability to make you feel that you are hearing the words for the first time. As I said earlier, I have experienced it in Branagh (a disgracefully under-rated and disparaged actor, in my view, a victim of the British resentment at early success), and it was frequently a feature of Gielgud's performances. For two generations of play-goers, Gielgud was simply the Hamlet of his time.

Act 3, scene 1: 'To be, or not to be …'

He slowly enters the vast palace hall and his footsteps echo as he crosses the black and white chessboard floor, the camera slowly tracking behind him. He stops, but the camera continues its movement so that we are watching him side on, when he turns to look at us.

Cut to a shot from behind his right shoulder, to see him staring into one of the hundred mirrors fixed to the hall's panelled doors, the very door behind which Claudius and Polonius are hiding, spying on him … For this particular mirror is two-way, as befits this repressive prison-like state.

'To be, or not to be', he whispers … And, as each thought comes, he slowly approaches his reflection.

The thin-bladed knife produced on 'bare bodkin' is a shock to us – and to Claudius, who flinches behind the glass, for a moment forgetting that he cannot be seen. Hamlet holds the dagger's point to his cheek, only lowering it to tap gently on the mirror at the thought of enterprises of great pitch and moment turning awry and losing the name of action …

Writing about this moment in Kenneth Branagh's film of *Hamlet*, Samuel Crowl commented:

> The device of shooting the 'To be, or not to be' soliloquy with the

camera peering over Hamlet's right shoulder capturing the famous words in multiple layers of reflection is inspired. Hamlet is fragmented and fractured; his psyche is troubled by the way in which he not only opposes but reflects Claudius; and while he keeps trying to hold the mirror up to both Gertrude's and Claudius's natures it keeps throwing back more and more images of his turmoil than of their transgression.[39]

Each director approaching this speech, unquestionably the most famous in world drama, is faced not only with the usual challenge of conveying Hamlet's thoughts effectively, but also with the problem of having to stage a soliloquy whole chunks of which many people can recite by heart. When Al Pacino walked the streets of New York asking passers-by if they'd heard of Shakespeare,[40] the standard response was a cry of 'To be, or not to be'; for, as actor Michael Pennington observes:

It has become an identification tag, together with Yorick's skull, in cartoon, headline or soundbite, a sort of universal shorthand.[41]

And actors anguish over how to approach it. Here is Steven Berkoff recalling his own method of dealing with the soliloquy:

'To be, or not to be.'

A hard walk downstage, stop and deliver the words as if I had said 'stand and deliver' … then lower my voice:

'that is the question'.

Sometimes I would find this a way of starting to get over the self-consciousness at the beginning of a purple passage, and so I was in it before the audience had noticed, and then I rested to let them take it in. Other times I might start in very slowly indeed, as a kind of confession of my problem, but always directed to them. If I started it hard and quickly then it would appear to be the apotheosis of many hours of thought – as if bursting through the skin of my thoughts it reveals itself: after all the Angst of indecision, life is condensed finally into *To be or not to be* ... There are times in the play when Hamlet can drop the act, and this is one of them – when all character falls away and one is left merely with the man ...[42]

Berkoff is here recalling his own stage performance from 1979; and it is noticeable that he refers throughout to his relationship with the audience, the live audience sitting in front of him. On screen, soliloquy presents an altogether new set of problems. And central among them is the key directorial question: to voice-over, or not to voice-over.

Since the earliest days of the talkies, voice-over has been available to movie-directors as a convention which allows an audience to hear a character's thoughts. So I am always intrigued by the variable extent to which it is exploited in filmed Shakespeare soliloquies. The Branagh 'To be, or not to be', for example, is totally spoken out loud. In contrast, director Grigori Kosintsev chose to have all the soliloquies performed in voice-over for his 1964 film (the 'Russian' *Hamlet*).* Olivier, different again, opted for a mixture of the two, electing to begin the soliloquy with speech, go into voice-over on line five for 'To die ...'; and return to speech on 'Perchance to dream ...', when, as though awoken from his suicidal reverie, Hamlet is jolted into thoughts of the consequences.

This mix of speech and voice-over is also a feature of the Ethan Hawke *Hamlet* movie, directed by Michael Almereyda (2000).[43] In this modern American setting of the story, the soliloquy takes place in a New York Blockbuster Video store (see Figure 18), the hero's vacillating introspection ironically contrasted with the high-explosive action

---

*Hamlet was played by Innokenti Smoktunovsky, an actor who, having fought against the Nazis, had been sent by Stalin to the Gulag Archipelago.

movie showing on the screens above him. And, despite the contrasts with Olivier's more traditional setting, Almereyda makes very similar choices to the 1948 director when it comes to the use of voice-over. Here the soliloquy begins in voice-over as Hamlet walks down the aisles, barely taking in what he sees, but transfers into speech when the destructive scene showing in the store's sample action-movie prompts him to declare: 'Ay, there's the rub.'

Although a logic could be found to underlie Olivier's and Almereyda's choices (voice-over for more introspective and inconclusive thoughts, speech for the more urgent and troublesome ones), I remain unconvinced. It seems to me that cinema has not yet arrived at an easy relationship with voice-over as a mechanism for dealing with soliloquy in Shakespeare. And I can see why Branagh might elect to speak the whole of 'To be, or not to be' out loud, albeit mostly in a whisper.

Act 4, scene 4: Enter Hamlet, Rosencrantz, Guildenstern, and attendants

GUIL: … What's he doing?

Ros goes upstage and returns.

ROS: Talking.

GUIL: To himself?

Ros makes to go, Guil cuts him off.

Is he alone?

ROS: No, he's with a soldier.

GUIL: Then he's not talking to himself, is he?

ROS: Not *by* himself … Should we go?

GUIL: Where?

ROS: Anywhere.

GUIL: Why? …

Hamlet enters behind them, talking with a soldier in arms. Ros and Guil don't look round.

ROS: They'll have us hanging about till we're dead. At least. And the weather will change. *(Looks up.)* The spring can't last for ever.

HAMLET: Good sir, whose powers are these?

SOLDIER: They are of Norway, sir …

. . . .

… Ros gets up quickly and goes to Hamlet.

ROS: Will it please you go, my lord?

HAMLET: I'll be with you straight. Go you a little before.

Hamlet turns to face upstage. Rosencrantz returns down. Guil faces front, doesn't turn.

GUIL: Is he there?

ROS: Yes.

GUIL: What's he doing?

Rosencrantz looks over his shoulder.

ROS: Talking.

GUIL: To himself?

ROS: Yes.[44]

This scene is typical of Tom Stoppard's *Rosencrantz and Guildenstern Are Dead* (1966), a comically reflective take on *Hamlet* in which the two attendant lords are elevated to the centre of the drama while the events of Shakespeare's plot are played out in the background. As the extract above shows, Stoppard interpolates short sections of Shakespeare's text into the new dialogue written for Rosencrantz, Guildenstern and the Player, the leader of the tragedians who come to Elsinore. As the Player explains:

> 'We do on stage the things that are supposed to happen off. Which is a kind of integrity if you look on every exit being an entrance somewhere else.'[45]

Looked at another way, it might be said that Stoppard's play turns *Hamlet* inside-out – in the sense that the conversations between Stoppard's Rosencrantz and Guildenstern take place while their equivalent characters in Shakespeare's play are offstage. As critic Harold Hobson explained:

> Shakespeare looked at the matter from Hamlet's viewpoint, with the Prince at the centre and everything revolving around him. How would these events appear to someone not at their centre, but on the periphery; someone such as Guildenstern or Rosencrantz? This is the question that Stoppard answers. To Rosencrantz and Guildenstern, what happens in Shakespeare's play seems totally baffling and incomprehensible.[46]

The extract above gives an example of the games Stoppard is playing with Shakespeare. Here he has inserted into some modern dialogue between the two courtiers Hamlet's conversation with the soldier (in 4.4), who informs him that the army they can see crossing Denmark is led by Fortinbras. For anybody who doesn't know Shakespeare's *Hamlet* terribly well (and even for those who do), it can all be extremely confusing, not least because, every time Rosencrantz and Guildenstern speak to Hamlet or the court, they slip into Shakespeare's script.

I recently directed this play with an amateur company, the Oxford Theatre Guild, in the Oxford Playhouse. And it was only the experience of rehearsing it with some extremely perceptive and talented actors that made me realise just how many things are going on. Take the scene above. As far as the two courtiers are concerned, Hamlet is simply 'Talking ... To himself ...'. But it's only when you check with Shakespeare's text that you realise what he is silently saying. It's the 'How all occasions do inform against me' soliloquy, the one that ends on a pretty determined note: 'O, from this time forth / My thoughts be bloody, or be nothing worth!' And unless you know this, you miss a great gag at the end of the scene ...

The extract above continues with Rosencrantz and Guildenstern debating *Godot*-like, whether to go or stay. All the while Hamlet is silently cogitating. As written, Stoppard's scene ends with the two courtiers deciding that they might as well remain where they are:

ROS: We've come this far.

He moves towards exit. Guil follows him.

And besides, anything could happen yet.

They go.

Blackout.

When the lights come up on Act 3, they are on board ship, bound for England and death. Insert Hamlet's concluding line, and the audience get the irony: Rosencrantz finds a scrap of optimism just at the very moment when Hamlet adopts the determined spirit that will enable him to substitute the forged letter that sends Rosencrantz and Guildenstern to their deaths:

ROS: We've come this far.

He moves towards exit. Guil follows him.

HAMLET: O, from this time forth
My thoughts be bloody, or be nothing worth!

ROS: And besides, anything could happen yet.

They go.

Blackout.

Stoppard's play is an example of a *Hamlet* spin-off that requires a pretty detailed knowledge of Shakespeare's play for it to be fully appreciated (though friends who attended our Oxford production assured me that it can be enjoyed without being fully understood). And the same, to a greater or lesser extent, applies to the many other off-shoots of Shakespeare's most famous play.

At the less serious end of the spectrum are a host of 19th-century burlesques of *Hamlet* (including a W. S. Gilbert *Rosenkrantz and Guildenstern* from 1874, evidence that Stoppard wasn't the first to see dramatic potential in the attendant lords); and a number of movies. I am indebted to Daniel Rosenthal[47] for introducing me via his informative *Shakespeare on Screen* to the 1919 cartoon short *Oh 'phelia* (in which Hamlet threatens to cut off his girlfriend's hair with the words 'To bob or not to bob?'); and the 1993 Hollywood flop *Last Action Hero* in which a schoolboy imagines his own *Hamlet* movie, with Arnold Schwarzenegger asking 'To be or not to be?', lighting a cigar, and, with the words 'Not to be', blowing Elsinore to smithereens.

Also under the 'ironic' label is a 1987 Finnish film, *Hamlet Goes Business*,[48] in which old Hamlet's brother Klaus (interesting just how many variations on these names you can get) is ambitious to buy a majority holding in Swedish Rubber Ducks and Pikka-Pekka Petelius

(Hamlet) is killed by the Horatio figure, Simo, who turns out to be a trade union spy ... The effect is described by Tony Howard:

> Whereas adaptors normally invoke classical literature to remind us of enduring ethical certainties, these characters have the Shakespearean names because this is what Shakespeare's characters have become: today's Hamlet stages *The Importance of Being Earnest* (with interpolated homicide), escapes death by poisoned chicken and then turns out to have killed his father. In a pseudo-Marxist finale Hamlet's chauffeur kills him, saves the millworkers, runs off into the sunset with the maid and leaves us to decide how ludicrous this is. Kaurismäki's lugubriously funny *film noir* is a post-industrial epitaph for a dying system doomed indefinitely to repeat its tragedies as farce.[49]

Other movie directors have traded on audiences' familiarity with the *Hamlet* story, or at least its outline, to present their critique of a post-war world in which Elsinore represents all that is worst about a corrupt and materialistic status quo. In Germany, Helmut Käulner directed *The Rest is Silence* (*Der Rest ist Schweigen*, 1959), in which the Claudius figure was a Rhine–Ruhr industrialist; Akira Kurosawa used the Hamlet outline to attack civic corruption in *The Bad Sleep Well* (*Warui Yatsu Hodo Yoko Nemeru*, 1960); and Claude Chabrol set his 1962 *Ophélie* partly in a country château where the uncle lives protected by a gang of neo-fascist thugs.

Polonius would have been in his element categorising the many films which have been based on, have drawn on, or have alluded to, *Hamlet*:

> ... The best play in the world, either for tragedy, comedy, history, pastoral, pastoral-comical ... comical-sentimental (*In the Bleak Midwinter*), sexual-comical (*Outrageous Fortune*), comical-pedagogical (*Renaissance Man*), comical-theatrical (*Withnail and I*), satirical-

comical-historical (*To Be, or Not to Be*), factual-historical (*A Letter to Timothy*), animal-allegorical (*The Lion King*), fantastical-astronomical-illogical, Jim *(Star Trek VI: the Undiscovered Country)* ...[50]

On stage, Hamlet thrives upon quirky interpretation and free adaptation. In one season alone (1999), Buenos Aires hosted four productions. There was director Andrés di Stefano's traditional *Hamlet*; a long-running version of Heiner Müller's *Hamlet Machine*; a manic, heavily psychoanalytical adaptation called *Hamlet: the One and the Other*; and *A Hamlet of the Suburbs*, which transferred the action of Elsinore to the southern outskirts of 1920s Buenos Aires. Chris Moss explains:

> Controversial director Alberto Félix Alberto's [*A Hamlet of the Suburbs*] alters the characters, the language and plot details to create a version which taps into local myths and enriches the familiar story of regicide and revenge. Claudius becomes small-time mafia boss Don Claudio Reyes, Polonius is a prostitute called Polonia, a profession Ophelia seems to be considering too, and even Horatio loses his whiter-than-white character, luring sailors into his corrugated-iron shack ...[51]

Again, the question arises – why, given a rich and disturbing local history and mythology, does an Argentinian director turn to the archetypal Dead White European Male? For Tulio Stella, who adapted the text, it's because he can see parallels between Shakespeare's England on the edge of Europe and the violent outskirts of 1920s Buenos Aires:

> Wasn't 16th-century England a suburb of the world? An impatient suburb with designs on copying, occupying and competing with the centre of the world: that great empire where the sun never set. Hamlet is the prince of a sub-suburban kingdom, created by a writer on the fringe.[52]

Supporting this thesis, there is a chilling look forward to the dark decades of 20th-century Argentina, when Stella's Hamlet dies with the words: 'The rest is in the shadows.'

Different forms encourage different emphases; and it's understandable that an operatic version of the play should focus heavily on Hamlet's relationship with Ophelia, given its potential for some terrific duets. Such is certainly the case with Ambroise Thomas's *Hamlet*, premièred in Paris in 1868 and recently performed in the Royal Opera House,[53] its first showing at Covent Garden since 1910. The jury remains out on whether Thomas's opera is actually any good. Written for a bourgeois Second Empire audience, the work was 'accordingly straitjacketed into the values of the time with a consequent narrowing of its emotional range'.[54] Discussing his approach to the opera's love scenes, singer Simon Keenlyside observed: '… there's really no room for nuance. The relationship between Hamlet and Ophelia is so *thin* …'[55] Shakespeare fans might be more perturbed by the ending, in which Hamlet survives (as does Polonius) and dispatches his mother to a convent. As one reviewer put it:

> A few of the best couplets survive, but not many, and the rest of the text is reduced to stock mid-19th-century libretto clichés; it may be Shakespeare, but not as we know it.[56]

Elsewhere, *Hamlet* has reappeared in plays as diverse as Chekhov's *The Seagull* (1896), whose characters quote directly from Shakespeare's play, and Samuel Beckett's *Endgame* (1958) with its central character Hamm. It has inspired poems from France (Arthur Rimbaud's 'Ophelia'), Poland (Zbigniew Herbert's 'Elegy of Fortinbras') and Russia (Boris Pasternak's 'Hamlet'); and the character famously helps to define the voice in Prufrock's

> No, I am not Prince Hamlet, nor was meant to be;
> Am an attendant lord, one that will do

To swell a progress, start a scene or two,
Advise the prince.[57]

And, as Nicola Watson observes:

> *Hamlet* underpins mainstream novels as diverse as Laurence Sterne's
> *Tristram Shandy* (1759–67) and *A Sentimental Journey* (1768),
> Johann Wolfgang von Goethe's *Werther* (1774) and his *Wilhelm
> Meister* series (1777–1829) … Virginia Woolf's *Between the Acts*
> (1941), Iris Murdoch's *The Black Prince* (1973) and John Updike's
> *Gertrude and Claudius* (1999).[58]

Looking back over the last page or two, I see that I have referred to
Hamlet-inspired works from the USA, Finland, Germany, Japan,
France, Argentina, Russia and Poland. They bear out Coleridge's
claim from 1808:

> I believe the character of Hamlet may be traced to Shakespeare's
> deep and accurate science in mental philosophy. Indeed, that this
> character must have some connection with the common funda-
> mental laws of our nature may be assumed from the fact that
> Hamlet has been the darling of every country in which the liter-
> ature of England has been fostered.[59]

Act 5, scene 2: 'The rest is silence'

*There remains enough forcefulness in his voice to make Horatio give up
the poisoned drink that he threatens to finish: 'Let go. By heaven, I'll
ha' it.' But Hamlet's speech is slowing by now, the venom taking effect, as
he fears what a wounded name he will leave behind him, and he briefly
touches Horatio's face, asking him to tell his story to a yet unknowing
world.*

There is a long pause and then he slowly sinks to his knees.

And smiles. And says: 'The rest is silence.'

Still smiling in his death, he slowly topples into his friend's arms ...

This was Adrian Lester, a youthful, sensitive Hamlet, with Scott Handy as Horatio, in Peter Brook's moving interpretation.[60] And Lester's enigmatic smile at the end might be taken to bear out Michael Pennington's view of Hamlet, that he

> ... goes with a riddle, 'the rest is silence' ... striking out of two nouns multiple meanings: nihilistic, romantic, heroic, humorous, restrained, defeated and triumphant at once. Glimpsing the undiscovered country at last, literature's most loquacious hero promises 'silence': and the 'rest' is both his and our release from his efforts ...

The actor adds:

> Among actors, the role is supposedly the object of much professional rivalry; among those who have played it, it is the source, surprisingly often, of regret, and occasionally of real self-definition. It's also said that nobody can quite fail in it, because Hamlet becomes the man (or woman) who plays it.[61]

While I might quibble with the notion that nobody can quite fail in the role, I would certainly endorse the reasoning behind it: that the personality of the actor always determines the nature of the Hamlet they give us. Laurence Olivier, for example, based his virile 1937 interpretation on that of the American John Barrymore, whose Hamlet had enjoyed 101 consecutive performances (New York, 1922 and London, 1925), and who, Olivier felt, had 'put the balls back' into the part. Disabled actor Nabil Shaban, on the other hand,[62] decided that [although] Hamlet's is a personal grievance, rather than a political grievance … as a disabled person I think I made it political. In all the plays and films I've seen, no one has ever made sense of his treatment of Ophelia – if he's just a nutter, then what's the play trying to say? But Hamlet is disabled because of this feeling of impotence and powerlessness …

For Ben Kingsley (directed by Buzz Goodbody at The Other Place in 1975), Hamlet is

the greatest part for a young actor – there are so many beautiful mysteries locked in there about boyhood becoming manhood that coincide with any young man's development – it's a visceral experience … To me Hamlet is not hosed in thought – to me he is a prince of light, a sweet delicate young man whose sensibilities have been very damaged.

And Mark Rylance (directed by Ron Daniels in 1988) took yet another view of the role, believing that:

One of the most interesting things in it is the way it encompasses the problem of being an actor – which is really the problem of living – to be in the present and not to hold on to what is behind you – 'The readiness is all'.[63]

Often described as the heir to Gielgud, Derek Jacobi played Hamlet for BBC Television in 1980. Twenty-three years on, and an hour before curtain up on his Prospero at the Old Vic, I ask him whether he feels that an actor playing Hamlet needs a kind of wisdom which can be acquired only through an age and maturity that disqualify him for the part. 'Ah! Absolutely, absolutely!', he declares.

'I mean, I've played it lots of times now. I've played it in two different productions on stage, I played it as an undergraduate at

Cambridge, then I played it for BBC Television … And, well, it's like most of Shakespeare: there are no definitives. You can get bits of them right, but you never get them all right all the time. And then I directed it. I directed Ken [Branagh] when he first did it on stage; and *lots* of things occurred to me, you know, watching … Getting a performance out of somebody else in a part that I knew, triggered lots of things in my head. And curiously enough, I in a sense resented giving them to Ken, because I felt – no, I need those for the next time I play it … But of course I'll never do it again, I'm too old now … But I *do* take your point about the more understanding you become, the richer your own life experience has been which you can draw on … But the time has to come when people won't accept you as that essentially young man.'[64]

And Jacobi is right: an ageing Hamlet has become as embarrassing as an ageing Romeo; and it is the young men who have rightly dominated the Hamlet scene in recent years. Critic Max Beerbohm once said that Hamlet was a hoop through which every eminent actor must sooner or later jump. These days it tends to be sooner. In the past few years the aspiring young actors of their generation – people like Sam West, Alex Jennings, Simon Russell-Beale and Adrian Lester – have all made notable success of the part, each in his unique way. And young actors will surely continue to queue up to jump through that hoop; to play this 'gifted hero, cruelly wasted, [who] leaves us with both benediction and emptiness'.[65]

CHAPTER 8

Kate

'The situation of poor Katharine ... becomes at last almost as pitiable as it is ludicrous'

William Hazlitt

'Her name is Katharina Minola', says Petruchio's friend Hortensio (1.2.97).

But is it? It's certainly what Hortensio and others, including her father, usually call her. But when she introduces herself, she says: 'They call me Katharine that do talk of me.' (2.1.183); and Petruchio later declares. 'I must, and will, have Katharine for my wife.' (2.1.272) – the metre, by the way, suggesting that the name is here given two syllables, with the stress on the first: *Káth-rin.* The two names, Katharina and Katharine, seem to be interchangeable, so there's no great problem. But, when you add in 'Kate', Petruchio's other name for her, you can see how an actress might view this varying nomenclature as an element of the character's confused identity.

And it doesn't stop there. Is Kate the only major Shakespeare character whom we refer to more commonly by her descriptive title – 'the Shrew' – than by her name? There are 'the Fool' in *Lear*, and 'the Ghost' in *Hamlet*, I suppose. But neither of those labels is judgemental in the way that 'Shrew' is. Nor is 'the Bastard' in *King John*, whose illegitimate connection to his father the Lionheart is a mark of honour rather than a slur. Set alongside that other deeply problematic play, *The Merchant of Venice*, it's inconceivable that we would these days unthinkingly call Shylock 'the Jew'. 'The Shrew' defines and reduces her. I shall call her Kate.

The *Concise Oxford Dictionary* is very interesting on the subject of shrews. Turn to the fifth edition of 1964 and you'll find:

> **shrew** *n*. 1. Scolding woman, whence shrewish … 2. Small, long-snouted mammal …

By the tenth (2001) edition, the definition is:

> **shrew** *n*. 1. Small, mouse-like insectivorous mammal … 2. A bad-tempered or aggressively assertive woman.

Clearly, lexicographers have come to take the view that, by the 21st century, 'scolding woman' is no longer the word's primary usage. And for that we thank both the feminist movement and four decades of TV wildlife programmes.

But what *is* a shrew in its 16th-century sense? What do shrews look like? How do they behave? If we are to judge by early impressions in Shakespeare's play, a shrew is a 'devil' (1.1.66, 119, 121 …), a 'fiend of hell' (1.1.88), 'the devil's dam' (3.2.152). Called a 'hilding of a devilish spirit' by her father (2.1.26), and considered by those who know her to be 'shrewd' and 'cursed',* this particular shrew is regarded – by a first-time viewer – as 'stark mad or wonderful froward' (1.1.69), and – by two of her sister's suitors – as 'too rough' (1.1.55), and unmarriageable unless she be 'of gentler, milder mould' (1.1.60). Observation of

---

* Within the opening few scenes, Kate is repeatedly called 'curst' (see, for example, 1.1.175; 1.2.68, 87 and 125–6; 2.1.185). The connection in meaning between the two words 'curst' and 'shrew' is seen in the oath 'beshrew [= curse] me', as, for example in Desdemona's 'Beshrew me if I would do such a deed for the whole world' (*Othello*, 4.3.81–2).

her behaviour shows that she shouts at her father (1.1) ties up and beats her sister (2.1), and breaks a lute over her teacher's head (2.1).

A 19th-century illustration by George Cruikshank shows Kate at the end of the play. She is seated and feebly gesturing, a huge padlock clamped over her mouth. This disquieting image – in fact from an edition of David Garrick's 18th-century version, *Catharine and Petruchio* – acknowledges both the violent nature of Kate's taming and the traditional definition of a shrew as a woman 'renown'd … for her scolding tongue' (1.2.98). For shrews make a row. They 'raise up such a storm / That mortal ears might hardly endure the din' (1.1.167–8). Time and again in the opening acts of Shakespeare's play, Kate's boisterous noisiness is contrasted with her sister Bianca's quiet restraint, a demure mildness that so exasperates Kate that she flies at Bianca in public, crying: 'Her silence flouts me and I'll be revenged' (2.1.29).

But shrewishness is not just a question of noise. In their 'scolding' (1.1.167) and 'loud alarums' (1.1.125), shrews rebel against male authority. Angrily resenting her father's order that she must stay behind while he goes off for a talk with her sister, Kate cries:

Why, and I trust I may go too, may I not?
What! Shall I be appointed hours, as though, belike,
I know not what to take and what to leave, ha? (1.1.102–04)

Shrews assert their independence; they will not accept the sovereignty of men. And, in taking that stance, they threaten to undermine the whole network of existing hierarchies. This is why shrews such as Noah's wife in the Mystery Plays – challenging her husband's actions, ridiculing his decision to build the ark, refusing to climb aboard even when the rains start – are seen as deeply subversive elements who dispute God's word and threaten His established order. Shrews are wildcats (1.2.193). Such women are dangerous and have to be subdued. This is the message we find reiterated throughout the shrew literature that precedes or is contemporary with Shakespeare's play.

Here, for example, is Chaucer's Wife of Bath – herself a shrew type – recalling the story read to her by her scholar husband of Socrates' wife Xantippe, the archetypal shrew:

> No thyng forgat he the care and the wo
> That Socrates hadde with his wyves two;
> How Xantippa caste pisse upon his heed ...[1]

Elsewhere, an anonymous husband rues his shrewish wife's noise and violence:

> What hap had I to marry a shrew,
> For she hath given me many a blow,*
> And how to please, alack I do not know.
> From morn to e'en her tongue ne'er lies.
> Some time she brawls, some time she cries,
> Yet can I scarce keep her talons from my eyes.

Later, in 16th-century ballads such as 'A Merry Jest of a Shrewd and Cursed Wife', 'The Patient Husband and the Scolding Wife' and 'The Scolding Wife's Vindication', we see a range of 'shrewish' behaviour from assertiveness to adultery.

And there is also the other shrew play, *The Taming of a Shrew*. Nobody is clear about the relationship between this play, first published in quarto in 1594, and Shakespeare's, which doesn't appear until the First Folio of 1623. Some people see it as a source for Shakespeare's version, some as an earlier draft of *The Taming of the Shrew* by Shakespeare himself. It could also be a 'bad quarto' of Shakespeare's play. (Also known as a 'memorial reconstruction' or 'reported text', a bad quarto was a pirated version cobbled together

---

* This rhyme, and the one at the end of 4.1 in Shakespeare's play, are evidence that 'shrew' rhymed with 'blow' and 'show'.

12. 'EVERY NERVE AND MUSCLE … IN ACTION': William Hogarth's painting
of David Garrick's performance of Richard the Third.

13. RICHARD IN A DECADE OF TYRANNY: Ian McKellen's 1930s dictator
in the 1995 film.

14. THE BOTTLED SPIDER: Antony Sher as Richard the Third
for the RSC in 1984.

15. 'SHAKESPEARE'S PAINTER': Henry Fuseli's 'Garrick and Mrs Pritchard as Macbeth and Lady Macbeth after the murder of Duncan'.

16. 'STOOGES PLAYING BIG-SHOTS': the poster for the 1955 gangster movie, *Joe Macbeth*, showing Paul Douglas and Ruth Roman as Joe and Lily.

17. THE TEUTONIC GODDESS: John Singer Sargent's monochrome oil sketch of Ellen Terry as Lady Macbeth in her 1888 performance.

18. THE MANHATTAN HAMLET: Ethan Hawke as a modern heir to 'Denmark Corporation' in the 2000 film.
19. THAT ICONIC MOMENT: Arnold Schwarzenegger contemplating the skull in the spoof movie trailer from *Last Action Hero*, 1993.

20. ANGRY AND ABUSED: Josie Lawrence as Kate and Michael Siberry
as Petruchio in the 1995 RSC production.

21. AWKWARD BUT NO SHREW: Alexandra Gilbreath as Kate and
Jasper Britton as Petruchio for the RSC in 2003.

22. 'TEMPESTUOUS' OR 'HEINOUS BITCH'?: Julia Stiles as Kate, with Heath Ledger as Petruchio, in the 1999 US high school spin-off *10 Things I Hate About You.*

23. 'SHAKESPEARE'S FORGOTTEN ROCK AND ROLL MASTERPIECE': *Return to the Forbidden Planet,* the 1981 rock musical, loosely based on *The Tempest.*

24. SHAKESPEARE'S *ALTER EGO*: Sir John Gielgud as Prospero
in Peter Greenaway's 1991 *Prospero's Books*.

from memory by people who had seen, or possibly acted in, the original 'authentic' version.) Nobody knows for sure what the relationship between the two plays is, but the similarities are intriguing.

Both plays are about the taming of an unruly wife, both have a romantic intrigue sub-plot, and both include Christopher Sly. Brian Morris lists further similarities:

> In both plays the husband behaves scandalously at the wedding, starves his wife afterwards, rejects the work of a Haberdasher and a Tailor, and misuses his servants. In both the wife is brought to submission, asserts that the sun is the moon and pretends an old man is a young girl. Each play culminates in a feast at which men wager on their wives' obedience.[2]

Surveying the period's shrew literature, Frances E. Dolan writes:

> However we interpret Katharine's shrewishness, reading Shakespeare's play against other texts reveals that the play, like most other depictions of shrews, is full of resistant, disorderly self-assertions, not just outspokenness.[3]

This idea of 'resistant, disorderly self-assertion' was a striking feature of Sinead Cusack's 1982 Kate. As she recalls:

> 'When I played Kate, I actually wanted to shave my head. Now that seems a very silly thing to want to do, but the reason I wanted to do it was, I could not believe that a woman of her strength and character would submit to the indignity of a father who was *selling* her. Which is precisely what he does – you know, dressing her in gorgeous gowns and putting her up for auction. That is in effect what he is doing. And I wanted to *destroy* Kate. I wanted her to have taken scissors to her head, shorn all her hair, taken away every female attribute she had. Now in the end the director

[Barry Kyle] said, "I don't want it to be known as 'the punk *Shrew*', so I won't let you do it". And I was devastated. I said, "But that's what I want to do. I want to make her in some way *foul*, because she will not allow this to be done to her."

'And so in the end what he allowed me to do – and it was the most *extraordinary* experience … We had a very famous designer called Bob Crowley, who designed these – you could call them "Elizabethan/Zandra Rhodes" – beautiful creations in silk. And, you see, during the rehearsal period I'd discovered things about Kate. But the thing about Stratford is that the designs are done pretty well on day one. You're shown the costumes and then you come, after an exploration of five weeks, to actually *know* that the person you've discovered *would not wear that dress*. And I had to go to Bob Crowley on the dress rehearsal and say, "I can't wear that dress. She simply wouldn't wear it. It's beautiful, it's obviously been crafted with extraordinary care and a huge amount of money spent on it. But she simply wouldn't wear it to be sold at auction – she simply wouldn't do it."

'And he said, "Well, what do I do?"

'And I said, "I don't know, *I don't know*." And I said, "Well, what if I desecrate it?"

'He said, "What do you mean?"

'I said, "Well … take scissors to it. Like *she* would. And … And wear wellingtons with it … And … er … just … *destroy* it …"

'And he was fantastic. And we took it up to my dressing-room and I said, "Shall you make the first cut, or will I?" And we took a pair of huge scissors, and we slashed the dress everywhere, and then I teased my hair out and I looked a fright. And I wore wellingtons. So that's the sort of creature I'd discovered …'

Act 1, scene 1: Enter Baptista with his two daughters, Katharina and Bianca …

The house is beautifully decorated, the walls subtly yet richly patterned with fleur-de-lys, the ornately mullioned windows looking on to a rose-garden. On the oak table are some playing cards … Someone has been enjoying a quiet game of patience …

Preceded by flying chairs, pots, saucepans and servants diving for cover, she erupts onto the scene, the original five-foot-nothing blonde bombshell, dressed wholly in black, a whip in her hand, glowering fiercely into the camera …

When 'America's sweetheart' Mary Pickford agreed to play Kate in 1929, it was as part of the first feature-length 'all-talking' Shakespeare movie.[4] Co-starring with Douglas Fairbanks, they formed a real-life husband and wife pairing of a kind later to be famously replayed by another internationally-famous star couple, Elizabeth Taylor and Richard Burton. Mary Pickford played Kate as 'a truculent vamp'.[5] But most recent interpreters of the role have been much more interested in what makes Kate behave as she does, and I have spoken to three of them. All three have played the character with the RSC: Sinead Cusack (1982), Josie Lawrence (1995) and Alexandra Gilbreath (2003).

Sitting on the roof terrace of the Swan theatre at Stratford a couple of hours before she is due to go on stage, Alexandra Gilbreath is telling me about her interpretation of Kate for the RSC. For her, the 'shrew' label simply isn't right:

'… She's not … I don't see her as a shrew. We talked a lot in rehearsals about propaganda, that if enough people tell you you're shrewish, cursed, you either behave like that or it is inevitable that you will be perceived in that way. I think that's what's happened to her … I mean, she's an awkward person, but I don't see her as a complicated person, I find her very uncomplicated. It's just that she has been denied fundamentals like parental love … Bianca has absolutely learned instinctively how to use her power, and Kate resents the fact that she has to play the game, and also resents that she's being sold off to a lowest bidder because she's the "difficult" one.'

Josie Lawrence echoes this interpretation:

'It must have been so frustrating in those days if a woman did have wit, did have intelligence, and was not allowed to use it in any shape or form, or she was called a shrew. And that's what I took on board, that's where I got my anger from …

'I always felt that my Shrew was, first of all, unloved … We wanted to get that across, to make sense of the bondage scene where she's teasing her sister (who drives her up the bloody wall) when her father comes on and berates her and sends Bianca off to do the sewing, and she says, "Oh, I see: she's your favourite. I'm the one who must lead apes to hell, I must be the sad spinster …" And she's also motherless, which I think is very important …'

This idea of Kate being motherless reminds me of two things. The first is the family biographies which Henry Goodman and a variety of Shylocks have created to make sense of that troubled character and his feelings. In these constructions the absent wife (who is usually the 'Leah' of 3.1) is imagined as recently dead, the widower still coming to grips with his bereavement.[6] Similarly, both Josie Lawrence and Alexandra Gilbreath factor in the absence of the mother – never referred to in Shakespeare's script – to help account for Kate's emotional deprivation and the damage caused by Baptista's open favouritism towards Bianca.

The second is the puzzling shortage in Shakespeare's plays of families which have two living parents *and* more than one child. It seems that, if both parents are alive, they have only one offspring (Juliet, Romeo, Anne Page, Marina …); and, if there is more than one child, they have only one living – or present – parent (Baptista, Lear, Gloucester, Lady Faulconbridge, Henry the Fourth, Priam …). There are several families in which the father's death is significant, and the mother dead or absent (Petruchio, Portia, Orlando and Oliver, Viola and Sebastian, Olivia, Richard the Third, Henry the Fifth …); and a number of one-plus-one families in which the relationship between the lone parent and the only child is an important feature of the play (Prospero–Miranda, Leonato–Hero,* Egeus–Hermia, Brabantio–Desdemona, Shylock–Jessica, Volumnia–Coriolanus, Constance–Arthur …). To that category we should also add Gertrude–Hamlet, given that Claudius hardly qualifies as a parent. In *The Winter's Tale*, Shakespeare seems to be so obsessive about observing this rule (you can't have two living parents and two children) that it's not long after Leontes and Hermione have produced a second child (Perdita), that their first (Mamillius) dies of grief. In fact, as far as Leontes is con-cerned – who denies that the baby is his until Apollo punishes him with Mamillius's death – he *does* have only one child living at any one time. And Hermione never gets to enjoy both together. In *The Comedy of Errors* there *is* a two-plus-two family, but the parents have spent most of their married life split up, believing each other dead, and each twin has been ignorant of the other's whereabouts. There are, of course, the ill-fated Macduffs (they don't last long), the family of Edward the Fourth (intact at the beginning of *Richard III*, but the father soon dies and his sons are butchered in the Tower), and possibly the Macbeths if you count that odd business about having given suck …

---

* Hero might, in fact, have a mother living. Leonato's wife 'Innogen' is listed in the opening stage direction of the quarto *Much Ado*, but then disappears in the First Folio.

Perhaps it's the case that neat, two-plus-two families don't make for good drama. All the same, you would expect *some* to survive and prosper. It's all very strange ...

Act 2, scene 1: 'Good morrow, Kate – for that's your name, I hear ...'

He is extremely nervous and, after a long journey to Padua, still deeply affected by the death of his father (he wears a black arm-band), emotional and unsettled. His public declaration, that he will 'woo her with some spirit', is precisely that: a public declaration – a piece of bravado for the benefit of the chaps. He really does not know how to approach this woman, and Hortensio's warnings are fresh in memory as he plans his tactics.

'Say that she rail ... ', he ponders. How do I deal with that? Well ... 'why, then ... ' (here's a possibility) —

> *'I'll tell her plain*
> *She sings as sweetly as a nightingale ... '*

That might work. Then again ...

That was Jasper Britton's very uncertain Petruchio at Stratford in 2003. Talking about her first scene with him, Alexandra Gilbreath recalls a key discovery. Unusually, it arose out of a moment of high vulgarity, towards the end of their opening round of fast, give-and-take verbal sparring, where, having been called a wasp, Kate replies: 'If I be waspish, best beware my sting.' The exchange continues:

PETRUCHIO: My remedy is then to pluck it out.

KATE: Ay, if the fool could find it where it lies.

PETRUCHIO: Who knows not where a wasp does wear his sting? In his tail.

KATE: In his tongue.

PETRUCHIO: Whose tongue?

KATE: Yours, if you talk of tales; and so farewell.

PETRUCHIO: What, with my tongue in your tail? Nay, come again,
Good Kate, I am a gentleman.[7]

In pretty well all the productions that I have seen, Kate is deeply
offended by this cunnilingus quip, and uses it as a motivational lead-
up to her striking him a line later. Alexandra Gilbreath's Kate stopped
on her way out, her hand on the door, turned, and then – bent double with mirth – burst into the most gorgeous fit of filthy laughter that
it has been my pleasure to hear in the theatre. Talking about the
moment (and she is exactly what you see on stage – funny, ebullient,
totally engaged), the actress says:

'I guess that, when we were rehearsing the wooing scene – this
very famous scene where there's lots of slapstick comedy – we
ended up realising that they fall in love with each other. Petruchio
comes up with this very rude joke, and instead of it upsetting her,
she roars – she's just a regular girl. I mean it's just so disgusting,
how dare he? It's hilarious. And for me, you know, that's why I said
she's an ordinary girl that's got caught up in certain situations
beyond her control. She has personality and is awkward and
angry; but she wasn't born angry – it's her response to the situations that she finds herself in. And she's powerless. And I think
that when Petruchio tells her she's beautiful – twice (and Jasper
says that, when Shakespeare uses a word like "beauty" at the end
of a sentence and at the beginning of a sentence, you need to take
notice) – I feel it's the first time someone has said, you know, "My,
you're really rather lovely!" I mean, of course, it's not that clichéd.
But she suddenly feels comfortable. She's not this tyrant.'

I want to pick out of that commentary a small detail concerning the rehearsal process and actors' preparation. The actress reported her Petruchio, Jasper Britton, as having commented on Shakespeare's use of language, and the fact that there might be some significance to be drawn from the repetition of key words in strategic positions. The lines in question are:

> For, by this light, whereby I see thy beauty,
> Thy beauty that doth make me like thee well … (2.1.265–6)

My point is not to support or argue with Britton's observation – that we should 'take notice' of the echoing of *beauty* at the end of one line and the beginning of the next (though that seems plausible to me). It's rather to highlight it as an example of the approach to the script that many actors take. Here he shows a keen (and some might say academic) response to word order and versification. Elsewhere, we learn that his interpretation was informed – and in an extremely significant way – by an awareness of text history …

> 'Also Jasper works from the First Folio. And there's an entrance for Baptista, Gremio and Tranio in all our versions at the end of the speech. But in the First Folio it's earlier …'

What Jasper Britton had noticed is that the Folio has a stage direction, '*Enter Baptista, Gremio & Trayno*', at line 267, immediately after Petruchio says: 'Thou must be married to no man but me.' So what you get is:

> For, by this light, whereby I see thy beauty,
> Thy beauty that doth make me like thee well …
> Thou must be married to no man but me.
>
> (*Enter Baptista, Gremio and Tranio*)

For I am he am born to tame you, Kate,
And bring you from a wild Kate to a Kate
Conformable as other household Kates.
Here comes your father. Never make denial;
I must and will have Katharine to my wife.[8]

In most modern editions, the entrance doesn't come until the end of Petruchio's words to Kate: at line 270, just before 'Here comes your father'.[9] The implications of following the Folio are considerable. It means that the rest of the speech – 'For I am he am born to tame you, Kate …' – is spoken, not privately to her, but for the benefit of the male audience who have re-entered; and an actor playing Petruchio can pretend, if it fits the interpretation, not to have registered their arrival …

> 'And suddenly it was like – oh, it was this wonderful discovery, purely by a change in entrance, that we obviously discovered that 'I am he am born to tame you, Kate' is not telling her 'I am going to smash you into submission' – it's *for effect*, because the men are coming back in and he's got to assume the position. And that was a great discovery, the fact that Kate and he are in cahoots, and they are two supposedly – in inverted commas – "mad" people who are outsiders, who are more individual than anyone else, and they do kind of meet each other. And, whether or not it works out, they fall in love …'

Stage directions are not a feature of Shakespeare's scripts that have traditionally received much attention. Set in a contrasting type (usually italic) in the original quartos and folios, they give indications of entrances, exits, actions, gestures and special effects. But because they are merely functional, and were for a long time believed to have been inserted by the book-keeper anyway, there has tended to be limited interest in them. According to Eric Rasmussen, however, 'recent studies of extant dramatic manuscripts have established that stage directions are more likely to be authorial than to be additions by playhouse personnel',[10] and people are beginning to take them a little more seriously.

But they are far from unambiguous. For example – and in relation to Jasper Britton's observation – there are stage directions for entrances which appear in the text a few lines earlier than one would expect. Some commentators have explained this on the grounds that, given the size of the original stage, it would take an actor entering through an upstage door a line or two to reach actors downstage and formally 'enter' the scene. In that event, the stage direction for the entrance would therefore need to be marked early. Alan C. Dessen finds that explanation 'highly suspect (given the large number of "normal" entrances with no such allowances made)', and says this of Petruchio's entrance in 2.1:

> The scene *can* be played effectively with the [stage direction inserted at line 270: just before 'Here comes your father'] ... but the earlier entry, especially if Petruchio is immediately aware of the observers, provides some rich comic possibilities. For example, the actor can change his tone and posture, visibly adjusting his role for the benefit of such an onstage audience. Or, to gain a broader effect, the three entering figures, fearful of Kate's wrath, may tiptoe onto the stage, setting up a decided contrast to Petruchio's bold lines.[11]

The fact is that editors often reposition a stage direction if they judge that the Folio has got it wrong. And this, of course, can have a profound effect on how the scene is played in the theatre. It's odd to think that the choice of edition could so influence an actor's interpretation and performance, but it plainly does.

Act 3, scene 2: 'No shame but mine …'

The family are waiting at the church, but the groom is late, unpardon-ably late. Kate is wearing a new dress. Pathetically unaccustomed to select-ing clothes that show off her beauty and femininity, she has chosen an absurd number with a vast circle of material that juts out from her waist in a stiff horizontal ledge and hangs down all round like some elaborate table-cloth. Baptista feels shamed and mocked – 'To want the bridegroom when the priest attends' – Kate humiliated.

'No shame but mine', she says, her voice betraying anger, disillusionment and sadness.

> *'… Now must the world point at poor Katharine,*
> *And say, "Lo, there is mad Petruchio's wife,*
> *If it would please him come and marry her!".'*

That was the scene in the 2003 RSC production. Talking about Kate's 'journey', Alexandra Gilbreath says:

> 'I didn't expect it to be as painful as it is. I expected her to be tougher. And I know that I read various pieces by Sinead [Cusack] and Fiona [Shaw] and others who have played her, about how they worked out that Kate fought her way through it. But Kate for me is … is …'

Striving to describe Kate, she encapsulates the character's needs surprisingly in the statement: 'She wants to be a *bride*.'

It's such an unusual way of looking at her. But it accounts for so much of the earlier fury and frustration she feels at seeing her sister desired and wooed:

> 'You know she sees her sister looking so beautiful. That's why ear-lier she takes all those favours off Bianca that Gremio's sent. She thinks – I want that. Why doesn't somebody send me something?'

And when she finally seems to be fulfilling that ambition, to be a bride, it all goes badly for her: 'She so gets it wrong at her wedding.'

I comment that the wedding dress is ridiculous ('It should be ridiculous', she says), and Kate's misjudgement in taste oddly touching.

'Good, it's what we wanted. Instead of being forced, she *wants* to get married, and her fury with herself is that he doesn't turn up …'

Eventually, of course, he does …

Act 3, scene 2: 'Signior Gremio, came you from the church?'

The scene: the interior of a beautiful Italian Renaissance church. Bright, colourful murals surround the splendidly costumed congregation, choir-boys sing and the tinny tinkling of the bell signals the entrance of the priest. Chubby and nervously perspiring, he carries a huge Bible. In the congregation, Baptista sniffs emotionally into his hankie (though from what emotion is not made clear) and the choir falls silent …

At which point, Petruchio, already the worse for drink, snatches the communion wine with the exclamation 'Hey, by Gog's wounds!', and downs it in one.

The uproar having calmed, the priest summons his courage, turns to Petruchio and calls his name. Then calls it again, more loudly, to wake him from a gentle slumber.

'Petruchio. Wilt thou take Katarina to be thy lawful wedded wife?', he asks, hopefully.

'I —' But Petruchio's response is interrupted by a belch and a prolonged coughing fit.

The priest repeats his question, and the groom again embarks upon an answer. This time he breaks off to search for the ring – pockets, wallet, sleeves; finally retrieving it fumblingly from the carpet – an act that he, and the congregation with him, seems to find hilariously funny. 'Marry, I will!', he exclaims brightly, to more general laughter, applause and relief.

The priest turns to Kate. 'Katarina', he begins beatifically, then takes a shuddering step back as he confronts her angry glare. Rallying, he forges on. 'Katarina, wilt thou take Petruchio as thy lawful, wedded husband?'

Silence. Whispered consternation in the pews. Slowly she lifts her veil and smiles at the priest. His relief, of course, will be short-lived. The smile metamorphoses into the most fearsome and terrible scowl, as she erupts into a defiant 'I WILL N—'

But the smacking kiss Petruchio plants upon her lips cuts off her reply, the priest hastily and desperately gives the blessing, the congregation joyfully erupts, and bells ring out over Padua ...

This sequence, from Franco Zeffirelli's 1966 film version, isn't actually played out in theatre performances, of course. It's one of those off-stage reported scenes[12] that film-makers find irresistible. This, frankly, isn't the best example: it's crude, knockabout stuff. But think of the murder of Duncan in Polanski's *Macbeth*, the failure to deliver the Friar's letter in Baz Luhrmann's *Romeo + Juliet*, and the death of Falstaff in Olivier's *Henry V*. Brilliant moments that Shakespeare denies us because they are not *required* on stage and would distract.[13]

But in the cinema, a visual medium, we demand to see them – sometimes as a replacement for the report, sometimes to augment it. And it doesn't end at reported scenes. Think of those great film moments which arise from ideas no more than hinted at in 'the text': the dangerously sexual presence of Pamela Brown's Mistress Jane Shore at the opening of Olivier's *Richard III*, a character merely referred to on stage, but who has a devastating influence on both Edward and Hastings; the brutal hanging of Bardolph in Branagh's

Henry V, a character described in the script as '*like to be* executed'; the sinister sealing of Shylock's bond in the Channel 4 *Merchant*; and the controlled departure of Malvolio, carrying his suitcase but having discarded his toupee, at the end of Trevor Nunn's *Twelfth Night*. None of these exists as scenes on the page; but their screen versions – and our awareness of each character's possibilities – would be infinitely the poorer without them.

Act 4, scene 1: 'Come Kate, sit down. I know you have a stomach …'

Kate staggers into Petruchio's house after a terrible journey which has ended with her having to push his ancient car through the mud. Her wedding dress torn to shreds, she now sits in her underwear, exhausted, frozen and starving. When the food finally arrives, it looks and smells delicious. Hungrily she dives forward; but is held back by her new husband who asks with nauseating unctuousness: 'Will you give thanks, sweet Kate, or else shall I?'

But before she can summon the energy to reply, Petruchio has angrily rejected the mutton on the (groundless) grounds that it is burnt and therefore 'engenders choler, planteth anger', declaring, to her dismay, that 'for this night we'll fast for company'.

I interview Josie Lawrence (Kate in the 1995 RSC production, described above) in the garden of the Hackney home she affectionately calls Yoghurt Villa (she purchased it with the proceeds of a TV commercial; and I don't know why I mention it, unless it be because the name has an irreverence which is in tune with her reputation as a stand-up comic, but at odds with her profoundly serious and thoughtful interpretation of Kate). Talking about the scenes in Petruchio's house, she recalls:

'Gale [Edwards, the director] wanted it to be extremely dark, which was easy to do because it's all there. Kate doesn't know why this is happening to her and her fighting spirit is leaving her because she's hungry. It's still there – she still finds time to beat Grumio – but she's incredibly, incredibly weak. And then all the stuff with the tailor, when she's presented with this beautiful dress that Petruchio rips apart ... When we did it, Petruchio sits her down on a chair because she is completely weak. And she gives up. She watches him ripping this dress apart and she says very little. And then, when she does speak, it's completely dignified. It's not 'shrewish' in any way:

> "Why, sir, I trust I may have leave to speak,
> And speak I will. I am no child, no babe.
> Your betters have endured me say my mind.
> And, if you cannot, best you stop your ears ..."

'You know, she's very dignified. She's a fantastic character.'

Audiences can feel very uncomfortable watching these scenes. We observe Petruchio first bring his bride into a remote and chilly hall peopled by grotesques and threatened horrors such as the unseen 'uncle Ferdinand', one that Kate 'must kiss and be acquainted with'; we watch as he tempts the cold and hungry woman with food, which is summarily removed; and then treats his servants to what looks like a show-beating. We're told that the bewildered bride's wedding-night is spent listening to a railing sermon on continence, and we listen to Petruchio informing us that his plan is to 'tame' her by denying her both sleep and food. Grumio taunts her by offering and then with-holding various dishes; on Petruchio's whispered instructions, Hortensio scoffs a meal for which she has been required to say, 'I thank you, sir'; and she is presented with a beautiful dress and cap which are torn to shreds before her eyes. Her chance to return to her father's house will be denied her unless she agrees to say that it is seven o'clock, as Petruchio asserts, even though she knows it to be 'almost two'. Many people would call this abuse. 'It *is* abuse', says Josie Lawrence.

> 'It's physical and mental torture. You don't see him – in our production anyway – physically harm her at all. I mean, he'll pick her up and move her about; but there are no thumps, or anything like that. But the scene I really had to work on was the starvation scene. Many audiences found it painful. I think Mike [Siberry, who played Petruchio] even showed at times that he knew what he was doing and knew it was becoming too much …'

By selecting words such as 'torture' and 'starvation', Josie Lawrence reveals here how seriously she took Kate's treatment. For her, Petruchio's behaviour is unquestionably abuse, painful to contemplate and disturbing for the audience to witness.

Rather like Antonio's treatment of Shylock in *The Merchant of Venice*, Petruchio's tactics provoke strong responses these days. I say 'these days' because it's not so long ago (the mid-1960s, in fact) that a trailer for the Zeffirelli film could advertise it as 'a motion picture for every man who ever gave the back of his hand to his beloved and for every woman who deserved it', tempting audiences with the offer 'if you haven't tamed any good shrews lately, she's just what you've been waiting for'.[14] As Deborah Cartmell observes of the 1966 movie:

> It's not only [Elizabeth] Taylor's sixties hairstyle and make-up that dates the film; Zeffirelli includes shots of her throughout lovingly gazing at Petruchio unobserved; the shot of her famous eyes gazing through a keyhole … epitomises the message of the film: here is a woman who secretly wants to be abused (or tamed).[15]

Sinead Cusack doesn't see Petruchio's treatment of Kate as abuse at all.

'Not to my mind, it isn't!', she roundly asserts when I put it to her.

'I know what you mean by the abuse element and I know it has to be treated very carefully. But, you see, my belief about Petruchio and Kate is that they're two sides of one coin. They're both anarchic, rebellious, angry and *conspiratorial*. They want something other than what convention and tradition decree ... I would be inclined to agree that the "taming" process comes very close to abuse. But I think there is an understanding which those two people arrive at through combat.'

She recalls that, in the 1982 production, director Barry Kyle had picked up on Petruchio's falconry speech, in which he proposes to 'tame' Kate as one would tame a falcon, by keeping it hungry and denying it sleep.

'Well, we had a rather interesting image – that he was a falconer. Petruchio [Alun Armstrong] had a hawk which he hooded during the course of that great speech he has about taming Kate. And it's necessary, in order for the falcon to fly to the lure, for certain disciplines to be imposed. Now it was a slightly dodgy image, but I liked it – that actually certain things have to happen before you can fly, certain disciplines have to be observed before your heart can fly, your soul can fly, your spirit can fly. And then, when I was doing *Our Lady of Sligo* – this is absolutely by-the-by, but it might interest you, because it's *à propos* having a discipline imposed upon you, a really strict, straitjacketing discipline imposed upon you in order that you can fly ...'

And she explains a principle that she had been introduced to when being directed by Max Stafford-Clark. Briefly, the director required her in early rehearsals to declare the purpose of every sentence she spoke before uttering it. For example, she would introduce a line with a verb such as 'persuade', or 'agree' or 'amaze'. This procedure, she explains, goes on for two weeks, and, though initially sceptical – she describes herself as an intuitive actress – she quickly became convinced.

> 'You see, most actors, we make a terrible mistake in thinking that how we say the line is the important thing. It isn't. You see, everything I'm saying to you now is to *persuade* you of something, make you hear what I'm trying to tell you. So we colour phrases in order that we have an effect on our listener – to excite, or entrance, or bore, or shock, or whatever. So, what it is, you say the verb "shock". Then you play the line as *shocking* the audience or person. And then, after about two weeks, you drop saying the verb and you just play …'

It was this process that helped throw a light on what she had been doing with Kate.

> 'And it's a fantastic lesson with Shakespeare. And it seemed to me, now that I was so into the idea of a discipline that seems to constrain but actually allows you to fly – that that's what I always felt about Kate. That disciplines were imposed because it was the only way her spirit could be released. And then' – she thumps her fist on her palm – 'then her spirit was released *gloriously*.'

Act 4, scene 5: 'Good Lord, how bright and goodly shines the moon!'

Having humoured him by agreeing that two o'clock is seven, she now has to declare the sun to be the moon before he will go a foot further.

'Now, by my mother's son, and that's myself', he swears,

> *'It shall be moon, or star, or what I list,*
> *Or ere I journey to your father's house.'*

'Say as he says', mutters a fed-up Hortensio, 'or we shall never go'.

So she agrees:

> *'… But sun it is not, when you say it is not,*
> *And the moon changes even as your mind.*
> *What you will have it nam'd, even that it is,*
> *And so it shall be so for Katharine.'*

Many actresses have taken this as a turning-point in Kate's understanding of what Petruchio is about. Alexandra Gilbreath says:

> 'And for me the biggest moment is in the sun and moon scene. She realises … it's not … it's a kind of a *joke*, isn't it? It's such an emotional realisation: 'OK, I get it. Enough. I see where you're going with it.'

Josie Lawrence takes a similar view:

> 'Here's this bloke once again doing this mental stuff. We all know it's the sun. And we did it … I remember going right up to Petruchio and saying it very quietly: *If you want it to be this way, it will be this way.* And Kate picks up on that early banter again, and she thinks, this is how it's got to be if it's going to work. It's not – oh, he's my lord and master and I've got to say this. It's – this is how *I'm* going to manage it myself.
>
> 'You see, it's very difficult. Because you have had the abuse, and I'm of the opinion, obviously, as everyone is, that abuse should not be tolerated – if this was a modern situation, then I would have left as soon as I could from that cell that he kept me in. But she can't do that. She has to create a way out, using her own wit, her own intelligence.
>
> 'So then we had a moment of silence where he is looking at me and I'm looking at him. And you get a feeling from Petruchio

that he's thinking: "Here's a fantastic woman. Quite what have I been doing here?" It could almost have been a kiss, but it wasn't.

'And then, of course, when Vincentio comes on and Petruchio tells her to embrace this "gentlewoman", she thinks, OK, I will. I'll play this game and I'll do it bloody well ...'

Act 4, scene 5: 'Young budding virgin ...'

At this moment on the road to Padua, Vincentio enters. Anxious to get to the city and check on his son Lucentio, the old man is little prepared for Petruchio's salutation:

> 'Good morrow, gentle mistress, whither away?
> ... Fair lovely maid, once more good day to thee.
> Sweet Kate, embrace her for her beauty's sake.'

Now determined to play the game for all it's worth (and do it 'bloody well'), Kate addresses 'her' in a similar vein:

'Young budding virgin', she begins (the old man by now bewildered and a little scared),

> '... Happy the parents of so fair a child,
> Happier the man whom favourable stars
> Allots thee for his lovely bed-fellow.'

Predictably, Petruchio interrupts:

> 'Why, how now Kate, I hope thou art not mad,
> This is a man, old, wrinkled, faded, withered,
> And not a maiden, as thou sayest he is.'

And she replies, feigning remorse:

> 'Pardon, old father, my mistaking eyes,

That have been so bedazzled by the —'

— and she stops. And looks to Petruchio for confirmation —

'... Sun?'

He smiles at her ...

'And that's us coming together again', says Josie Lawrence. 'And we take this old bloke off and we're on our way. And if the play ended then – I know there has been abuse, but you feel that, if he left it at that, if he left her being this powerful, witty woman, who could make him laugh and make him feel proud – then it would be the most fantastic relationship ever ...

'But he blows it completely ...'

Act 5, scene 2: 'I am ashamed that women are so simple / To offer war where they should sue for peace ...'

At Bianca's wedding, the conversation between the men turns on the allegation that – of the three husbands, Petruchio, Lucentio and Hortensio (now married to his lusty widow) – it is Petruchio who has 'the veriest shrew of all'. Confident in the new-found relationship with his wife, Petruchio suggests a bet:

'Let's each one send unto his wife,
And he whose wife is most obedient,
To come at first when he doth send for her,
Shall win the wager which we will propose.'

Lucentio and Hortensio readily agree. But after Bianca and the widow have each sent frosty refusals, Kate obediently enters and then returns, at Petruchio's request, to bring the other two recalcitrant wives into their new husbands' presence. With a stupefied audience of wedding guests and

Baptista's amazed declaration that Kate is 'chang'd as she had never been',
the scene is set for her big speech ...

But how does she deliver it? Sincerely? Ironically? (Mary Pickford famously winked at Bianca in the 1929 film.) As many critics have pointed out, this speech is something of a paradox – a sermon on submission delivered by a character who takes centre stage, dominates the audience and lectures her fellow women in the longest speech in the play. But that isn't the actress's problem. For her, what is important is how she delivers the speech; and that depends heavily on the nature of the newly-formed relationship with Petruchio, the attitude Kate has adopted, and the factors which underlie her apparent transformation.

Josie Lawrence's belief that the 'sun and moon' moment had established an understanding between them led her to a feeling of the profoundest disillusionment when Kate realises that her husband has gambled on her obedience. And this turns to bitter resentment at the humiliating moment when he requires her to remove her cap and tread on it:

> 'It should have just been a game that these two played in the world of etiquette – these two could have become rather wonderful, rebellious creatures. You could even have a point where she quite enjoys saying, you know, "What is your will, my lord?" Then the cap incident happens, and that is humiliation all over again. That's the slippery slope, stepping on the cap. It should be really embarrassing for everyone to watch, it should be completely humiliating.
>
> 'And then he doesn't stop there. This stupid idiot doesn't stop there. He then asks her to tell these women how to be beholden, and how to honour their husbands.
>
> 'And I thought, right, I will do this speech and I won't stop. I'll carry on. And I'll carry on and I'll carry on. Because I know

this is the end now, what you're doing here. You've fucked up, you've made a mess of it. I shall carry on. It might make me cry, it might make me frustrated, but I shall really do it. And I loved the fact that Gale directed the people watching to become really embarrassed by it. Then, when I placed my hand down, he walked towards me and knelt down beside me and put his head in his hands, completely shamed.'

The actress is now back in the moment. Listen to the present tense ...

'And that's when Kate becomes the actress again. That's when I stand up, so that I'm looking down on him. I walk away. I turn round one last time ... "You blew it." And I'm off.'

I remember that moment very clearly. There wasn't a sound in the auditorium. I think we were all shocked that the play could end on such a downbeat note. But there was one small glimmer of salvation. Gale Edwards had decided to include a version of the Induction, in which a drunken Christopher Sly is thrown out of the house by his wife and then 'dreams' the shrew-taming story as a kind of wish-fulfilment. And, while Shakespeare doesn't complete the frame, by bringing Sly on again at the end, Edwards did. And it was here that we were allowed a little optimism, as Sly, possibly changed by his dream-memory of Kate's last moment, once again encounters his wife. Slumped on the ground, he bows his head as she approaches, then holds onto her legs for comfort and support as she places a hand on his shoulder and the lights dim ...

Other productions have been considerably more upbeat.

Basing her interpretation on the fact that Kate and Petruchio have become 'absolute soul-mates', Sinead Cusack says:

'Those two people have the same methods – they operate in the same way. And when she does the speech at the end, I think it's such a two-fingers up to society, to her sister and those suitors and her father. These two are embarking on one of the great adventures of all time ... So that within the speech, there is indeed submission, there is indeed. But it's a submission that she *wants*, because she knows that it's actually to her huge advantage to go along with this man. Because he is part of her. He's like, as I say, the other side of the coin. But it's a very difficult battle that they've fought, to arrive at that understanding.

'I used to love that. People used to walk out. But I used to love that speech, and I never thought of it as the fact that, you know, you place your foot on my hand. It was the biggest joke they had. Can you just imagine those two looking at everybody – her sister Bianca, what she must have thought! But it's their secret, their complicity – they're totally complicit in that last speech. I thought I was going to have huge difficulty with it. But during the course of rehearsals it became very clear to me that this was a very feisty, opinionated, passionate woman; and she finds her mirror-image – somebody who has all those attributes as well, and is prepared to flout every rule in the book.'

So Sinead Cusack found an accommodation with Kate's 'submission' speech by seeing it in the context of the couple's shared rebelliousness and contempt for convention. For Alexandra Gilbreath, the speech became acceptable if seen as the culmination of Kate's liberation:

'He does liberate her. And I think the final speech for me – of course, it's intimidating to start off with, but she's got things to say to those people. And it's not about being submissive, because it's not a speech for every woman and every man. It's Kate's opinion, and at that stage Kate is fully prepared to obey her husband because she feels bigger and better for it. And I know that [director Gregory Doran's] uncle, I think, was a Benedictine monk and that when he was growing up there was the sense of the joy of service – the more you give, the more you receive. And I know that my John (my chap), when we were rehearsing, said: "I've been looking in my golf book" – he's a golfer – "and I think what might happen in that final speech is that, to gain control, one must give up control."'

She chuckles at the putting reference, but it reminds me of Petruchio's falcons and Max Stafford-Clark's verbs.

'You realise that, if you do give up control, life is great.

'So when Biondello comes out and summons Bianca and the Widow, she just thinks, what game are you boys playing? So it's not – yes, I'm submissive. It's: you want me to take the hat off? OK, I'll take it off – it doesn't mean anything. Because I'm *bigger*. I don't have to fight any more.

'And that's a liberation. But it's *her* liberation. It doesn't mean that every woman has to do the same. The others say that's disgusting, I'm not going to obey my husband. OK. *Don't*. Kate *wants* to. Because she feels great about herself.'

Now I can hear a lot of people echoing Mercutio's 'O calm, dishonourable, vile submission!'[16] After all, it's one thing to *choose* obedience, quite another to have it forced upon you. And our feelings about the ending of *The Taming of the Shrew* depend at least in part on the extent to which we believe that Kate has made an independent choice, and how far Petruchio's 'taming' has contrived not to look like abuse.

Though *The Taming of the Shrew* is among the most commonly performed plays in the Shakespeare canon (in the early years of the Memorial Theatre at Stratford, performances of *The Shrew*, *The Merchant of Venice* and *The Merry Wives of Windsor* were so frequent that some wag suggested simply putting on *The Merry Shrews of*

Venice), it is these days regarded as a deeply problematic play, not least because of Kate's final speech. Germaine Greer argued in *The Female Eunuch* that the speech is 'the greatest defence of Christian monogamy ever written' – take that how you will; and George Bernard Shaw famously described Kate's statement as 'altogether disgusting to modern sentiments' (*modern* being 1897). It's not surprising that actresses offered the chance to play this character think long and hard about how to accommodate the speech in ways that do not compromise their integrity.

The end of Act 5: The Swan, Spring 2003

Alexandra Gilbreath approaches the front of the stage and addresses the audience:

> '… *But so as nor the men*
> *Can find one just cause to complain of when*
> *They fitly do consider in their lives*
> *They should not reign as tyrants o'er their wives,*
> *Nor can the women from this precedent*
> *Insult or triumph, it being aptly meant*
> *To teach both sexes due equality;*
> *And, as they stand bound, to love mutually.*'[17]

This is not, of course, the ending of Shakespeare's *The Taming of the Shrew*, but the epilogue to his fellow-dramatist John Fletcher's irreverent sequel, *A Woman's Prize*. Played in repertory with *The Shrew* in the 2003 Stratford season, Fletcher's comedy was advertised under its more eye-catching sub-title *The Tamer Tamed* – a title which helpfully proclaims its links with Shakespeare's play.

John Fletcher (1579–1652) is best known for being half of a highly successful play-writing double-act with his off-stage partner,

Francis Beaumont (who died the same year as Shakespeare, 1616). But he collaborated with Shakespeare on at least three plays: the lost *Cardenio* (c. 1612–13), *All Is True* (*Henry VIII*) (1613), and *Two Noble Kinsmen* (probably 1613–14, almost certainly the last play that Shakespeare wrote); and he took over as the King's Men's principal dramatist after Shakespeare died. The fact that the two men were collaborating only two years after *The Tamer Tamed* (first performed in 1611, and by the King's Men) suggests that Shakespeare couldn't have been too put out by Fletcher's cashing in on his shrew story. (In fact, it's a fair guess that, as a businessman, he was probably delighted, as it would give the company a chance to revive his own play.)

Fletcher's sequel takes place a few years after the events recorded in *The Taming of the Shrew*. Kate has died (in what circumstances we are not told) and Petruchio is about to remarry a young woman called Maria. Interestingly, the word is that Kate was never quite as fully 'tamed' as the conclusion to the earlier play suggests, for his friends recall her 'daily hue and cries upon him', which so 'turned his temper' that even now

> The bare remembrance of his first wife
> Will make him start in's sleep, cry out for cudgels,
> And hide his breeches out for fear her ghost
> Should walk, and wear 'em yet.[18]

'Since his first marriage', reports Tranio, 'He is no more the still Petruchio / Than I am Babylon'.

As it turns out, fears that Maria's youth, her 'modesty and tenderness of spirit' will be crushed by Petruchio's angry domination prove spectacularly unfounded, as she sets about taming him. Lysistrata-like, she first denies him sex, and then turns each of his ruses against him. When he feigns illness, she locks him out and has a plague cross painted on the door. When he threatens to leave, she helps pack his bags and expresses the hope that he will return many years later a better person; when a coffin is brought in bearing his corpse, her valedictory speech over it expresses the view that

> The memory of this man, had he liv'd
> But two years longer, had begot more follies
> Than wealthy autumn flies.

— concluding (in a comment which causes him – predictably – to leap from his coffin, a broken man):

> But let him rest;
> He was a fool, and farewell he.[19]

Fletcher's play, in addition to being extremely funny and pointed, is a fascinating historical phenomenon, revealing as it does that we need to rethink easy assumptions about women's ready acceptance of an inferior role in Shakespeare's England. Greg Doran, director of the 2003 production (the first revival since Fletcher's lifetime) says:

> The role of woman in society was certainly changing. You need only read the huge number of pamphlets and broadsheets railing at the way women were asserting themselves to grasp the intensity of the debate. It reached its climax in Joseph Swetnam's fiercely misogynistic 1615 diatribe, *The Arraignment of Lewd, Idle, Froward and Inconstant Women*. The very title reveals its essential male paranoia.[20]

Contemplating the evidence that Fletcher might have been a homosexual,* Doran offers an interesting speculation. While aware that, as a gay man himself, he might be 'appropriating' Fletcher, he says:

---

* Fletcher's sexuality is difficult to determine. He and Beaumont seem to have had a ménage-à-trois with a woman until Beaumont's death; but Fletcher then seems to have had a close relationship with the young playwright Philip Massinger.

Perhaps I see in his perspective on male–female relationships and bully-boy chauvinism in *The Tamer Tamed*, for example, an outsider's objectivity which I assign to his sexuality because I am myself gay … I wonder: if I do claim Fletcher's place among the pantheon of writers who share my sexuality, will it alter the audience's perception of his work one jot?

Well, I think it will, if it is shared, as was the case in 2003, with the actors who are giving life to Fletcher's plays.

That season, the company made theatre history as the first to stage both shrew plays in repertory – Shakespeare's *The Taming of the Shrew* and Fletcher's *The Tamer Tamed* – since 1633. And the fact that essentially the same group of actors performed in the two plays (Jasper Britton playing both Petruchios, Alexandra Gilbreath Kate and Maria) enabled them to feel that Kate's Act 5 speech need not be viewed as the last word on the subject of marriage, and *The Taming of the Shrew* no longer labelled 'a problem play'. Alexandra Gilbreath says:

'Well I know that Greg has this wonderful quote about "the problem plays" – that the plays aren't the problem, it's our problem with them, or something along those lines. And I don't see *The Taming of the Shrew* as a problem play at all. But maybe it's that I've been released from the problem of having to solve the final speech, knowing that I've got *The Tamer Tamed* as the answer.'

So you haven't quite completed the story at the end of *The Shrew?*, I ask.

'Exactly. I feel as if I can play Kate in the way I do because I have this wonderful role called Maria who, at the end of the play – in an epilogue that was written 400 years ago – says that men and women should live together in "due equality / And, as they stand bound, to love mutually".

(*Animated*) 'It's positively revolutionary. I get such a thrill from that.

(*Appalled*) 'And we still have TV programmes like *Wife Swap*! We're still fascinated by all that! (*Amazed*) He wasn't only ahead of his time for 400 years ago – he's still ahead of his time now! But those two lines … And we're still dealing with issues of inequality! That's why we have programmes where a wife can't quite believe that her husband can insist that she makes him porridge at six o'clock!

(*Incredulous*) 'We're not past that yet? So, when people say, you know, let's talk about why people find *The Taming of the Shrew* offensive, I don't find it offensive at all. Because at the end it's one person's point of view. It's Kate's point of view, she's not speaking for all women. Maria *does* speak for all women, because it seems to me that Maria doesn't have the amount of self-doubt that Kate has. And she's completely determined to fulfil her ambition, for want of a better word. But it's not about reigning tyrant over Petruchio. It's about – you and I have to be equals, you know, we stand together and face the world.

(*Radiant*) 'And that for me is extraordinary.

'She says, "I've tamed you. It's OK, don't worry, it's not a problem. But now you'll understand, I didn't intend to spend your money, I didn't intend for you to die, I didn't intend for you to leave. I intended to behave as badly as possible so you could see there are possibilities. It's a two-way street. You can't behave badly to me and expect me to take it – I can behave badly to you." That's why it's such a strong story.'

Playing Fletcher's sequel in tandem with *The Taming of the Shrew* also allows a different perspective to be taken on the 'abuse' scenes in Shakespeare's play. While Shakespeare is content to allow the possibility of wife-beating to emerge at a remove – when Petruchio strikes his servants rather than Kate – Fletcher raises the issue openly. It is an extraordinary moment, and one that Alexandra Gilbreath cherishes as a favourite in performance:

'It's when he says, do you not beg that I should beat you? —

> If I should beat thee now as much may be,
> Dost thou not well deserve it? O' thy conscience,
> Dost thou not cry "Come, beat me"?

'It's such a shock that he might hit her; and she says: the first time you touch me, it's over —

> I defy you,
> And my last loving tears, farewell. The first stroke,
> The very first you give me, if you dare strike,
> I do turn utterly from you. Try me
> And you shall find it so, for ever,
> Never to be recall'd. And so farewell.[21]

'We still have women who have to leave their homes because they're being battered by their husbands. But Maria says, no, I won't just take a beating and then perhaps we'll come back and talk about it. The very first stroke you lay on me – I'm talking about *the first stroke* – I am gone for ever, never to come back. And, because it's considered, I suppose, a light-hearted sit-com (of course, for me it's a play about human rights), at that point it suddenly becomes something completely different. And I love the fact that the audience think they're sitting down to a comedy – they're enjoying the fact that Petruchio has to blow his way out of the house and it's all very funny – and then she says: no, this is serious stuff, I'm not kidding around here. And I find that a very powerful moment.'

There is a significant sector of the academic establishment these days unhappy with Shakespeare's pre-eminence. Some dislike the notion of 'genius' which he seems to represent, seeing it as a distorted view of how plays of that period came about; some the fact that the writer and his work have been co-opted by a conservative establishment to reinforce the status quo; others that he represents all that is reprehensible in cultural imperialism. While I can see what they're getting at (and also, patently, where they're 'coming from'), I don't share most of their concerns – except one. That, by giving so much attention to Shakespeare, we ignore the work of contemporaries who, condemned to languish in his shadow, receive nothing like due acknowledgement. Fletcher is a case in point. His two extant collaborations with Shakespeare have seemed only to confirm how inferior he is. Yet *The Tamer Tamed* is a play which opens up at least as many interesting perspectives on human relationships as *The Taming of the Shrew*; features a central character in Maria who deserves at least as many stage outings as Kate; and contains some extraordinary and unexpected moments. If only for that shockingly defiant 'Try me', this play and its remarkable heroine deserve more attention.

The end of the final Act: Goes forward with Catharine in his hand

As the stage direction indicates, Petruchio turns to the audience and continues his speech. The war is over, he has dispensed with his whip and can now conclude proceedings on a contented note:

> 'Such duty as the subject owes the prince,
> Even such a woman oweth to her husband ...
> How shameful 'tis when woman are so simple
> To offer war when they should sue for peace.
> Or seek for rule, supremacy, and sway,
> Where bound to love, to honour, and obey.'   *Exeunt omnes.*

When John Philip Kemble delivered this speech in the 1780s* at the end of David Garrick's *Catharine and Petruchio* (1754; 'altered from Shakespeare's *The Taming of the Shrew*, with alterations and additions'), he was of course uttering lines which in Shakespeare's version are spoken by Kate. Restoration (and later) audiences don't seem to have minded changing Shakespeare to fit their sense of decorum – witness Nahum Tate's famous happy ending to his adaptation of *King Lear*.† And Garrick's version, itself adapted in Kemble's 1810 acting edition, became the standard performance version of *The Taming of the Shrew* for most of the 19th century.[22]

Adaptations of the play since that time have been many and various. But none has been more radically disruptive than Charles Marowitz's *The Shrew*. Marowitz, an American director, dramatist and critic, staged a series of revolutionary re-workings of Shakespeare's plays from the mid 1960s, including *Hamlet*, *Macbeth*, *Othello*, *Measure for Measure* and *The Merchant of Venice*. Each adaptation might as accurately be described as a collage, given that Marowitz's method involves re-assigning speeches and re-arranging the text. The effect is to bring to the surface meanings which are not normally apparent in more traditional interpretations. The Marowitz Shakespeares also force us to confront the plays' contemporary implications. In the case of *Variations on The Merchant of Venice*, this involved opening the play with the terrorist bombing of the King David Hotel, Jerusalem, in

---

* In the prompt-book for the 1788 production, Kemble had written 'whip for Petruchio' in the margin next to Petruchio's entrance in the wedding scene. (See Arthur Colby Sprague, *Shakespeare and the Actors* (Harvard University Press, 1944), p. 57.)

†Nahum Tate (1652–1715) was made Poet Laureate in 1692 and, among other achievements, wrote the libretto for Purcell's *Dido and Aeneas* (1689). His adaptation *The History of King Lear* – in which the King is restored and Cordelia survives to marry Edgar – held the stage for a century and a half from its first performance in 1681.

1946 (see page 146). For *The Shrew*, it meant looking afresh at what society does to people like Kate.

Josie Lawrence dolefully recalls playing Kate in the Marowitz *Shrew* at drama school: 'She was drugged at the end – he flicks a whip.' This was the climax to an adaptation which, as Marowitz explains, 'involved a careful reassessment of the play's ideology'.[23] Marowitz believed that:

> If Katharine can be made to represent breeding and elegance, and one is able to discard the tirades of the traditional termagant, her downfall becomes truly pathetic, for it then represents the abandonment of personal style in the face of a brutalising conformity …
>
> The only victory available to the Petruchio–Baptista–Bianca axis is the artificially induced spectacle of a mesmerised or drugged victim droning the words her tormentors could not make her speak voluntarily.

So, in Marowitz's version, Kate is drugged, and Petruchio *does* crack a whip.

Marowitz's re-workings prompt many people to ask: why doesn't he simply write a new play? Daniel Rosenthal surveys some 20th-century cinematic spin-offs of *The Taming of the Shrew* which have done just that:

> The play has inspired numerous movies about bachelors 'taming' wild women, such as the musical comedy *You Made Me Love You* (UK, 1933) and *Second Best Bed* (UK, 1938), and although few people would associate John Wayne with the Bard, he twice appeared in Petruchio-and-Katharina-style double-acts.
>
> In John Ford's *The Quiet Man* (1952), Wayne was ex-boxer Sean Thornton, who returns to Ireland and marries his neighbour

Will's fiery sister, Mary Kate (Maureen O'Hara), after winning a fist-fight with Will to secure her dowry. Then, in 1963's *McLintock!*, Wayne's cattle baron sparred with his tempestuous wife, Katharine (O'Hara again). The poster's tagline asked 'He tamed the West, but could he tame her?'.[24]

He might also have included in that list the 1929 *Taming of the Shrew* Pickford–Fairbanks 'talkie' with the famous credit title: 'Written by William Shakespeare with additional dialogue by Sam Taylor.' 'Sure we're making *The Taming of the Shrew*', a spokesman for United Artists is reported to have said, 'but we're turning it into a comedy'.

The best-known *Shrew* spin-off of all, of course, is Cole Porter's Broadway musical *Kiss Me Kate*. In the hugely successful 3D film version, released in 1953,[25] Kathryn Grayson starred alongside Howard Keel as Lili Vanessi, wild-tempered and uncontrollable ex-wife of actor-director Fred Graham, whose task it is to persuade her to star in a new show as 'a perfect shrew'. Given songs such as 'I Hate Men', Grayson's 'shrew' is allowed to pummel her Petruchio figure when she realises that his gift of pre-show flowers was intended for 'Bianca'; and the physical stuff is reciprocated when he gives her an on-stage spanking. You'd have to be pretty po-faced to object to this, or to the generally tame 'taming', not least because Lili's equivalent of Kate's final speech is perfunctory and formulaic. Generally, *Kiss Me Kate* is a witty and joyous celebration of its forerunner – and I might have said 'irreverent', were it not for the fact that the reverence for Shakespeare is always (seemingly irreverently) implied. It's a bit like school-children impersonating their teacher; though ostensibly sub-versive, the act itself is a tacit acknowledgement of her authority. This is especially noticeable when, for no very obvious reason, a couple of New York gangsters hoof their way down the city's back streets singing:

Brush up your Shakespeare, start quoting him now.
Brush up your Shakespeare, and the women you will wow.

A recent spin-off which draws more obviously on the details of Shakespeare's plot and cast of characters is the 1999 teen-movie *10 Things I Hate About You*.[26] Based in present-day Seattle, it stars Julia Styles and Heath Ledger as the Kate–Petruchio equivalents. Showing a keen awareness of late 20th-century gender politics that is nonetheless never allowed to become preachy, the film's shrew plot centres upon Kat Stratford, an aggressively feminist senior at Padua High School who reads Plath and the Brontës, plays a mean soccer game and has a reputation for giving boys a tough time. (When she claims that she is not badly behaved, merely 'tempestuous', her guidance counsellor airily replies: 'Heinous bitch is the term most often used.') Kat's Petruchio is Pat Verona, an almost stereotypically Australian macho wild boy, sexy and caustic – a brooding mix of Jim Morrison and Heathcliff, rumoured to have 'sold his own liver on the black market for a new set of speakers'. ('I heard he ate a live duck once', says another admirer, keen not to be out-done. 'Everything but the beak and feet.')

But, in a witty rethink, Pat's strategy is not to tame Kat, but to tame himself. And, as this is late-century USA, his taming involves conversion into a 'new man' who stops smoking, starts to read feminist novels and listen to girl rock-bands, and caringly looks after Kat when she gets drunk at a party and vomits into his lap. Fittingly, there is no last-act submission speech from Kat. Instead, she writes a sonnet on her new boyfriend's flaws, the '10 things' she hates about him. Meanwhile, the nastier aspects of Petruchio are transferred into Joey 'Eat Me' Donner (a combined Hortensio–Gremio figure chasing Bianca, Kat's sister). Narcissistic and misogynistic, it's Joey who is finally tamed – kicked in the balls, he lies writhing on the ground. 'Is he in pain or having an orgasm?', asked one reviewer; 'It's hard to tell … it's clear that if anyone here has masochistic tendencies, it's the macho male.'[27]

The film comments amusingly on its Shakespearean source. The wise-cracking Tranio figure, Michael, is constantly quoting Shakespeare and parodying the language ('The shit hath hitteth the fan'). A black English teacher, setting the rewriting of a sonnet as homework, remarks: 'I know Shakespeare was a dead white guy, but he knows his shit.' But alongside respect for Shakespeare is some splendidly genuine irreverence. When one character sees a picture of the playwright in a fellow-student's locker, he points to the ruff around the Bard's neck and asks: 'Is that to stop him licking his stitches?'

Most interestingly, the film turns its heroine and hero into like-able non-conformists, too bright and individual for the society in which they find themselves – which is exactly how Kate and Petruchio are being played on the Stratford stage as I write. It also gives Kat psychologically plausible motivations for her anti-male behaviour: a bad early sexual experience; and the belief that, if she represses her sexuality and remains a child, her absent mother will return home. This again parallels the kind of background-history work that stage Kates in the contemporary theatre perennially find themselves engaging in.

Reviews of this film were highly favourable – and also fascinating for the deep dislike they revealed for Shakespeare's original. Here is a representative selection:

So, in many ways, I suppose the film cheats. It's everything you wish the play was, free of its hoods and traps, its pandering to the status quo, its low expectations.[28]

… debut screenwriters Karen McCullah Lutz and Kirsten Smith simply grab what they fancy and ditch the rest, which mercifully includes most of the 'Women! Know Your Place!' theme.[29]

... what [the screenwriters] have done is chosen a Shakespeare play that actually needs rewriting. Shakespeare's tale of two sisters ... is not only conservative, but psychologically unbalanced.[30]

[*The Taming of the Shrew*] has been all but unstageable since the 1960s – the merry fun seems indistinguishable from the breaking of a female spirit. The simplest way of salvaging the play is to omit the extremes of Kate's submission, but it's still not a comfortable piece.[31]

My feeling is that these reviewers have probably read the *text* of *The Taming of the Shrew* and have maybe seen the Burton–Taylor film; what they plainly have not done is experience a perceptive stage version.

One further point about *10 Things*. A major reason for taking a period analogue or modern-setting approach to a Shakespeare play is to bring out a key feature which otherwise might remain obscure or buried in a traditional 'Elizabethan' or 'historical' production. This element is often the rigid social hierarchy within which the characters interact, and its effect upon sexual mores, marriage arrangements and courtship. Audiences find it easier to tune in to this alien culture if they are given a period or modern analogy. And there seem to be two cultural contexts favoured by cinema and stage directors at the moment which are seen as effective parallels for Elizabethan society and its strict conventions: the Mafia and the American education system. The Mafia has provided a basis for two brilliantly effective *Romeo and Juliet*s, for example – the 1986 RSC production and the 1996 Baz Luhrmann film; as well as a Buenos Aires *Hamlet* (see pages 251–2). The US high school, having stood in as a substitute for Jane Austen's England in *Clueless* (based on *Emma*),[32] seems to offer useful reference points for an audience striving to understand the social and sexual pressures that make Kate, Bianca, Petruchio and Baptista tick. The *Othello* remake, *O*, exploits the same context, setting its story of sexual jealousy in the world of US college basketball.[33]   It's interesting to speculate on what the next cultural reference-point will be.

10 Things I Hate About You showed that the shrew as a figure in popular culture is as vividly alive as ever. From Socrates' Xantippe to Noah's wife in the Mysteries, and in every threatening female from the Wife of Bath to Lady Bracknell, she returns time and again as a figure of fear and ridicule in equal measure. She was alive and kicking throughout the golden age of seaside postcards, when an army of muscular-forearmed wives stood behind doors, sleeves rolled up, rolling-pin in hand, grimly waiting for the midnight return of the small, timid, tipsy, red-nosed husband. She re-emerged unwillingly as 'my mother-in-law' on the stereotyping lips of every lazy music-hall comedian from the Glasgow Empire to Clacton Pier. She was the Joan Sims character in the *Carry On*s, a powerful unseen presence as the other half of Captain Mainwairing's telephone calls, and the restraining hand of Arthur Daley's 'her indoors'. There was more than a touch of her in Hyacinth Bucket and Norah Batty. Pre-eminently, she was there in Sibyl Fawlty.

Despite changes in the status of women and the nature of marriage, the unruly, domineering woman has proved to be a durable stereotype and a major challenge for any actress offered the role of Shakespeare's Katharina Minola.

CHAPTER 9

Prospero

'The stately magician'

William Hazlitt

The old man is a Prospero and the music is his all-encompassing island. The tempest has blown itself out and his last, most enduring act will be to bequeath a life's magic to his Miranda. But not quite yet ...[1]

This is the conclusion to a newspaper article about the musician Ravi Shankar and his teenage daughter Anoushka. And it intriguingly opens up the question of what a journalist means when he describes someone as 'a Prospero'. What impression does he expect his audience to have of Shakespeare's character? What is 'a Prospero' like? And how identifiable is he, as compared with, say, 'a Romeo' or 'a Lady Macbeth'?

If we try to list the character's identifiable qualities, then clearly 'a Prospero' must be skilled in 'magic' of some kind; he has to possess the wisdom of mature years; and – if the appellation means anything more than 'clever old magician' – he will have exploited his skills in the pursuit of some grand design. If he is linked with 'a Miranda', then we are encouraged to think about a father–daughter relationship characterised by a more or less benign paternal control on the one hand, and an Edenic innocence on the other.

So it's easy to see why journalist Alan Franks has lighted on the Prospero–Miranda parallel as a fitting conclusion to this particular article. Like Prospero, Ravi Shankar is an elderly man venerated for his genius; to many musicians (most famously George Harrison), he has been regarded as a kind of guru; now in his 80s, the passion of his earlier years is past (his storm blown out); and when we think of his sitar music – to Western ears, exotic and mysterious – we have a sound-track for *The Tempest* which is so obviously fitting as to be a cliché.

But look again at Prospero's relationship with his daughter. For it is here that interesting questions bubble to the surface about what happens when media people draw upon Shakespeare's characters as reference-points for their audience.

In this particular case, the *Times* journalist clearly wants us to understand that the great musician is in the process of handing down to his daughter skills that have taken him a lifetime to acquire – he is 'bequeath[ing] a life's magic to his Miranda' – and that Anoushka, actually the subject of the interview, will consequently become a notable performer in her own right. But we don't have to examine this parallel very closely before cracks start to appear. For one thing, Shakespeare's Prospero specifically does not hand his 'rough magic' on to Miranda: having served their purpose, Prospero's staff is broken and his book thrown into the sea 'deeper than ever did plummet sound'. Equally importantly, the bizarre Prospero–Miranda relationship is quite unlike that enjoyed by Ravi and Anoushka Shankar, characterised as theirs appears to be by its healthy, happily adjusted normality.

Clearly Alan Franks does not expect us to take the parallel that far. I'm doing so only to explore the ways in which character allusions of this kind work and don't work. In this case, the ageing genius/guru aspect of Ravi Shankar makes 'Prospero' an apt reference; but the Miranda idea works only if you don't know Shakespeare's play that well, or don't think too carefully about it. And this wouldn't be a problem were it not that both Prospero's relationship with his daughter, and the fact that he abjures his magic at the end, are key elements of our conception of the character. We can call somebody a Hamlet figure in confidence that our audience will think 'brooding, tortured intellectual' rather than 'multiple killer', because his violence isn't iconologically what Hamlet is 'about'. But Prospero's special relationship with his daughter and final abjuration of his magic are too bound up with our conception of him to make 'a Prospero' a helpful allusion much of the time.

To see a Prospero reference which works more successfully, examine this by Lesley Jackson in an article on glass-maker Dale Chihuly:

> Chihuly has emerged as a kind of Prospero, masterminding the staging of indoor and outdoor spectaculars ...[2]

Or this, in which novelist J.G. Ballard states that the Shakespeare character with whom he most identifies is Prospero, adding: '... if only I could find his wand.'[3]

The first works because it focuses on highly specific and related elements of the Prospero myth – Prospero as grand illusionist; the second because it sees literary genius as a kind of magic, while not taking either genius or magic too seriously.

There's another factor, too, which places a limit on the use of 'Prospero' as a readily identifiable allusion. Check through the newspaper cuttings collection at the Shakespeare Institute, Stratford, and you'll find dozens of examples where a woman is 'a Lady Macbeth', or a couple finds itself in 'a Romeo and Juliet' situation; very few where someone is called 'a Prospero'. This is largely because Prospero is simply not that well known – stop a hundred people in the street and ask them to name ten Shakespeare characters, and not many will include Prospero. But, as I have suggested, the low reference count is also partly because you can't take the Prospero parallel very far before it ceases to be a helpful one.

So, if Prospero cannot be said to be in the popular consciousness in the way that the other characters in this book are, why is he here? For three reasons: because Prospero is a particularly good example of the way in which interpretations of Shakespeare's characters change with the times; because he illustrates something important about the actor's method; and because he is the only Shakespearean character who is traditionally associated with the playwright himself, the magician's renunciation of his art commonly taken as an expression of the dramatist's retirement from the theatre.

Act 1, scene 2: 'Twelve year since, Miranda, twelve year since, / Thy father was the Duke of Milan ...'

I am sitting in the circle of the Old Vic in London's Waterloo, looking into a set which is designed to represent the abandoned stage and proscenium arch of an old theatre. This is a productively disorienting experience, as the stage set looks curiously like the actual Old Vic proscenium which frames it; so that there is constantly the impression that we are watching, if not a play-within-a-play, then a production-within-a-production, Shakespeare-within-the-Old Vic, with the magician Prospero becoming the impresario of his own story.[4]

The scene 1 tempest over, Prospero the magician removes his mantle to reveal Prospero the man; and we see a figure off a Father's Day card, all sloppy cardigan and slippers. While we are never allowed to forget his awesome power, this is a largely benign Prospero, characterised by a great gentleness towards his daughter, with a twinkling humour never far below the surface – the audience laughs approvingly as he admonishes her with a 'How now, moody?', and as he complains that the boat in which they had, twelve years before, been set adrift was so rotten that 'the very rats / Instinctively have quit it'.

He lulls her asleep, imposing 'a good dullness', and the spirit Ariel informs him that he has whipped up the storm on his master's orders, and Prospero's usurping brother Antonio is now marooned on the island, along with his supporter, Alonso, King of Naples, the King's son Ferdinand, and their ally, Antonio, Duke of Milan. All are now in Prospero's power ...

So it is time to awaken Miranda. And it is here that one of those moments happens which, for me, help to define a performance. They are frequently insignificant in the context of the plot, and usually thematically inconsequential; often the actor will not even have noticed what he is doing. Which, as it turns out, is the case here, when Sir Derek Jacobi wakes his Miranda (Claire Price) with the words:

Awake, dear heart; awake. Thou hast slept well;
Awake.

And, in response to her puzzled explanation that

The strangeness of your story put a heaviness upon me,

he says:

Shake it off.

When I later comment on the manner in which he delivered that simple line 'Shake it off' – uttered with extraordinary tenderness and love – the actor is unaware of it. It clearly had not been a line which in rehearsal had been given great thought (or, I should say, *consciously* addressed); but it was one of those lines which, when you hear them delivered by a particular actor in a particular performance, seem to be totally fresh – it's as if you've never heard them before. And, for me, that freshness draws attention to the underlying emotion, in this case a mix of gentleness, warmth and great paternal love, which can inform the whole interpretation of the role.

Later on, sitting with Prospero in his Old Vic dressing room is a bit surreal in itself, not least because the furnishings – Regency-style drapes, a little staircase leading up to a raised couch, a pervasive faded elegance – seem an extension of the *Tempest* stage set. But, in contrast to the dream-like surroundings, the conversation is grounded in practical things – what makes theatre work, what the actor actually *does*. Helping to account for his delivery of 'Shake it off', he says:

> 'I have always tried, whatever Shakespeare I've done – and I'm still trying – to make it sound like it's the way I speak all the time, and to infuse every phrase with a sort of emotion. That kind of approach for me is very attractive, because for me that's what it's all about – it's about the characters and the people and their relationships ...'

Act 1, scene 2: 'This island's mine ...'

Before the gang of assorted travellers were tempest-tossed onto the island, it had just four inhabitants: Prospero, his daughter Miranda, the spirit Ariel, and a strange being called Caliban. Before Prospero's arrival, the territory was Caliban's alone. But, for reasons as yet unknown, Prospero now calls him 'my slave ... earth ... tortoise'; Miranda describes him as 'a villain ... I do not love to look on'.

When Caliban appeared in the 1988 Old Vic production,[5] we saw that the actor, Rudolph Walker, was Afro-Caribbean ...

'This island's mine', he defiantly declares, then reminds Prospero of the succour he, Caliban, had given when the Duke and his daughter were first cast upon the island, and how little he has deserved his present treatment:

> *'For I am all the subjects that you have,*
> *Which first was mine own king; and here you sty me*
> *In this hard rock, whiles you do keep me from the rest of the island.'*

But Prospero is quick to justify his treatment of the islander. 'Thou most lying slave', he cries:

> *'... I have used thee*
> *(Filth as thou art) with humane care, and lodged thee*
> *In mine own cell till thou didst seek to violate*
> *The honour of my child.'*

This particular stage interpretation brings to mind an observation once made by director Terry Hands – that each Shakespeare play seems to go through phases when it comes in and out of focus. One year it will be full of urgent and important contemporary meanings; the next it will seem to have less to say of immediate relevance to the cultural and political climate.

As I write this, for example, the United Kingdom has just invaded Iraq; and the RNT production of *Henry V* (see pages 51–3) is very much 'in focus' for a public that has become accustomed to hearing politically loaded arguments for going to war. Shakespeare's script of *Henry V* allows for upbeat, patriotic, pro-war interpretations as much as it does pessimistic, sceptical anti-war ones; the approach will be influenced by the context in which the play is performed.

This, of course, applies equally to *The Tempest*, and especially to the relationship between Prospero and Caliban, radically reconceptualised throughout its performance history in ways which have made it a touchstone for determining the spirit of the times.

Take, for example, the mid-19th century. For evidence that *The Tempest* was being read as a parable of social change and revolution, we can go back as far as the 1840s when Robert Brough, in his serious burlesque *The Enchanted Isle*, depicted Caliban as a figure with a highly developed political consciousness. Only seven months before this production opened at the Adelphi, the Chartists workers' movement had been prevented by troops and Special Constables from holding a massed rally in London, and audiences would readily have recognised in Caliban a character who had developed 'from oppressed slave to disaffected worker to militant revolutionary'.⁶* Actively resisting Prospero's autocratic rule, this Caliban pointedly asks Miranda: 'Ain't I a man and a brother?', a question which evokes the slogan of the Anti-Slavery Society. Yet slavery had been abolished throughout the British Empire in 1838; and it is as a militant revolutionary Chartist that Caliban comes to the fore, expressing a 'disaffection' (as Brough's Prospero terms it) which is only partly checked by his embodiment of the forces of law and order, Ariel. At the peak of his power, Caliban turns European revolutionary, donning a Cap of Liberty, waving the red flag, giving a spirited rendition of *La Marseillaise* and declaring: '[I will] have a revolution ... Proclaim my rights, demand a constitution.'

Caliban dominated the mainstream theatre in the late 19th century too. He overshadowed Prospero in the first production at Stratford's Shakespeare Memorial Theatre in 1891 and was still the focus of interest in Beerbohm Tree's production at His Majesty's Theatre in 1904.†

---

*Richard W. Schoch points out that a *Theatrical Times* review employed the terms 'fraternise' and 'fraternity' – recognisable codewords for French-style revolution – with specific and exclusive reference to Caliban, confirming the character as an active revolutionary. (*Not Shakespeare: Bardolatry and Burlesque in the Nineteenth Century* (Cambridge University Press, 2002).)

†The earlier stage history of the play is a blank, then undistinguished. After its first recorded performance in 1611, there is no evidence of outings at either the Globe or Blackfriars, though it must have been performed at one or both. In 1667, Samuel Pepys enjoyed watching an adaptation by William Davenant and John Dryden called *The Tempest; or The Enchanted Isle*, a version which, as the most popular show of its time, held the stage until well into the 19th century. Shakespeare's version was not properly restored until William Charles Macready staged it, with lavish special effects, in 1838. (See Michael Dobson, *The Oxford Companion to Shakespeare*, p. 473.)

Moving to the post-colonial era, there have been many productions in which the relationship between Prospero and Caliban is conceptualised as one of European master and black slave. When, for example, ethnographer Octave Mannoni published his 1956 English-language version of *Psychologie de la colonisation*, it was titled *Prospero and Caliban*. Mannoni posited that Prospero was in the subconscious of the archetypal colonial – 'as he was in Shakespeare's' – and that Caliban had 'fallen prey to the resentment which succeeds the breakdown of dependence'. In other words, Prospero had failed to establish a satisfactory colonial–native relationship with Caliban, and was now attempting to justify his oppressive subjugation of the islander:

> ... did Caliban not attempt to violate the honour of his child? After such an offence, what hope is there? There is no logic in this argument. Prospero could have removed Caliban to a safe distance or he could have continued to civilize and correct him. But the argument: you tried to violate Miranda, *therefore* you shall chop wood, belongs to a non-rational mode of thinking. In spite of the various forms this attitude may take ... it is primarily a justification of hatred on grounds of sexual guilt, and it is at the root of colonial racialism ...[7]

Fiercely interrogating Mannoni's inferiority–dependence theory of colonialism, the Martinican Aimé Césaire's 1969 dramatic adaptation *Une tempête* saw Caliban as the exploited native in a sinister dictatorship, a character whose opening line is 'Uhuru!' – the African liberation cry 'Freedom!'.* In Jonathan Miller's 1988 parable of colonialism (represented in the scene described on pages 306–7), an enslaved black Caliban was freed of the oppression of his white master, only to be

---

* Aimé Césaire (b. 1913) is a Martinican poet, playwright and political leader. He founded the black French-language *négritude* movement. *Une tempête* was published in English as *A Tempest* in 1986.

309

re-enslaved by a black Ariel, who, at the end of the play, re-assembled Prospero's broken staff and held it ominously over Caliban's head. By 1990, Peter Brook was able to apply the same colonial interpretation, but by reversing the colours, and portraying a white Caliban as an outsider in the black world of the master and his attendant spirit.[8]

But social anthropology has provided only one angle on Prospero and his complex relationships. His two servants, Ariel and Caliban, can be interpreted quite differently. Looked at psychologically, they can be seen as representing conflicting and complementary aspects of Prospero's (and humanity in general's) make-up: the imaginative, creative, intellectual part; and the animal, emotional, sexually unruly part – a development of the Friar's 'two opposèd kings ... grace and rude will'.[9] Re-conceptualising these polarities, the post-Freudian age has found much to exploit in this play.

For example, cross psychoanalysis with science fiction, then graft it onto *The Tempest*, and you get *Forbidden Planet*, a 1956 film in which, as the London *Evening Standard* put it, 'Shakespeare takes a journey into space'.[10] In this thoroughly engaging sci-fi movie, set in the year 2257, Prospero becomes Doctor Morbius, living on planet Altair IV with his daughter Altaira and a robot, Robby (the multi-talented Ariel figure – who speaks 187 inter-galactic languages and can produce bottles of bourbon on demand – evidently created by some-one in props by bolting a juke-box onto the Michelin Man). Spotting the essentials of Shakespeare's plot, we learn that Morbius and Altaira are the only survivors of the crashed ship *Bellerophon* and have been on the planet for twenty years; while the arriving rescuers include equivalents for Ferdinand (Commander Adams, who falls in love with Altaira); and Stephano (the vessel's drunken cook). Most interestingly, there is the Caliban-equivalent, an unseen but massively destructive 'monster from the Id', which turns out to be a product of Morbius's own subconscious. (It becomes apparent that Freud is almost as great an antecedent for this movie as Shakespeare, when we start to deduce that Morbius's Id monster attacks only men with designs on his daughter ...) If they'd been working with a better screenplay, Morbius might well have said: 'This thing of darkness I / Acknowledge mine.' But even with its shaky dialogue and an outstandingly wooden performance from *Naked Gun*'s Leslie Nielsen, *Forbidden Planet* makes an interesting contribution to the debate over what exactly Caliban *is*, and how he connects with Prospero.

These post-colonial and post-Freudian *Tempest*s are happily complemented by Bob Carlton's postmodern *Return to the Forbidden Planet* (1981), described in one press-release as 'Loosely based on The Tempest, Shakespeare's Forgotten Rock and Roll Masterpiece'.[11] This rock musical, whose 1999 revival 'Had the crowd bopping in the aisles and me standing on my seat screaming along to all the songs' (*me* being a critic from the *Daily Telegraph*), is a joyously unabashed cocktail of the 1956 movie, Shakespeare's works, and the world of rock. (The production, we are told, is 'Busting at the seams with red hot hits including Good Vibrations, Monster Mash, Great Balls Of Fire, It's A Man's World and Hey Mister Spaceman'.) These disparate elements conspire to produce a storyline in which we are invited to:

> Join Captain Tempest and his interplanetary buccaneers on their unexpected journey to Planet D'Illyria, where they encounter the dastardly Doctor Prospero, his beautiful daughter Miranda and their roller skating robot Ariel.

With its Olivier Award for Best Musical and extensive cult following, *Return to the Forbidden Planet* has given Prospero an afterlife in mainstream popular culture that even the magician himself could not have foreseen.

One interesting feature of the *Forbidden Planet* movie and its rock musical spin-off is that in both versions, the Prospero figure is seen as dangerous and threatening. In the film, he himself is the origin of the devastating Id monster; in the musical, he is a kind of James Bond villain – 'the dastardly Doctor Prospero'. In both these 'Doctor' incarnations, Shakespeare's character has transformed from magician to scientist, to 'mad and bad scientist', thereby epitomising an increasingly pejorative view of the scientist which we can observe in literature (Doctor Frankenstein, Doctor Jekyll …), the popular media (Doctor Strangelove, Doctor Evil …) and society itself (Dr Harold Shipman, the Raelians clone cult …). This might seem an odd development for a character whose name is evocative of 'prosperity' or 'making happy'. But the control he exercises over his fellow human beings in *The Tempest* has been a growing source of disquiet to audiences who have come to recognise that the dividing line between benign dictator and tyrannous despot is hard to draw.

Act 3, scene 1: 'Poor worm, thou art infected …'

As planned by the magician, they have fallen in love – Miranda, his adored daughter, and Ferdinand, son of the Neapolitan King. They plight their troths and depart, leaving the unseen watching father to declare:

> *'So glad of this as they I cannot be,*
> *Who are surprised with all, but my rejoicing*
> *At nothing can be more.'*

On the surface, this appears to be a celebratory speech: 'I can't share their joyful surprise, as I knew this would come to pass – but nothing could make me happier!' However, the convoluted syntax may be exploited by the actor to convey more mixed feelings and a confused state of mind.

For example, Octave Mannoni's ideas about Prospero, Caliban and Miranda (see page 309) suggest one way in to an interpretation of Prospero's emotions:

The 'inferior being' always serves as scapegoat; our own evil intentions can be projected on to him. This applies especially to incestuous intentions; Miranda is the only woman on the island, and Prospero and Caliban the only men. It is easy to see why it is always his daughter or his sister or his neighbour's wife (never his own) whom a man imagines to have been violated by a negro; he wants to rid himself of guilt by putting the blame for his bad thoughts on someone else …[12]

Derek Jacobi says:

'Well, I feel Miranda's been his companion for the last twelve years, he's overseen her growth and her gradual maturity, her growing up. And then he's had to listen to her saying to Ferdinand "I would not wish / Any companion in the world but you". And I think there's a sexual frisson – I'm not talking paedophilia, I'm talking father–daughter, alone, a man who's still sexually active. She was three when they were exiled, it could have been difficult for him. He's really ruined Caliban because Caliban's attack on Miranda, as far as Caliban was concerned, was perfectly natural – nothing wrong with that at all, it's what happens. And, until that point, I had treated Caliban well, he'd been living with us. I'd turned him into a monster – "This thing of darkness I / Acknowledge mine", he says at the end. Yeah, I turned this thing into something of darkness, because he did something that he, Caliban, didn't know was wrong. I didn't play it right. I punished him for doing something he thought was right. I should have taught him that it was wrong. Instead I chained him to a rock – for which, I think, Prospero feels incredibly guilty. And also, in that very punishment of Caliban, there is a sexual quality in it, and a sexual guilt to it as well, I'm sure. And all these things are spinning around in his mind …'

I love listening to actors talk about their work. Not just to gain an insight into how they approached a role or what meanings they found in it; but to listen out for those unconsidered bits of phraseology that offer brief glimpses into the actor's mind. I'm fascinated, for example, by the way Jacobi seamlessly drifts in and out of the first person in that last extract. He begins by discussing Prospero as a character ('He's really ruined Caliban ...'). And then, in mid-thought, *he is* Prospero, speaking for himself, describing experiences as though they befell *him* ('I had treated Caliban well ...'). And this jumping between third and first person becomes more intensified as the thought develops, so that twice he switches in mid-statement – from third to first and back to third:

> '"This thing of darkness I / Acknowledge mine", *he* says at the end. Yeah, *I* turned this thing into something of darkness ... I didn't play it right. I punished him for doing something he thought was right. I should have taught him that it was wrong. Instead I chained him to a rock – for which, I think, Prospero feels incredibly guilty.'

The other fascinating thing about these comments is the way in which the actor has lighted upon an interpretation for which there is actually no explicit evidence in Shakespeare's script: '... for which, I think, Prospero feels incredibly guilty.' *Prospero never expresses guilt*, and other characters never allude to his guilt; so where does this idea come from? Almost certainly from a very contemporary attitude towards this Jacobean play which reminds us that Caliban, as the character himself declares, was master of the island before Prospero's arrival, had helped the newcomers by showing them where to drink and what to eat, and had never asked to be 'civilised'. In other words, by feeling Prospero's guilt, the actor has applied to his interpretation of the role his own responses to the scenes from colonial history of which the Prospero–Caliban story has become a parable: scenes in which white Europeans land on foreign shores, are assisted by the native people, and then exploit and brutalise them. What Jacobi's guilt shows is a historical shift in the balance of sympathy from Prospero to Caliban, in that a modern actor playing this role can no longer be innocent of what happened to the Inca, the native American, the Australian aborigine* – any more than a 21st-century Shylock can ignore the Holocaust.

Looking at the two very different Prosperos played by Sir Derek Jacobi, it is tempting to see his harsh 1982 version[13] as a product of the early Thatcher years and the more gentle and benign 2002–3 interpretation as a reflection of an era in which the magician ('tough on the *causes* of crime ...') has some sympathy for a Caliban warped by birth and circumstance. But such a categorisation would be crude and simplistic, for Jacobi's own analysis of his more recent performance is informed by concerns which have been predominant at least since the 1960s: an interest in *understanding* Caliban; a sense of Prospero's *guilt*; and an awareness of the ambiguous territories of a father's psychology. These characteristics of Jacobi's performance are integral to a gentle and tender interpretation which bucks the recent trend of darker Prosperos, who have ranged from puritanically vengeful (Sir John Gielgud), to tyrannical (Timothy Walker), to dangerously necromantic (Michael Bryant), to pained, insecure and irritable (John Wood), to avuncularly patronising (Alec McCowen – a production in which Simon Russell Beale's freed Ariel venomously spat upon his master as he departed).[14] Jacobi's 21st-century Prospero was a welcome re-establishment of the character's humanity.

Act 4, scene 1: 'Some vanity of mine art ...'

Having promised Miranda and Ferdinand that he will offer them an example of his magic powers, Prospero conjures spirits to represent the

---

* This drawing of particular parallels with colonialism goes back at least to the mid-19th century, when a play like Charlotte Barnes's *The Forest Princess* (1844) could combine *The Tempest* with the story of Pocahontas.

goddesses Iris, Juno and Ceres, who sing a marriage blessing and evoke nymphs, 'Naiades of the windring brooks'. They in turn call forth 'certain Reapers, properly habited' who 'join with the Nymphs in a graceful dance ...'.

Miranda sits absorbed, still decked in her tattered and dated pink ball-gown, her hair spiked and untidily braided, as a chorus line of twenty extremely fetching white-uniformed sailors dance camply onto the set and perform a nicely choreographed hornpipe. When the even camper Stephano enters, dragged through the mire by a giant and shaven-headed Caliban, the sailors greet his arrival with a chorus of admiring wolf-whistles, before jazz diva Elisabeth Welch, a spectacle of golden drapes, diaphanous high collar and wispy feathers, sings, in knowing reference to the play's meteor-ological title, the classic cabaret number 'Stormy Weather' ...

Director Derek Jarman's 1979 film of *The Tempest* is set in 'an island of the mind', in which the initiating storm is both dreamt by Prospero and real to those who experience its aftermath. This interiorising of the story leads to some extremely gloomy scenes, and audiences have found it difficult to engage with Heathcote Williams's young and somewhat subdued Prospero. Frequently speaking in hushed tones, he is a world away from the lavish and spectacular movie interpretation of the character which followed twelve years later: by Sir John Gielgud in Peter Greenaway's *Prospero's Books* ...

Act 5, scene 1: 'I'll break my staff'

Seated in his cell – an oak-clad study lined with ancient volumes – Prospero is a Renaissance doge, decked in white cap and sumptuous blue and gold robes, cataloguing the creations of his magic art:

'... *Graves at my command / Have wak'd their sleepers', he boasts, 'and let 'em forth / By my so potent art'.*

'But —', slamming each volume shut amidst a cloud of dust, 'this rough magic / I here abjure ...', and an army of attendant spirits creates a stage from which he magically advances, followed by a team of strange, bare-breasted automatons, dancing a staccato ballet among scarlet-plumed banners.

'... And when I have required / Some heavenly music – which even now I do' – the sounds of the re-awakened tempest grow in intensity, naked attendants roll out a huge sheet of paper before him, a tiny Ariel supports the foot of a giant pair of compasses while two adolescent Ariels describe a broad circle – 'I'll break my staff, / Bury it certain fathoms in the earth, / And deeper than did ever plummet sound / I'll drown my book.'

And the great magician's final words are almost obliterated by the howling wind and a cacophony of bells.

For all the beautiful acting – and Gielgud speaks almost every line from Shakespeare's script, including those of the other characters – *Prospero's Books* is a film which gives me visual indigestion. Based on a central detail in the pre-history of the action – that Prospero had been set adrift in a small boat with only Miranda and some books from his library supplied by the kindly Gonzalo – Greenaway's interpretation sees the story as though through 24 of the treasured volumes from which Prospero might have learned his magic. It is an intriguing and fruitful concept, but, for many people, over-lavishly materialised in ways that are evident from this description by film-writer Daniel Rosenthal:

> As each book becomes relevant – the *Book of Water* when Prospero summons the storm, the *Book of Games* when Ferdinand and Miranda play chess – its pages come to life. Through a vivid combination of computer animation (using the revolutionary Quantel Paintbox program) and high-definition video, text writes itself, diagrams rotate, and bodily fluids splash onto the screen ...[15]

317

Or from this by David Benedict of *The Guardian*, who naughtily called it:

> an absolute must-see for trainee art directors and any member of the Greenaway family ... an embarrassment of riches, the stress being on the word 'embarrassment'.[16]

Greenaway felt that Gielgud's all-encompassing role provided 'a still centre around which everything revolve[d]'.[17] Equally, having Prospero provide all the characters' voices, write their dialogue in one of his books, and entitle the final volume *Thirty-six Plays by William Shakespeare*, makes it abundantly clear that Prospero and the playwright are equated in this interpretation.

Greenaway, of course, is by no means the first person to see Prospero as Shakespeare's *alter ego*. The identification of the magician with the playwright must have started as soon as the first audiences watched the rightful Duke of Milan break his staff and bid farewell to a life of 'rough magic'. *The Tempest* is probably the last play that Shakespeare wrote unaided (he went on to collaborate with John Fletcher on *The Two Noble Kinsmen*, *All Is True* (*Henry VIII*) and the lost *Cardenio*), so it is tempting and satisfying to think that the playwright might have been speaking through his character, the master illusionist, and saying his public goodbyes to the stage. In the past, Shakespeare seems to be saying, I have created a myriad amazing sights to awe and intrigue you; but now I lay aside my genius, set down my pen and prepare for a quiet retirement in Stratford. In an earlier speech, to Ferdinand, Prospero has explained that 'Our revels now are ended'; predicting that 'the great globe itself' (or Globe?) will one day 'dissolve / And, like this insubstantial pageant faded, / Leave not a rack behind'. The party's over, he says, things are changing.

This equation of Prospero with the author has been going on a long time. John Middleton Murry, for example, wrote:

Because I am by temperament averse to reading Shakespeare as allegory, I am struck by my own impression that *The Tempest* is more nearly symbolical than any of his plays. I find it impossible to deny that Prospero is, to some extent, an imaginative paradigm of Shakespeare himself in his function as a poet; and that he does in part embody Shakespeare's self-awareness at the conclusion of his poetic career ...

When I reach the conclusion that Prospero is, in some sense, Shakespeare, I mean no more than ... that it is remarkable and impressive that Shakespeare should have given his last play this particular form, which carried with it this particular necessity; which is no other than that of coming as near to projecting the last phase of his own creative imagination into the figure of a single character as Shakespeare could do without shattering his own dramatic method.[18]

More recently, Park Honan, contemplating whether we should 'run away from the identification of Prospero with Shakespeare', answers:

Probably not. Rather as the dramatist does, the magician assembles and disciplines an almost unmanageable world, heads his people along certain paths, and gives them situations to which they must react ...[19]

On stage, the Prospero–Shakespeare link was strikingly played out in the RSC's 1995 touring production, when the play was performed in tandem with Edward Bond's *Bingo*,* Paul Jesson playing both Prospero and Shakespeare.

For director Peter Brook, there is a kind of identification between the author and his creation, but it is not a comfortable one:

* Bond's 1973 play was a portrait of Shakespeare which condemned him for lack of political commitment in his local Stratford community. The 1995 double-bill was directed by David Thacker.

When we see how nothing in the play is what it seems, how it takes place on an island and not on an island, during a day and not during a day, with a tempest that sets off a series of events that are still within a tempest even when the storm is done, that the charming pastoral for children naturally encompasses rape, murder, conspiracy and violence; when we begin to unearth the themes that Shakespeare so carefully buried, we see that it is his final statement, and that it deals with the whole condition of man.[20]

Needing to shape their Shakespeare to fit the troubled and ambiguous times in which they live, many people are reluctant to accept Prospero's 'I'll break my staff ...' as a serene and happily resigned farewell by the author. But whether or not Shakespeare consciously put himself into Prospero doesn't really matter; the parallels exist, and I can't see that *The Tempest* is materially harmed if it pleases audiences to think of the playwright talking directly to them in this way.

More interesting to me is the way in which Prospero concludes the substance of his earlier speech to Ferdinand:

> We are such stuff
> As dreams are made on, and our little life
> Is rounded with a sleep.

Seemingly aware that this is a strange and unsettling message for these young lovers, he uncharacteristically offers an excuse:

> Sir, I am vexed.
> Bear with my weakness; my old brain is troubled.
> Be not disturbed with my infirmity.[21]

The habit of finding whatever meanings we want to find in Shakespeare does not end with equating the playwright's biography with Prospero's. Both Catholics and Protestants cite unequivocal evidence in the plays to show that Shakespeare was one or the other; he is, according to your reading, a conservative and a liberal; a war-monger and a pacifist, a monarchist and a republican. You pays your money and you takes your choice. But the surprising thing is, he usually turns out to hold a world view remarkably similar to your own. For example, from my own perspective as a card-carrying rationalist, Shakespeare was unquestionably a closet non-believer in a Christian afterlife; and here's a selection of my evidence:

1. Hamlet, who, after a dramatic lifetime spent questioning what death is all about (*viz* seeing a ghost, pondering 'the undiscovered country', playing with skulls, etc.), selects as his dying, conclusive words: 'The rest is silence'[22] (see also pages 231–2, 254);

2. Claudio in *Measure for Measure*, terrified, not by the physical fact of his impending execution, but by what follows: 'Ay, but to die, and go we know not where; / To lie in cold obstruction and to rot ...';[23]

3. Prospero, as above: 'We are such stuff / As dreams are made on, and our little life / Is rounded with a sleep.'

There you have it: three key moments in three major plays, and they all imply that death is little more than rotting bodies and a silent unknown nothingness. Nobody mentions heaven.

The problem is, of course, that the writer – Shakespeare, Shaks-pere, whoever – is not speaking these lines. The people whose philo-sophies, doubts and speculations are expressed in these perplexed and perplexing utterances are Hamlet, Claudio and Prospero – and they have minds of their own. Shakespeare isn't necessarily speaking through Prospero, any more than he is speaking through Iago, Ulysses or the gardener in *Richard II*.

Except, of course, when their beliefs and opinions happen to coincide with my own. As the man said, Shakespeare doesn't necessarily *mean* this or that; or rather, he means this *and* that: we select the meanings that please us: we *mean by* Shakespeare.[24]

So, pursuing my own chosen meaning, I ask Derek Jacobi whether Prospero and Hamlet are indeed saying that this life is all you get. He replies:

'I think they are ... Here certainly it seems that death leads into a kind of benign coma, as Hamlet's does ... With Prospero, I think he can do all those wonderful things ... but ultimately there's going to be nothing, there's going to be nothing left. And all the palaces, all the cloud-capped towers, all the temples ... there's going to be absolutely nothing left. And it's deeply nihilistic.'

And, focusing on Prospero's prediction that —

> the great globe itself,
> Yea, all which it inherit, shall dissolve,
> And like this insubstantial pageant faded,
> Leave not a rack behind ...

— he offers a very personal interpretation of the word 'dissolve':

'It's a strange word ... It's like he's foreshadowing Hiroshima. And "rack" means a wisp of cloud. But strange that the words "dissolve" and "cloud" ... when you think of the atom bomb and mushroom clouds – it's almost as if he's describing an atomic bomb ... It's very strange ...'

And the actor tails off, deep in thought ...*

---

* Jacobi's interpretation is an echo of Jan Kott's observation that 'We hear in [Prospero's final] soliloquy an apocalyptic tone. It is not, however, the poetic Apocalypse of the romantics, but the Apocalypse of nuclear explosions and the atomic mushroom.' (See *Shakespeare Our Contemporary* (Methuen and Co., 1964), p. 200.)

This fascinating flight of fancy shows how difficult it is to do anything more with an actor's performance than just describe it as it appeared to the observer on a given day in a particular theatre. Jacobi's Prospero had been formed by all manner of influences, from the experience of having played it twenty years before, to persistent and disturbing images of Hiroshima and the atomic bomb. In one performance – perhaps the one I saw that day – those images might have been consciously present, subtly influencing the way the actor enunciated Prospero's nihilistic predictions of a dissolving globe; in another they might have been suppressed, while more immediate concerns jostled for attention in the actor's consciousness.

It is for reasons like this that no single performance can ever be fully analysed; and no two performances can ever be exactly the same. Nor, for that matter, are any two audience members; which means that the 500 or so people in the Old Vic the evening I was there saw as many different Prosperos. My own Prospero was particularly moved at the thought of having to give up his daughter to Ferdinand; and that was only partly down to the skill of the actor. A whole other part of it was in the fact that my own daughter Lucy was in the middle of her gap year in Japan, and I was missing her. It is upon such indeterminate and personal factors that our response to an actor's performance commonly depends.

Act 5, scene 1: '… whom to call brother / Would even infect my mouth …'

Prospero approaches Antonio, the brother who had twelve painful years before stolen his dukedom, and callously set him and his three-year-old daughter adrift in a barely seaworthy craft …

'For you, most wicked sir …' – his anger and bitterness are proving hard

to control, and he is tempted to smash Antonio's face with the staff in his trembling hand —

> *'— whom to call brother*
> *Would even infect my mouth, I do forgive*
> *Thy rankest fault ...'*

And the brother says not a word.

That was Max von Sydow's reaction as Prospero in 1988. And I was thinking about it on my journey up to the Old Vic, happening to be reading an interesting article in the *Shakespeare Newsletter* entitled '"Gracious silence" in Shakespeare'.[25] In it, the writer, John W. Velz, makes the point that 'Silence in Shakespeare is declarative', and that 'in certain morally significant moments it can convey more meaning than prolix speech'. Velz doesn't mention *The Tempest*, so I asked Derek Jacobi what we should construe from the fact that the usurping brother Antonio says virtually nothing in the 200-plus lines between the moment when Prospero reveals himself – 'Behold ... The wronged Duke of Milan, Prospero' – and the end of the play. For Jacobi, it's all linked up with the nature of Prospero's forgiveness ...

> 'The forgiveness, I think, is kind of wrenched out of him. It's done – but he'll never forget. Forgiveness also depends on people asking to be forgiven. Alonso does – he says "[I] do entreat / Thou pardon me my wrongs" – but the brother [Antonio] doesn't say anything, except some comment about Caliban being like a fish.* He says nothing. He doesn't say sorry; neither does Sebastian ... So I grew to interpret lines like "And thence retire me to Milan, where / Every third thought shall be my grave" to mean that he's

---

* In answer to Sebastian's jocular question about curiosities such as Caliban ('... Will money buy 'em?'), Antonio replies: 'Very like. One of them / Is a plain fish, and no doubt marketable.' (5.1.265–6)

saying to Antonio: "You're not going to get away with it again. From what I've seen, you are the same man, the same man who kicked me out and tried to murder me … So, when we get back, every third thought will be the knife in the back …" – "my grave" meaning "you putting me *in* my grave". I think it's a much harsher forgiveness and he's still very much unforgiving in his forgiveness … it's very harsh.'

But surely, I ask, the last plays are usually taken to be all about forgiveness, aren't they?

'Oh, you can play them that way. You can suddenly become Jesus Christ if you want to do that. But … curiously the lines allow themselves to be played the way I'm doing it. For instance, when Alonso goes towards Miranda and says: "How oddly it will sound that I / Must ask my child forgiveness!" And Prospero has this line: "There, sir, stop." Well, you can say: "Oh, don't go down that path again, please don't say sorry again." But it's the idea of Alonso calling Miranda *his* child, and (as we're performing it) walking up to her about to *KISS HER!* No way, *NO WAY*, is Prospero about to allow that to happen.'

And that leads us back again, first to the complex nature of Prospero's love for his daughter, and then to some interesting thoughts from the actor which take us far outside the written text of Shakespeare's play and into the realm of speculation and conjecture …

'And then, of course, there's that terrible closure when he loses Miranda, he loses Caliban, he loses Ariel, he loses them all, and he's going back into a dangerous situation – he's not going back to somewhere they're all going to love him, welcome him home. What's happened over the last twelve years? What sort of Duchy is he going to find? How's he going to cope with his brother?'

Jacobi's questions (which, in their urgency, recall those 'see next week's thrilling episode' moments in 1950s movie serials) are a compelling response to those people who declare that Shakespeare's characters have no existence whatever outside the text, that it's naïve and misguided to think about them as though they are 'real', and that we should adopt a position of superior disdain towards anyone silly enough to ponder how many children Lady Macbeth might have had.

I know that, stripped down, a Shakespeare character is only 'words, words, words'. But the fact remains that, when an actor speaks Prospero's lines with skill and conviction, he becomes a tired and aged father losing his daughter; he doesn't remain merely 'a text'; still less 'a site for competing discourses'. And, if Prospero is a person, rather than 'a construct', then we have a right to speculate on what will happen to him after his final speech has been spoken; and I for one would feel severely let down if the actor did not engage in such speculation himself.

Speaking about his experience of playing Shylock at the height of the trial scene, Henry Goodman said: 'I see my wife sitting next to me, saying "Be reasonable".'[26] And the actor contemplated what fate would befall Shylock after leaving the court, sure that the man would be 'thinking it's my fault and God has taught me a lesson and if Leah had been here it would have been different'. Leah, of course, doesn't even appear in the *dramatis personae* of *The Merchant of Venice*; and the one reference we have is vague as to her identity.* But I don't think it's idle to hypothesise, as Goodman did, that she might be Shylock's wife, that she had died within the past year, and that she was so constantly in his thoughts that his obsessive adherence to the daily act of prayers for the dead had turned his household into the claustrophobic 'hell' that had driven away his only daughter. Early rehearsals, he

---

* Bewailing the loss of a ring that his daughter had exchanged for a monkey, he says: 'I had it of Leah when I was a bachelor.' (*The Merchant of Venice*, 3.1.114)

said, 'completely affirmed my sense that he's living on his own without his wife ... and I just built up a whole picture of his personal life which I found liberating'. In Goodman's case and Jacobi's and a thousand other actors', this construction of a character's biography, built up from the tiniest textual hints, vague, highly ambiguous and open to interpretation, is an essential part of the process of understanding the role and creating a believable human being on stage.* Goodman's Shylock and Jacobi's Prospero were memorable, for me, because they were real people. I too feared for this restored Duke of Milan once he got home ...

The Epilogue: 'Let your indulgence set me free'

With a sound effect that evokes the actor's role as the Chorus in the Branagh film of Henry V, *when he threw a switch to activate the studio power to the accompaniment of a dull, metallic thud, the Old Vic stage lamps go off, and Sir Derek Jacobi stands in front of the audience no longer as Prospero, but as himself, lit only by overspill from the house-lights that illuminate the audience ...*

Now that his plans have come to fruition, what does Prospero do, left only with whatever strength a frail old man might possess? Equally, the play being over, what does the actor do, to make the transition from Prospero's island, 'full of noises / Sounds, and sweet airs, that give delight and hurt not', to the traffic and the cold night air of the Waterloo Road? These are some of the questions posed by *The Tempest*'s concluding words.

---

* I recently attended a workshop given by the Oxford Stage Company director Dominic Dromgoole, in which he explained how he always dedicates the first few days of any rehearsal period to seeing actors individually or in pairs, in order to discuss their 'back-histories'. In the context of the period in which the play is set, he asks questions such as: 'Did you get on with your parents? What was your childhood like?'

The speech from which they come enjoyed one of its more unexpected incarnations in the summer of 1982 at the end of the Falklands/Malvinas war. Throughout the conflict, television viewers had been treated to the urbane and cultured contributions of Sir Ian McDonald, the Ministry of Defence spokesman, who was as likely to quote Shakespeare as military jargon. It was wholly fitting then that, striving to find an apt way in which to sign off at the end of the conflict, he lighted upon Prospero's

> Now my charms are all o'erthrown,
> And what strength I have's mine own,
> Which is most faint ...[27]

McDonald recognised that the magic of televisual wizardry would no longer be his to deploy; and it was tempting to read in his chosen identification with Prospero a tinge of regret that he was now obliged to renounce screen glamour and return to the daily banalities of the Ministry of Defence.

Ten of Shakespeare's plays have epilogues,* and they can be a tricky moment to handle. Does the actor speak in character, or as him or herself? Or perhaps as a kind of hybrid figure, half in character, half out? Anne Righter, for example, is clear that

> Prospero does not cease to be Prospero in the moment that he turns to address the theatre audience, does not step out of the illusion of the play.[28]

But, as I have been saying throughout this book – that's just one way of doing it. And in the 2003 Old Vic production there was no doubt as to which option had been taken:

---

* None, interestingly, is a tragedy (though Marlowe's tragic *Doctor Faustus* does have one). Some plays might, of course, have had epilogues which are now lost.

'That, I have to say, was very much down to Michael Grandage. On and on, every time we rehearsed it, he said "Take away *any* performance – *NO* performance! This is *you* talking to the audience. Don't sound lovely, don't do anything vocally, it's Derek saying "I can't get off the stage unless you clap me".'

The effect was to remove any thought that we had witnessed 'Shakespeare's farewell to the stage'. With his back to the now dimmed set of a theatre proscenium, this was the theatrical knight explaining the conditions and conventions of being an actor, the contract that has to be fulfilled between the performer and the audience: *Watch what I do, believe I'm someone else for a while, and then, like Prospero releasing Ariel, set me free. Only when I hear your applause is the staff broken and the book drowned deeper than did ever plummet sound. Only then can I go back to being myself…*

It's a pleasing idea.

Notes

INTRODUCTION

1 Interview with the author, 7 February 2003.

2 RSC publicity booklet, March–November 2003.

3 See page 45.

4 For more on Bruce Springsteen and Shakespeare, see Stephen M. Buhler, 'Reviving Juliet, Repackaging Romeo: Transformations of Character in Pop and Post-Pop Music', in Richard Burt (ed.), *Shakespeare After Mass Media* (Palgrave, 2002), pp. 252–6.

5 See Craig Dionne, 'The Shatnerification of Shakespeare', in Richard Burt, op. cit., p. 185.

6 A term coined by Richard Burt to describe manifestations of Shakespeare in the mass media which have traditionally been excluded from academic attention. See Richard Burt, op. cit., p. 12 and passim.

7 See Charles Dickens, *Nicholas Nickleby* (1838–9), Chapter XXIV; and *Romeo and Juliet*, 1.3.41.

8 See Jonathan Bate, *The Genius of Shakespeare* (Picador, 1997), p. 252.

9 See L.C. Knights, *How Many Children Had Lady Macbeth?* (The Minority Press, 1933), pp. 10–11; and pp. 201–3 of this book.

10 See Stephen Greenblatt, *Shakespearean Negotiations: The Circulation of Social Energy in Renaissance England* (California University Press, 1991).

11 Harriet Walter, *Actors on Shakespeare: Macbeth* (Faber and Faber, 2002), p. 27.

12 Samuel Taylor Coleridge, *Biographia Literaria* (1817).

13 This position is also acceptable to an academic approach: see Janet Adelman, *Suffocating Mothers: Fantasies of Maternal Origin in Shakespeare's Plays:* Hamlet *to* The Tempest (Yale University Press, 1992).

14 *The Merchant of Venice*, 2.7.76–7.

15 Terence Hawkes, *Meaning by Shakespeare* (Routledge, 1992), p. 3.

16 Interview with the author, 2 June 2003.

17 John Morrish, 'A Mighty Clash of Wills', *Independent on Sunday*, 22 June 2003. Morrish is reviewing Paul M. Matthews and Jeffrey McQuain, *The Bard on the Brain* (Dana, 2003). Their book is subtitled *Understanding the Mind Through the Art of Shakespeare and the Science of Brain Imaging*.

18 Nicholas Hytner, talking on *Start the Week*, BBC Radio 4, 12 May 2003.

19 Chris Moss, 'Prince of the barrio', *The Guardian*, 28 July 1999.

20 *Henry V*, 4.8.119.

21 Gary Taylor, 'Cry havoc', *The Guardian*, 5 April 2003.

22 Nicholas Hytner, *The Guardian* Review, 12 April 2003.

23 Robin Headlam Wells, ibid.

24 Cartoon by Ros Asquith, ibid.

25 Interview with the author, 9 May 2003.

CHAPTER 1. ROMEO AND JULIET

1 Ghulam Hasnain, *Sunday Times*, 22 February 1998: 'Romeo and Juliet lovers face life in jail: They have been called the Romeo and Juliet of Pakistan. A young man and woman from rival ethnic groups who fell in loved and eloped are facing ... a possible lifetime in jail ...'

2 *Sunday Times*, 'Critics' Choice', 1 February 1998: the caption accompanies a photograph of a young couple from behind, gazing wistfully out to sea.

3 Suzanne Goldenberg, *The Guardian*, 6 January 1999.

4 *The Times*, 22 January 1988.

5 Joy Hall, 'TES Talkback', *Times Educational Supplement*, 17 April 1998.

6 'Unholy force': Judith Mackrell on a story choreographed by Darshan Singh Bhuller for his new show, *The Guardian*, 10 September 1998.

7 Richard Owen, *The Times*, 4 August 1999.

8 The extract is from the *Romeo and Juliet* Release Dialogue Script, dated 8 July 1968 and signed by Leonard Whiting, a copy of which is in the Shakespeare Institute Library.

9 *Romeo and Juliet*, 2.3.63–4.

10 *The Guardian*, 'The Week', 6 December 1997.

11 *Daily Telegraph*, 'Agony Atkins', 3 April 1998.

12 *Daily Telegraph*, 19 January 1999.

13 *The Guardian*, 4 January 1999.

14 *Daily Telegraph*, 8 February 2001.

15 Dalya Alberge and Alex O'Connell, *The Times*, 19 May 1999. It's pleasant to compare Sean Connery with 'Romeo, an ageing Lothario of the lizard world', the scaly lover featured in 'Blind Romeo sees his Juliet' (*The Times*, 6 May 1999).

16 Fiona McNeil, *Independent on Sunday*, 1 August 1999.

17 Adrian Lee, *The Times*, 11 May 1999.

18 Christopher Andrew, *The Times*, 13 September 1999. A similar article appeared in the *Sunday Telegraph*: 'Romeo targeted "Diana": A British woman, codenamed Diana, became the victim of an attempted "Romeo-style" recruitment by East German intelligence ...' (David Rose, *Sunday Telegraph*, 19 September 1999).

19 Mavis Cheek, *Daily Telegraph*, 22 May 1999.

20 Directed by Michael Bogdanov, this opened in the Royal Shakespeare Theatre on 31 March 1986. The lovers were played by Niamh Cusack and Sean Bean, with Michael Kitchen as Mercutio.

21 The article, by Lyn Gardner, appeared in the 11 March 2003 *Guardian* and was a review of Joe Calarco's *Shakespeare's R & J* (see pages 43–4).

22 *Sunday Telegraph* magazine, 14 March 1999.

23 Ray Galton and Alan Simpson, *Hancock's Half Hour* (Woburn, 1974), pp. 78–98. The extract is quoted in Derek Longhurst's '"You base football-player!" Shakespeare in contemporary popular culture', published in Graham Holderness (ed.), *The Shakespeare Myth* (Manchester University Press, 1988), p. 64.

24 Shreddies Cereals, UK, 2000.

25 In national newspapers, February 2000.

26 Keith Parsons and Pamela Mason (eds), *Shakespeare in Performance* (Salamander Books, 1995), pp. 192–3.

27 Created by Rennie Harris's Puremovement Company, founded in Philadelphia in 1992.

28 Judith Mackrell, 'Where are thou, Juliet?', *The Guardian*, 20 October 2001. A photograph was captioned 'Homie-oh, homie-oh …'.

29 Rennie Harris, quoted in 'Shakespeare takes a hip turn', *The Times*, 7 October 2000.

30 Quoted in Judith Mackrell's 'Modern Lovers', *The Guardian*, 1 May 2002.

31 It was first performed in September 1998.

32 Leonard Bernstein, quoted by Humphrey Burton in 'How the West Side was won', *Sunday Times*, 8 May 1994.

33 Brooks Atkinson, *New York Times*, 27 September 1957.

34 Marc Norman and Tom Stoppard, *Shakespeare in Love* (Faber and Faber, 1999), pp. 144–6.

35 Directed by John Madden (Miramax, 1998).

36 Marc Norman and Tom Stoppard, op. cit., p. 30.

37 Directed by Joe Calarco, the play opened in the Expanded Arts Theater, New York in September 1997 and transferred to the John Houseman Studio Theater in January 1998. It toured the UK in March 2003.

38 Joe Calarco, quoted by Lyn Gardner in 'Never mind the balcony', *The Guardian*, 11 March 2003.

39 Ibid.

40 *New York Times*, 24 May 1998.

41 Russell Jackson (ed.), *The Cambridge Companion to Shakespeare on Film* (Cambridge University Press, 2000), p. 324.

42 Published in 1972.

43 First UK performance in 1991.

44 Written by Iyoti Patel and Jess Simons, its first major performance was in the Battersea Arts Centre, July 1988.

45 Directed by Mike Sarne, its UK release was in December 1994.

46 Produced by Joel Silver, and released in the USA in 2000.

47 Produced by Robert Carsen with choreography by Meryl Tankard, it opened in London in September 2000.

48 Hector Berlioz, from an article written in 1832; in David Cairns, *Berlioz: the Making of an Artist* (Allen Lane, 1999); and quoted in John Gross, *After Shakespeare* (Oxford University Press, 2002), p. 308.

49 Hector Berlioz, quoted in Ian Kemp's '*Romeo and Juliet* and *Roméo et Juliette*', in *Berlioz Studies* (ed. Peter Bloom) (Cambridge University Press, 1992), p. 74; and quoted in Jonathan Bate, op. cit., p. 281.

50 Michael Church, *The Independent*, 21 February 2000.

CHAPTER 2. HENRY THE FIFTH

1 *Henry V*, directed by Kenneth Branagh, Renaissance Films, 1989; Branagh played Henry in an interpretation influenced by his 1984 performance with the Royal Shakespeare Company (directed by Adrian Noble).

2 Kenneth Branagh, *Beginning* (Chatto and Windus, 1989), p. 139.

3 William Hazlitt, *The Characters of Shakespeare's Plays* (1817; Oxford University Press, 1924), pp. 168–9.

4 Quoted in 'Once more unto the material breach, dear friends', Nigel Reynolds, *Daily Telegraph*, 24 January 2003.

5 Michael Billington, *The Guardian*, 14 May 2003.

6 Nicholas Hytner, speaking on BBC Radio 4's *Start the Week*, 12 May 2003.

7 'Electrifying PM goes into Churchill–Henry V–Custer mode', *The Guardian*, 19 March 2003.

8 *Henry V*, English Shakespeare Company, 1986–9; Henry was played by Michael Pennington.

9 Michael Bogdanov and Michael Pennington, *The English Shakespeare Company: The Story of The Wars of the Roses, 1986–1989* (Nick Hern Books, 1990), p. 24.

10 Ibid., p. 48.

11 Emma Smith, *Shakespeare in Production: King Henry V* (Cambridge University Press, 2002), p. 10.

12 Michael Dobson, *The Making of the National Poet: Shakespeare, Adaptation and Authorship, 1660–1769* (Oxford University Press, 1992), p. 148.

13 Emma Smith, op. cit., p. 15.

14 *The Times*, 2 February 1946.

15 Winston Churchill, *Hansard*, 20 August 1940, col. 1166.

16 Christopher Palmer, Introduction to a recording of William Walton's film music *Henry V* (Chandos Records, 1990), p. 4.

17 The Choristers of Westminster Cathedral and the Orchestra and Chorus of the Academy of St Martin in the Fields (Chandos Records, 1990).

18 *Henry V*, 3.2.1–19.

19 Ibid., 3.1.8–11.

20 David Jones, *In Parenthesis* (Faber and Faber, 1937); and quoted in John Gross, *After Shakespeare* (Oxford University Press, 2002), p. 128.

21 W. Macqueen-Pope, *Ghosts and Greasepaint: A Story of the Days that Were* (Robert Hale and Co., 1951), pp. 101–02; quoted in Emma Smith, p. 38.

22 Max Beerbohm in *The Saturday Review*, 24 February 1900, pp. 233–4.

23 Sally Beauman, *The Royal Shakespeare Company: A History of Ten Decades* (Oxford University Press, 1982), p. 40.

24 Lisa Jardine, 'The age of manly tears', *Daily Telegraph*, 10 September 1997.

25 Richard Olivier, *Shadow of the Stone Heart – A Search for Manhood*.

26 These details are reported in 'Into the breach', an article by Maggie Hartford in the *Oxford Times*, 22 March 2002.

27 Ibid.

28 Richard Olivier, *Inspirational Leadership* (The Industrial Society, 2001).

29 Ibid., pp. 121–2.

30 Ibid., p. 126.

CHAPTER 3. CLEOPATRA

1 First performance, Royal Shakespeare Theatre, Stratford-upon-Avon, 13 April 2002, directed by Michael Attenborough; the production later transferred to the Theatre Royal, Haymarket in London.

2 *The Guardian*, 'Pass Notes', 5 November 1996.

3 Michael Billington, 'Still the biggest asp disaster in the world?', *The Guardian*, 14 October 1998.

4 Jonathan Bate, op. cit., p. 12.

5 Lucy Hughes-Hallett, *Cleopatra: Histories, Dreams and Distortions* (Bloomsbury, 1990), p. 266.

6 USA, 1963; directors Joseph L. Mankiewicz and others.

7 Goscinny and Uderzo, trans. Anthea Bell and Derek Hockridge, *Asterix and Cleopatra* (Hodder Dargaud, 1965; UK, 1969), p. 27. Parodic allusions to the 1963 film begin with the front-cover subtitle printed in fake Hollywood-Egyptian letters: 'The greatest story ever drawn … 14 litres of Indian ink, 30 brushes, 62 soft pencils, 1 hard pencil, 27 erasers, 1984 sheets of paper, 16 typewriter ribbons, 2 typewriters, 366 pints of beer went into its creation!'

8 Francesca T. Royster, 'Cleopatra as Diva: African-American Woman and Shakespearean Tactics', in Marianne Novy (ed.), *Transforming Shakespeare: Contemporary Women's Re-Visions in Literature and Performance* (St Martin's Press, 1999), p. 114.

9 Ibid., p. 107.

10 Lucy Hughes-Hallett, op. cit., caption to Plate 33.

11 *Antony and Cleopatra*, 1.1.6 and 10; and 1.5.28.

12 *Love's Labour's Lost*, 4.3.243–71.

13 Shakespeare, Sonnet 127.

14 *Othello*, 1.1.63 and 89.

15 Janet Adelman, *The Common Liar: an Essay on Antony and Cleopatra* (Yale University Press, 1973), p. 186.

16 John Dover Wilson, Introduction to *Antony and Cleopatra* (Cambridge University Press, 1968), p. xi.

17 Richard Madelaine, *Shakespeare in Production: Antony and Cleopatra* (Cambridge University Press, 1998), p. 4. Madelaine cites Anthony G. Barthelemy, *Black Face Maligned Race* (Louisiana State University Press, 1987), pp. 33–4, 147n1.

18 *Titus Andronicus*, 5.1.27.

19 *Henry V*, 3.6.158–60.

20 J. P. Brooke-Little, *Boutell's Heraldry* (Frederick Warne, 1950; revised 1973), p. 27.

21 Janet Adelman, op. cit., p. 188.

22 Michael Neill, *Antony and Cleopatra* (Oxford University Press, 1994), p. 65.

23 Francesca Royster, op. cit., p. 110.

24 Derek Longhurst, '"You base football-player!": Shakespeare in contemporary popular culture', in Graham Holderness, op. cit., p. 65.

25 See Chapter 4, pages 109–11.

26 Edmund Wilson, 'The National Winter Garden', quoted in Lucy Hughes-Hallett, op. cit., p. 263.

27 *Carry on Cleo*, an Amalgamated film released through Warner-Pathé Distribution, 1964, screenplay by Talbot Rothwell.

28 George Bernard Shaw, *Caesar and Cleopatra*, Act 5, in *Bernard Shaw: Collected Plays with their Prefaces*, vol. II (The Bodley Head, 1971 edition), p. 291.

29 Priscilla Murr, *Shakespeare's Antony and Cleopatra: A Jungian Interpretation* (Peter Lang, 1988), p. 62.

30 Jane Lapotaire played Cleopatra in the BBC Shakespeare series. First shown in 1980, it was directed by Jonathan Miller.

31 Michael Scott, *Text and Performance: Antony and Cleopatra* (Macmillan, 1983), p. 60.

32 Margaret Lamb, *Antony and Cleopatra on the English Stage* (Associated University Presses, 1980), p. 196n12.

33 Keith Parsons, in Keith Parsons and Pamela Mason, op. cit., p. 43.

CHAPTER 4. SHYLOCK

1 Directed by Alan Horrox; Antonio was played by Benjamin Whitrow, Bassanio by Paul McGann.

2 *The Merchant of Venice*, 2.2.99.

3 Christopher Marlowe, *The Jew of Malta*, 1.955–63.

4 'A Funeral Elegy on the Death of the Famous Actor, R. Burbadge, who died on Saturday in Lent, the 13th of March, 1618'; quoted in J. Payne Collier, *Memoirs of the Principal Actors in the Plays of Shakespeare* (London, printed for the Shakspeare Society, 1846), p. 53.

5 Ibid., p. 22.

6 See William Archer and R. W. Lowe (eds), *G. H. Lewes: Dramatic Essays Reprinted from the Examiner* (London, 1894), p. 115.

7 George Granville (later Lord Lansdowne), *The Jew of Venice* (London, 1701; facsimile published by Cornmarket Press from the copy in the Birmingham Shakespeare Library, London, 1969).

8 I am following most current thinking, including that of Jay L. Halio (*The Merchant of Venice* (Oxford University Press, 1994)) in assuming a date of composition between summer 1596 and summer 1598.

9 Andrew Gurr, *The Shakespearian Playing Companies* (Oxford University Press, 1996), p. 291.

10 See T. W. Baldwin, *The Organization and Personnel of the Shakespearean Company* (Princeton University Press, 1927), pp. 228–9.

11 See Amiel Schotz, 'Who Played Shylock? A Note on *The Merchant of Venice*', *Shakespeare Newsletter* (Spring 1999), pp. 13–14.

12 First performance, 20 May 1998; directed by Richard Olivier. Shylock was played by the German actor Norbert Kentrup.

13 The description is by Downes, the Lincoln's Inn prompter for over 40 years, quoted in H. H. Furness (ed.) *The Merchant of Venice* (New Variorum Edition, 1888), vol. vii, p. 371.

14 William W. Appleton, *Charles Macklin: An Actor's Life* (Harvard University Press and Oxford University Press, 1961), p. 50.

15 Thomas Davies, *Memories of the Life of David Garrick* (London, 4th edition, 1784), vol. 1.

16 George Colman and Bonnell Thornton, *The Connoisseur*, no. 1, 31 January 1754, quoted in William Appleton, op. cit., p. 46. (Colman was manager of the Covent Garden theatre.)

17 Georg Christoph Lichtenberg, *Vermischte Schriften*, iii, p. 226 (Göttingen, 1867), in the translation by Margaret L. Mare and W. H. Quarrell, *Lichtenberg's Visits to England* (New York: Benjamin Blom Inc., 1938; revised 1969), p. 40.

18 Jonathan Bate, op. cit., Chapters 6 and 7.

19 Andrew Willet, *De Universali et Novissima Judæorum Vocatione* (Cambridge, 1590), page 25v; cited by James Shapiro in *Shakespeare and the Jews* (Columbia University Press, 1996), p. 168.

20 William Cooke, *Memoirs of Charles Macklin* (London: Asperne, 1804); see also William Appleton, op. cit., p. 46.

21 Charles Macklin, Diary, f7, Folger Library. Shakespeare's contemporary, the playwright Thomas Lodge, had published a translation of *The Famous and Memorable Workes of Josephus* in 1602. It was reprinted in 1632.

22 John Gross, *Shylock: Four Hundred Years in the Life of a Legend* (Chatto and Windus, 1992), p. 111.

23 B. W. Procter, *The Life of Edmund Kean* (London, 1835), vol. 2, p. 47. 'Bryan Waller Procter' was actually the actor and biographer Barry Cornwall. The digression on the recognition of Jewish suffering continues for a further two pages and concludes the chapter.

24 Charles Dickens, *Oliver Twist* (1837), Chapter VIII.

25 John Gross, op. cit., p. 117.

26 *The Theatrical Journal*, 1841.

27 Richmond P. Bond, *English Burlesque Poetry, 1700–1750* (Cambridge MA, 1952), p. 3.

28 Stanley Wells, *Shakespeare Burlesques*, vol. 3 (Diploma Press, 1977), p. viii.

29 Francis Talfourd, *Shylock; or The Merchant of Venice Preserved* (1849), in Stanley Wells, vol. 3, op. cit.

30 G. W. Griffin and Christy's Minstrels, *Shylock* (c. 1870), in Stanley Wells, vol. 3, op. cit.

31 *The Merchant of Venice*, 4.1.315–16 and 343.

32 Lionel Bart, *Oliver!* (1960).

33 The interview from which these quotations are taken took place on 25 October 1997.

34 Robert Smirke, 'Shylock, Jessica and Launcelot', in the library of the Georg-August-Universität, Göttingen, Germany; see Walter Pape and Frederick Burwick (eds), *The Boydell Shakespeare Gallery* (Verlag Peter Pomp, 1996), p. 225; Gilbert Stuart Newton, 'Shylock and Jessica from *The Merchant of Venice*', in the Yale Center for British Art, New Haven CT; see Richard Studing, *Shakespeare in American Painting* (Associated University Presses, 1993), p. 102.

35 David Calder, interviewed by Liz Gilbey in *Plays International*, May 1993.

36 Henry Goodman, interview with the author, 17 May 1999.

37 Paul Taylor, *The Independent*, 21 June 1999.

38 Susannah Clapp, *The Observer*, 20 June 1999.

39 William Winter, *Shakespeare on the Stage* (T. Fisher Unwin, 1912), pp. 186–7.

40 William Winter, *Henry Irving* (New York: George J. Coombes, 1885), p. 36.

41 *Stratford-upon-Avon Herald*, 30 April 1915.

42 Joseph Hatton, *Henry Irving's Impressions of America*, vol. 1 (London, 1884), p. 269.

43 H.A. Saintsbury to some extent echoes this chameleon portrayal when he recalls that Irving's Shylock reminded him of some Moroccan Jews he had once seen: 'impudent and cringing, insolent, cunning, and prone to self-pity …' (H.A. Saintsbury and Cecil Palmer (eds) *We Saw Him Act: A Symposium on the Art of Sir Henry Irving* (London, 1939), p. 166.)

44 A.B. Walkley, *Playhouse Impressions* (T. Fisher Unwin, 1892), pp. 159–60.

45 Joseph Hatton, op. cit., p. 265.

46 J.C. Bulman, *Shakespeare in Performance: The Merchant of Venice* (Manchester University Press, 1991), p. 31.

47 Henry Irving, *The Drama: Addresses by Henry Irving* (London, 1881), p. 31.

48 *The Times*, 10 October 1919.

49 *The Times*, writing about Beerbohm Tree's production, 6 July 1909.

50 Hubert Griffith, *The Standard*, 18 October 1927.

51 St John Ervine, *The Observer*, 23 October 1927.

52 These featured Henry Baynton at the Savoy, Ernest Milton at the Old Vic and Augustus Milner at the Duke of York's.

53 R.S. Wistrich, *Anti-Semitism: The Longest Hatred* (Mandarin, 1991), p. 66, citing J. Toland, *Adolf Hitler* (New York: Ballantyne, 1977), p. 157.

54 J.C. Bulman, op. cit., p. 102.

55 Ibid., p. 103.

56 Based on the 1970 National Theatre performance, directed by Jonathan Miller, this 1973 version was filmed for Associated Television in 1973, directed by John Sichel.

57 Komisarjevsky's production opened in the newly-built theatre on 25 July 1932. Shylock was played by Randle Ayrton.

58 *The Spectator*, 16 December 1932.

59 *The Times*, 17 February 1943, reviewing a production in which Shylock was played by Frederick Valk.

60 *The Times*, 4 October 1938, reviewing Wolfit at the People's Palace.

61 *The Times*, 3 December 1935.

62 Ibid.

63 *Daily Express*, 22 April 1938.

64 *New Statesman*, 7 May 1938.

65 *Daily Express*, 15 March 1934, reviewing a production of the play at the Alhambra.

66 *Birmingham Gazette*, 16 April 1936.

67 *New Statesman*, 7 May 1938.

68 *Evening Standard*, 27 April 1936.

69 *Evening Standard*, 26 April 1934.

70 *Evening Standard*, 28 April 1937.

71 *Evening Standard*, 19 August 1937.

72 *Daily Telegraph*, 2 August 1934.

73 *Daily Express*, 11 April 1933, 17 September 1935, 22 October 1931.

74 *Daily Express*, 11 March 1940.

75 Wilhelm Hortmann, *Shakespeare on the German Stage: The Twentieth Century* (Cambridge

University Press, 1998), pp. 134–5.

76 Gerwin Strobl, 'Shakespeare and the Nazis', *History Today*, May 1997.

77 The performance was advertised in the *Daily Express* on 9 September 1946. Myer Zelnicker played Shylock, and his daughter, Anna, Portia.

78 *Daily Express*, 29 December 1946. Earlier that year, a brief report had appeared in the same newspaper: 'TO BE – The German Shakespeare Society will be reestablished next Sunday. – Reuter.' (*Sunday Express*, 17 February 1946)

79 *The Times*, 14 July 1947, reviewing *The Merchant of Venice* at Stratford.

80 *Daily Mail*, 20 April 1948; and *Coventry Evening Telegraph*, 20 April 1948.

81 *Daily Express*, 18 March 1953; *Daily Herald*, 18 March 1953.

82 *Daily Telegraph*, 16 March 1953.

83 *Gloucester Echo*, 18 April 1956; *Financial Times*, 18 April 1956; *Leamington Spa Courier*, 20 April 1956; Samuel L. Leiter (ed.), *Shakespeare Around the Globe* (New York: Greenwood, 1986), p. 431; *Birmingham Post*, 20 April 1956; and *Birmingham Sunday Mercury*, 22 April 1956.

84 *The Observer*, 4 April 1965.

85 *Daily Telegraph*, 31 March 1971.

86 *Daily Express*, 31 March 1971.

87 *Daily Mail*, 20 April 1948; and *Birmingham Mail*, 20 April 1948. This portrayal also gave rise to the headline: 'Helpmann's Shylock is Not a Man', with the explanatory comment: 'it is a "character" …'. (*Daily Worker*, 20 April 1948)

88 *Evesham Journal*, 21 March 1953.

89 *Financial Times*, 18 April 1956; *The Guardian*, 1 April 1971; and *Daily Telegraph*, 31 March 1971.

90 *South Wales Argus*, 18 April 1956.

91 *Gloucester Echo*, 18 April 1956.

92 *Daily Telegraph*, 16 March 1953.

93 *Daily Herald*, 18 March 1953.

94 Reported in the *Daily Express*, 30 June 1948.

95 *Daily Telegraph*, 26 March 1949; and *Daily Express*, 28 March 1949.

96 *Stratford-upon-Avon Herald*, 23 April 1948.

97 Interview with the author, 16 April 2002.

98 Wilhelm Hortmann, op. cit., pp. 254–5.

99 Richard Westall, 'Shylock Rebuffing Antonio' (1795), in the Folger Shakespeare Library; see William L. Pressly, *A Catalogue of paintings in the Folger Shakespeare Library 'As Imagination Bodies Forth'* (Yale University Press, 1993), pp. 158–9 and Plate 4.

100 'He has made a pact with God; he is cold, committed': all the insights here into Shylock's and Portia's thought-processes were provided by Henry Goodman in an interview with the author, three weeks into performance, 14 July 1999.

101 As described by John Peter, *Sunday Times*, 27 June 1999.

102 First performance in the Cottesloe Theatre, RNT, 17 June 1999. The play, directed by Trevor Nunn, later transferred to the Olivier Theatre. Henry Goodman's performance as Shylock secured him the Olivier Award for Best Actor.

103 Patrick Stewart played Shylock with the RSC in The Other Place, first performance 11 May 1978. The production subsequently transferred to the Theatre Royal, Newcastle (from February 1979) and the Donmar Warehouse, London (from May 1979).

104 *Morning Star*, 16 May 1978.

105 John Caird's production for the RSC, with Ian McDiarmid as Shylock, opened in the Royal Shakespeare Theatre on 10 April 1984.

106 William Frankel, *The Times*, 17 April 1984.

107 In fact, McDiarmid's performance recalled several Shylocks at Stratford in the immediate post-Holocaust years, such as those by Robert Helpmann and Michael Redgrave (see pages 133–6 and 141).

108 With David Calder as Shylock, this production opened at the Royal Shakespeare Theatre on 27 May 1993.

109 Arnold Wesker, 'A nasty piece of work', *Sunday Times*, 6 June 1993. See also 'The trial of Shylock', *The Guardian*, 13 April 1994.

110 Preface to *Shylock*, the published version of *The Merchant*, first performed in Stockholm in 1976. The English-speaking première was at the Plymouth Theatre, New York, on 16 November 1977.

111 David Nathan, *Jewish Chronicle*, 26 December 1997.

112 *Inter alia*, the director John Barton.

113 Charles Marowitz, *Variations on The Merchant of Venice*, in *The Marowitz Shakespeare* (Marion Boyars, 1978).

114 Heinrich Heine, *Shakespeare's Girls and Women* (1838), in *Frankenstein's Island* (trans. S. S. Prawer) (Cambridge University Press, 1986).

CHAPTER 5. RICHARD THE THIRD

1 *Looking for Richard*, directed by Al Pacino (Twentieth Century Fox, 1996).

2 *Richard III*, directed by Laurence Olivier (London Film Productions, 1955).

3 *Henry VI Part 3*, 3.2.153–62.

4 From John Manningham's *Diary* (ed. J. Bruce) (Clarendon Press, 1868).

5 Jonathan Romney, *The Guardian*, 16 May 1996.

6 H. R. Coursen, 'Three films of *Richard III*', in the *Cambridge Companion to Shakespeare on Film*, op. cit., p. 112.

7 Ibid., p 110.

8 Chris Lawson, 'The Don who Would be King': Looking for Richard (USA, 1996) but finding "Al"', in *The Proceedings of: Shakespeare and his Contemporaries: A Postgraduate Forum* (ed. Jacqueline Hanham) (University of Hull, 1998), p. 48.

9 Ibid., p. 56.

10 From the screenplay of the Richard Loncraine film, reproduced in Ian McKellen, *William Shakespeare's 'Richard III': A Screenplay Written by Ian McKellen and Richard Loncraine, Annotated and Introduced by Ian McKellen* (Doubleday, 1996), pp. 207–08. This scene was filmed in The Royal Horticultural Hall, London, one of the many venues that helped to establish the 1930s art deco settings.

11 At the Royal National Theatre, 1990, directed by Richard Eyre.

12 Ian McKellen, op. cit., p. 13.

13 *Much Ado About Nothing* (dir. Kenneth Branagh, 1993); *Hamlet* (dir. Kenneth Branagh, 1996); *Love's Labour's Lost* (dir. Kenneth Branagh, 1999); *A Midsummer Night's Dream* (dir. Michael Hoffmann, 1999); *Twelfth Night* (dir. Trevor Nunn, 1995); *The Merchant of Venice* (dir. Trevor Nunn, Royal National Theatre, 1999); *The Merry Wives of Windsor* (dir. Rachel Kavanaugh, 2002); *Coriolanus* (dir. David Farr, 2002).

14 See, for example, H. R. Coursen, op. cit., pp. 107–08.

15 Antony Sher, *The Year of the King* (Methuen, 1985), p. 189.

16 John Everett Millais, 'The Princes in the Tower' (1878), Royal Holloway College, London.

17 *Richard III*, 1.4.51–5.

18 Ibid., 4.3.6–13.

19 *York Records* (ed. R. Davies) (London, 1843), p. 218. See Paul Murray Kendall, *Richard the Third* (George Allen and Unwin, 1955), p. 369.

20 *Henry V*, Epilogue, line 2.

21 E. A. J. Honigmann, Introduction to *Richard III* (Penguin, first edition, 1968), p. 8.

22 R. Chris Hassel Jr (*Songs of Death: Performance, Interpretation and the Text of Richard III*, University of Nebraska Press, 1987, p. 168) draws on Bullough's *Narrative and Dramatic Sources of Shakespeare* (3: 225–6, 228) to conclude that 'though both Hall and Holinshed derived their material from Sir Thomas More's *History of King Richard III* "almost word for word", Shakespeare is most likely to have used Hall'. Honigmann, citing further possible sources, is of the opinion that 'we cannot always say with certainty that one rather than the other was consulted' (op. cit., p. 13).

23 Professor Michael Dobson (University of Surrey), speaking on BBC Radio 4's *Start the Week*, 12 May 2003.

24 Josephine Tey, *The Daughter of Time* (Peter Davies, 1951). The title is based on the proverb: Truth is the daughter of Time. Rosemary Hawley Jarman, *We Speak No Treason* (Wm Collins Sons, 1971). For the title, see *Richard III*, 1.1.90–7: 'We speak no treason, man; we say the King / Is wise and virtuous ...'

25 Rev. John Trusler, *The Works of Hogarth* (Simpkin, Marshall, Hamilton, Kent and Co., date unknown), p. 131.

26 William L. Pressly, *A Catalogue of Paintings in the Folger Shakespeare Library* (Yale University Press, 1993), p. 186.

27 Catherine Alexander, in *The Oxford Companion to Shakespeare* (eds Michael Dobson and Stanley Wells) (Oxford University Press, 2001), p. 160.

28 Thomas Davies, *Memoirs of the Life of David Garrick* (London, fourth edition 1784), vol. 1, pp. 40, 44.

29 John Hill, *The Actor: A Treatise on the Art of Playing* ... (1750); quoted in George Winchester Stone Jr and George M. Kahrl, *David Garrick: A Critical Biography* (Carbondale IL: Southern Illinois University Press; London: Feffer and Simons Inc., 1979), p. 36.

30 Quoted in James T. Kirkman, *Memoirs of the Life of Charles Macklin, Esq.* (Lackington Allen and Co., 1799), vol. I, pp. 363–4.

31 See Scott Colley, *Richard's Himself Again: A Stage History of Richard III* (Greenwood Press, 1992), p. 39.

32 See Jonathan Bate, op. cit., p. 252.

33 Antony Sher, op. cit., p. 142.

34 Ibid., p. 217.

35 *Richard III*, 1.3.241.

36 At The Crucible, Sheffield; first performance 19 March 2002.

37 Mark Lawson, BBC Radio 4, *Front Row*, 20 March 2002.

38 See Ray Puxley, *Cockney Rabbit* (Robson Books, 1992), p. 158; Julian Franklyn, *A Dictionary of Rhyming Slang* (Routledge and Kegan Paul, 1960; reprinted 1987), p. 113; and Jonathon Green, *Slang Down the Ages* (Kyle Cathie, 1993), pp. 73, 208.

CHAPTER 6. LADY MACBETH

1 Roger Boyes, 'Inside Germany', *The Times*, 2 November 1998.

2 *Daily Telegraph*, 11 June 1993.

3 *The Times*, 11 June 1993.

4 Drudge's comment appeared in 'What happened when Michael met Maureen', *The Observer*, 29 November 1998.

5 Sarah Sands, 'Why Lady Macbeths get a bad press', *Daily Telegraph*, 11 February 2000.

6 Advertisement for *The Spectator*, *Daily Telegraph*, 28 July 2000.

7 Andrew Sparrow, 'Tories attack Cherie as "Lady Macbeth"', *Daily Telegraph*, 8 August 2000.

8 *The Guardian*, 'Pass Notes', 9 August 2000.

9 Marcus Tanner, *Independent on Sunday*, 8 April 2001.

10 John Simpson, *Sunday Telegraph*, 1 July 2001.

11 Neil Darbyshire, *Daily Telegraph*, 12 June 1993; Simon Hoggart, *The Guardian*, 3 July 2001; Sue Mott, *Daily Telegraph*, 4 December 1999; David Thompson, *Independent on Sunday*, 1 October 2000; Robert Philip, *Daily Telegraph*, 18 July 1998; and *The Times*, 'Bibliofile', 1 February 1998.

12 Jeanette Winterson, *The Guardian*, 21 August 2001.

13 Amanda Craig, *Sunday Times*, 29 December 1999.

14 *Macbeth*, 1.5.63–4.

15 John Mullan, *The Guardian*, 24 April 2003.

16 From the second volume of Raphael Holinshed's *Chronicles* (1587), p. 150. A.R. Braunmuller, editor of the New Cambridge *Macbeth* (Cambridge University Press, 1997), points out that 'aside from Holinshed's *Chronicles* and the dramatist's possibly direct use of Holinshed's own sources, such as Hector Boece's *Scotorum historiae* (1526, 1575) and Buchanan's *Rerum Scoticarum historis*, many other texts may have contributed to the language of *Macbeth* …' (p. 15).

17 Raphael Holinshed, op. cit., p. 171.

18 William Hazlitt, *Criticisms and Dramatic essays of the English Stage* (Geo. Routledge and Co., 1854), pp. 271–2.

19 H.C. Fleeming Jenkin, 'Mrs Siddons as Lady Macbeth. From contemporary notes by George Joseph Bell', in *The Nineteenth Century 3* (1878), pp. 296–313; and Jenkin, *Papers on Acting, III* (1915), pp. 35–6; cited by A.R. Braunmuller in his Introduction to the New Cambridge *Macbeth*, op. cit., p. 65.

20 See Suzanne Harris, 'Macbeth', in Keith Parsons and Pamela Mason, op. cit., p. 124.

21 Georgiana Ziegler, 'Accommodating the virago: Nineteenth-century representations of Lady Macbeth', in Christy Desmet and Robert Sawyer (eds), *Shakespeare and Appropriation* (Routledge, 1999), p. 124.

22 Sinead Cusack played Lady Macbeth for the RSC in 1986. The production was directed by Adrian Noble.

23 *The Times*, 31 December 1888. The version of Sargent's portrait in the colour plates of this book appeared in Ellen Terry's 1906 Jubilee programme.

24 Gabriel Egan, in the *Oxford Companion*, op. cit., p. 93.

25 See S. P. Cerasano, '"Borrowed Robes": Costume Prices and the Drawing of *Titus Andronicus*', in *Shakespeare Studies* 22 (1994).

26 Dennis Kennedy is author of *Looking at Shakespeare: Contemporary Performance* (Cambridge University Press, 1993), a fascinating and marvellously illustrated study of Shakespeare scenography. This quotation comes from his entry on Poel in the *Oxford Companion*, op. cit., p. 348.

27 See pages 158–61.

28 Alfred Jarry, *Ubu Roi*, from *The Ubu Plays* (trans. Cyril Connolly and Simon Watson Taylor) (Methuen, 1968), pp. 21–2.

29 *Joe Macbeth* was directed by Ken Hughes from a screenplay by Philip Yordan. The Macbeth couple were played by B-movie hard man Paul Douglas and tough gal Ruth Roman. *Men of Respect* was directed by William Reilly from his own screenplay.

30 Tony Howard, 'Shakespeare's cinematic offshoots', in the *Cambridge Companion to Shakespeare on Film*, op. cit., p. 302.

31 Kate Bassett, 'Damned spot? No worries, says soap star', *Daily Telegraph*, 12 August 1999.

32 The film, which came out in 1957, starred Toshiro Mifune as Washizu/Macbeth and Isuzu Yamada as Asaji/Lady Macbeth.

33 Daniel Rosenthal, *Shakespeare on Screen* (Hamlyn, 2000), p. 82.

34 Sinead Cusack, in Carol Rutter, *Clamorous Voices* (The Women's Press, 1988), p. 56.

35 Harriet Walter, op. cit., pp. 27–8.

36 L. C. Knights, *How Many Children Had Lady Macbeth?* (The Minority Press, 1933).

37 Tom Matheson, in the *Oxford Companion*, op. cit., p. 53. Matheson directs readers to Katharine Cooke's *A. C. Bradley and his Influence in Twentieth-Century Shakespeare Criticism* (1972).

38 See *The Merchant of Venice*, 4.1.303–9, and Ellen Terry's *Four Lectures on Shakespeare* (1932), pp. 119–20.

39 L. C. Knights, op. cit., pp. 10–11.

40 A. C. Bradley, *Shakespearean Tragedy* (1904; Macmillan, 1957), pp. 310–11.

41 Harriet Walter, op. cit., p. 31.

42 'Garrick and Mrs Pritchard as Macbeth and Lady Macbeth after the murder of Duncan' (c. 1766), in the Kunsthaus, Zürich. See Gert Schiff, *Johann Heinrich Füssli 1741–1825: Text und Oevrekatalog*, vols 1–2 (Prestel, 1973), no. 341.

43 Phyllis Hartnoll and Peter Found (eds), *The Concise Oxford Companion to the Theatre* (Oxford University Press, 1992), p. 395.

44 Johann Herder, in a letter to his mentor, Johann Hamann; see Eudo Mason, *The Mind of Henry Fuseli: Selections from his Writings* (Routledge and Kegan Paul, 1951), p. 69; quoted in Bate, op. cit., p. 266.

45 See Walter Pape and Frederick Burwick (eds), *The Boydell Shakespeare Gallery* (Peter Pomp, 1996), pp. 9–10.

46 See Eudo Mason, op. cit., p. 343.

47 J.H. Fuseli, Aphorism 96, cited in Walter Pape and Frederick Burwick, op. cit., p. 62.

48 Jonathan Bate, op. cit., pp. 267, 269.

49 Directed by Gregory Doran, it was later filmed for Channel 4 Television and shown in January 2001.

50 The production was re-staged in the main house at Stratford the following year, and was filmed for television in 1978, directed by Philip Casson.

51 See Michèle Willems, 'Video and its paradoxes', in the *Cambridge Companion to Shakespeare on Film*, op. cit., p. 39.

52 Pamela Mason, 'Orson Welles and filmed Shakespeare', in the *Cambridge Companion to Shakespeare on Film*, op. cit., p. 186.

53 Daniel Rosenthal, op. cit., p. 72.

54 Richard D. Altick, *Paintings from Books: Art and Literature in Britain, 1760–1900* (Ohio State University Press, 1985), p. 317.

55 All quotations are taken from the Assessment and Qualifications Alliance's specification document for English (specification A, 2004), p. 32.

56 Description based on Anna Picard's account of the Kirov Opera *Macbeth* (*Independent on Sunday*, 15 July 2001).

57 Gary Schmidgell, *Shakespeare and Opera* (Oxford University Press, 1990), p. 61.

58 Nick Kimberley, 'Good things come in trees', *The Observer* Review, 15 July 2001.

59 See Nick Kimberley, 'Behind every great maniac …', *The Observer* Review, 5 September 1999.

60 Andrew Clements, 'Raw power in ENO's superb revival', *The Guardian*, 18 June 2001.

61 See *The Oxford Dictionary of Music* (Oxford University Press, 1994; reprinted 2001), pp. 491, 807.

62 Charles Dickens, *Dombey and Son* (1848), Chapter LIX.

63 *Hamlet*, 1.2.216 (the line is actually 'It lifted up it head').

64 *Macbeth*, 5.1.32–3.

65 See Barbara Howard Traister, *The Notorious Astrological Physician of London: Works and Days of Simon Forman* (University of Chicago Press, 2001), p. 171.

66 *Macbeth*, 5.3.61–2.

67 Taken from the notebook later known as Manningham's *Diary*. It is in the British Museum (Harley ms 5353), and was edited for the Camden Society in 1868.

CHAPTER 7. HAMLET

1 Tom Stoppard, *Rosencrantz and Guildenstern Are Dead* (Faber and Faber, 1967), p. 108. (See pages 245–9.)

2 'Don't delay if you want to stay healthy – and sane', John Carlin, *Independent on Sunday*, 18 January 1998.

3 Laurence Olivier produced and directed the 1948 film, in addition to playing Hamlet.

4 *The Independent* Review, 5 February 2000.

5 *The Times*, 16 July 2001.

6 *Daily Telegraph*, 1 January 1997.

7 'The Hamlet of the weights room', *Independent on Sunday*, 19 January 2003.

8 Respectively: *The Guardian*, 7 January 2003; *The Times*, 23 January 2003; *The Times*, 19 January 1998; *The Guardian*, 7 June 1999.

9 Speaking on Channel 4 Television's *100 Best TV Advertisements*, made by Tyne Tees Television (2000).

10 Derek Longhurst, '"You base football-player!": Shakespeare in contemporary popular culture', in Graham Holderness, op. cit., pp. 67–8.

11 *Richard II*, 2.1.40–66.

12 Respectively: 'The curtain was going up, but yet again it was Hamlet without the Prince …' (Paddy Agnew, 'Inter's No 9 nightmare', *The Guardian*, 27 February 1999); '*It's Ulrika!* [BBC2, Monday] was Hamlet without the Prince …' (*Daily Telegraph*, 30 August 1997); Roger Bootle, 'Like Hamlet without the Prince', (*The Times*, 1 March 1999); Tim Hames, 'An education photo opportunity with no Blair is not so much Hamlet without the Prince as Macbeth minus all the Scots' (*The Times*, 20 March 1999).

13 Directed by Laurence Olivier.

14 See Sigmund Freud, 'Some character-types met with in psychoanalytic work' (1916), *Penguin Freud Library* (PFL) (Penguin, 1990), vol. 14, especially pp. 296–8 (on Richard the Third) and pp. 301–8 (on Macbeth and Lady Macbeth).

15 See Sigmund Freud, 'The theme of the three caskets' (1913), *PFL*, op. cit., vol. 14, pp. 233–49.

16 Sigmund Freud, *The Interpretation of Dreams* (1900), *PFL*, op. cit., vol. 4, p. 364.

17 Sigmund Freud, 'Psychopathic characters on the stage' (published 1942; written 1905–6), *PFL*, op. cit., vol. 14, p. 126.

18 Sigmund Freud, 'The Moses of Michelangelo' (1914), *PFL*, op. cit., vol. 14, pp. 254–5.

19 Sigmund Freud, 'Dostoevsky and parricide' (1927–8), *PFL*, op. cit., vol. 14, p. 454.

20 Sigmund Freud, *The Interpretation of Dreams* (1900), *PFL*, op. cit., vol. 4, p. 368.

21 For dating, see, among others, Anthony Davies (*The Cambridge Companion to Shakespeare*, Cambridge University Press, 2001, p. 179), Anne Barton (The New Penguin Shakespeare, 1980, p. 18), Kathleen O. Irace (*The First Quarto of Hamlet*, Cambridge University Press, 1998, p. 5), G. R. Hibbard (The Oxford Shakespeare, 1987, p. 5) and Philip Edwards (The New Cambridge Shakespeare, 1985, p. 8).

22 See Freud's address given to the Goethe House at Frankfurt in 1930 (*PFL*, op. cit., vol. 14, pp. 470–1).

23 *Hamlet*, 5.2.213–18.

24 Kenneth Muir, 'Some Freudian Interpretations of Shakespeare', in *Proceedings of the Leeds Philosophical Society* (July 1952), vol. VII, part I, p. 46.

25 Friedrich Nietzsche, *The Birth of Tragedy* (1872), in *The Birth of Tragedy and The Genealogy of Morals* (trans. Francis Golffing) (Doubleday Anchor Books, 1956), p. 51.

26 Philip Armstrong, *Shakespeare in Psychoanalysis* (Routledge, 2001), pp. 41–2.

27 Norman N. Holland, *Psychoanalysis and Shakespeare* (McGraw-Hill, 1964; revised 1966), p. 59.

28 Marc Norman and Tom Stoppard, op. cit., pp. 10–11.

29 *Lethal Weapon* directed by Richard Donner (1987); *Fatal Attraction* directed by Adrian Lyne (1987).

30 Directed by Franco Zeffirelli (1990), the film also featured Alan Bates as Claudius, Ian Holm as Polonius, Paul Schofield as the Ghost and Helena Bonham-Carter as Ophelia.

31 *The Shakespere Allusion-Book* (London: Humphrey Milford; Oxford University Press, 1932), vol. II, pp. 433–6; cited by Philip Edwards in his Introduction to The New Cambridge *Hamlet* (Cambridge University Press, 1985; revised 1995), p. 61.

32 See *The Letters of David Garrick* (ed. D.M. Little and G.M. Kahrl, 1963), vol. II, pp. 840–1.

33 William Hazlitt, *The Characters of Shakespeare's Plays* (1817; Oxford University Press, 1924), p. 92.

34 Directed by Kenneth Branagh, the film came out in 1996.

35 See Richard Foulkes, in the *Oxford Companion*, op. cit., p. 149.

36 John Gielgud with John Miller, *Shakespeare – Hit or Miss?* (Sidgwick and Jackson, 1991), p. 39.

37 Richard Findlater, *These Our Actors* (Elm Tree Books, 1983), p. 53.

38 James Agate, 'Their hour upon the stage', *Sunday Times*, 5 May 1930.

39 Samuel Crowl, 'Flamboyant realist: Kenneth Branagh', in the *Cambridge Companion to Shakespeare on Film*, op. cit., p. 234.

40 In the film *Looking for Richard* (see pages 153–7).

41 Michael Pennington, *Hamlet: A User's Guide* (Nick Hern Books, 1996), p. 80.

42 Steven Berkoff, 'Perchance to act', *The Guardian*, 11 August 1989.

43 The film also featured Diane Venora (Baz Luhrmann's Lady Capulet) as Gertrude, Kyle Maclachlan as Claudius, Bill Murray as Polonius and Sam Shepard as the Ghost.

44 Tom Stoppard, op. cit., pp. 85–7. The play was first performed by a student company, the Oxford Theatre Group, as part of the Edinburgh Festival fringe in 1966; its first professional performance was at the National Theatre in April of the following year. A film version appeared in 1991.

45 Tom Stoppard, op. cit., p. 19.

46 Harold Hobson, *The Christchurch Press* (3 May 1977).

47 See Daniel Rosenthal, op. cit., pp. 20–1.

48 *Hamlet Liikemaailmassa*, directed by Aki Kaurismäki, 1987.

49 Tony Howard, 'Shakespeare's cinematic offshoots', in the *Cambridge Companion to Shakespeare on Film*, op. cit., p. 302.

50 *In the Bleak Midwinter* (dir. Kenneth Branagh, 1996); *Outrageous Fortune* (Arthur Hiller, 1987); *Renaissance Man* (Penny Marshall, 1994); *Withnail and I* (Bruce Robinson, 1987); *To Be, or Not to Be* (Ernst Lubitsch, 1942; remake Alan Johnson, 1983); *A Letter to Timothy* (Humphrey Jennings, 1946); *The Lion King* (Roger Allers, Rob Minkoff, 1994); *Star Trek VI: the Undiscovered Country* (Nicholas Meyer, 1991).

51 Chris Moss, 'Prince of the barrio', *The Guardian*, 28 July 1999.

52 Quoted by Chris Moss, op. cit.

53 Directed by Patrice Caurier and Moshe Leiser, the opera was performed on 12, 15 and 20 May 2003, and featured Simon Keenlyside as Hamlet and Natalie Dessay as Ophelia.

54 Tim Ashley, 'Outrageous fortune', *The Guardian*, 2 May 2003.

55 Robert Thicknesse, 'The Hamlet with a happy ending', *The Times*, 6 May 2003.

56 Andrew Clements, *The Guardian*, 14 May 2003.

57 T.S. Eliot, 'The Love Song of J. Alfred Prufrock' (1917), in *T.S. Eliot: Collected Poems, 1902–1962* (Faber and Faber, 1963), p. 17.

58 Nicola Watson, in the *Oxford Companion*, op. cit., p. 138.

59 Samuel Taylor Coleridge, *Notes and Lectures upon Shakespeare* (1808).

60 A video recording of the performance was produced in 2001 by BBC/ARTE France/NHK/AGAT Films et Cie (France).

61 Michael Pennington, op. cit., p. 185.

62 Shaban played Hamlet in 1988, in a production directed by Alasdair Ramsay at the Half Moon, London.

63 The actors are quoted by Georgina Brown in 'To play the prince', *The Independent*, 17 March 1989.

64 Interview with the author, 28 January 2003.

65 Michael Pennington, op. cit., p. 150.

CHAPTER 8. KATE

1 From the Wife of Bath's Prologue, *The Canterbury Tales* (c. 1387), III (D), lines 727–9.

2 Brian Morris, Introduction to *The Taming of the Shrew* (Methuen, 1981), p. 13.

3 Frances E. Dolan, *The Taming of the Shrew, Texts and Contexts* (Bedford Books of St Martin's Press, 1996), p. 14.

4 It was directed by Sam Taylor.

5 Michael Hattaway, 'The comedies on film', in the *Cambridge Companion to Shakespeare on Film*, op. cit., p. 93.

6 See pages 113–15 and 326–7.

7 *The Taming of the Shrew*, 2.1.208–16.

8 Ibid., 2.1.265–72.

9 See the Arden, Cambridge and New Penguin editions, for example.

10 Eric Rasmussen, in the *Oxford Companion*, op. cit., p. 446.

11 Alan C. Dessen, *Recovering Shakespeare's Theatrical Vocabulary* (Cambridge University Press, 1995), pp. 65, 68.

12 See *The Taming of the Shrew*, 3.2.154–75.

13 See *Macbeth*, 2.2; *Romeo and Juliet*, 5.1 and 5.2; and *Henry V*, 2.3.

14 Quoted by Deborah Cartmell, 'Franco Zeffirelli and Shakespeare', in the *Cambridge Companion to Shakespeare on Film*, op. cit., pp. 213, 221.

15 Ibid., p. 213.

16 *Romeo and Juliet*, 3.1.72.

17 John Fletcher, *A Woman's Prize* or *The Tamer Tamed*, Epilogue, lines 1–7; in the edition prepared for the Royal Shakespeare Company (Nick Hern Books, 2003).

18 Ibid., 1.1.32–5.
19 Ibid., 5.3.72–5.
20 Gregory Doran, 'The antidote to Shakespeare', *The Guardian*, 2 April 2003.
21 *The Tamer Tamed*, 4.2.73–80.
22 Garrick's was the only version of Shakespeare's play performed in England and America between 1754 and 1844 (Frances E. Dolan, op. cit., p. 155).
23 Charles Marowitz, Introduction to *The Marowitz Shakespeare* (Marion Boyars, 1978), p. 17.
24 Daniel Rosenthal, op. cit., p. 135.
25 Directed by George Sidney from a screenplay by Dorothy Kingsley; music and lyrics by Cole Porter.
26 Directed by Gil Junger from a screenplay by Karen McCullah Lutz and Kirsten Smith.
27 Charlotte O'Sullivan, 'Shakespeare goes to the prom', *The Independent*, 9 July 1999.
28 Antonia Quirke, 'It's the best high-school movie for years', *Independent on Sunday*, 11 July 1999.
29 Anne Billson, 'Wacky teens love the Bard', *Sunday Telegraph*, 11 July 1999.
30 Charlotte O'Sullivan, op. cit.
31 Adam Mars-Jones, 'Poisoners of gender', *The Times*, 8 July 1999.
32 Directed by Amy Heckerling, USA, 1995.
33 Directed by Tim Blake Nelson, USA, 2001. In this version, Odin James is the only black student at a high school in the deep South. Widely popular and a star basketball-player, he is dating the Dean's daughter, Desi. But Odin's best friend Hugo is bitterly envious of Odin's success and plots to ruin him.

CHAPTER 9. PROSPERO

1 Alan Franks, 'Daddy's Girl'; interview with Anoushka Shankar, *The Times* Magazine, 17 April 1999.
2 Lesley Jackson, 'Master of the crystal vision', *The Independent* Weekend Review, 30 June 2001.
3 J.G. Ballard, 'Bibliofile', *The Times*, 1 February 1998.
4 This production of *The Tempest*, directed by Michael Grandage, opened at the Crucible, Sheffield and transferred to the Old Vic on 16 January 2003.
5 In that production, directed by Jonathan Miller (Old Vic, first performance 6 October 1988), Prospero was played by Max von Sydow and Caliban by Rudolph Walker.
6 See Richard W. Schoch, *Not Shakespeare: Bardolatry and Burlesque in the Nineteenth Century* (Cambridge University Press, 2002), p. 181.
7 Octave Mannoni, *Prospero and Caliban: the Psychology of Colonisation* (trans. Pamela Powesland) (Methuen, 1956; second edition, Frederick A. Praeger, Inc., 1964), p. 106.
8 In Peter Brook's 1990 production of *La Tempête* by the Théâtre des Bouffes du Nord, Paris, Prospero was played by Sotigui Konyaté and Caliban by David Bennett.
9 *Romeo and Juliet*, 2.3.23–4.
10 Screenplay by Cyril Hume from a novel by Irving Block, *Forbidden Planet* was directed by Fred McLeod Wilcox and starred Walter Pidgeon and Leslie Nielsen.

11 Press-release from the Belgrade Theatre, Coventry, for their July 1999 production.

12 Octave Mannoni, op. cit., p. 106.

13 Directed by Ron Daniels for the Royal Shakespeare Company. Caliban was played by Bob Peck.

14 National Theatre, directed by Peter Hall, 1973 (Gielgud); Cheek by Jowl, directed by Declan Donnellan, 1988 (Walker); National Theatre, directed by Peter Hall, 1988 (Bryant); Royal Shakespeare Company, directed by Nicholas Hytner, 1988 (Wood); Royal Shakespeare Company, directed by Sam Mendes, 1993 (McCowen).

15 Daniel Rosenthal, op. cit., p. 156.

16 David Benedict, 'William Shakespeare: The Man, The Myth and The Movies', *The Independent*, 18 September 1999.

17 Peter Greenaway, interviewed in Brian McFarlane (ed.), *An Autobiography of British Cinema* (London, 1997), p. 241; cited by Russell Jackson in the *Cambridge Companion to Shakespeare on Film*, op. cit., p. 16.

18 John Middleton Murry, *Shakespeare* (Jonathan Cape, 1936), pp. 391–2.

19 Park Honan, *Shakespeare: A Life* (Oxford University Press, 1998), p. 372.

20 Peter Brook, *The Empty Space* (Macgibbon and Kee, 1968), pp. 94–5.

21 *The Tempest*, 4.1.156–60.

22 *Hamlet*, 5.2.350

23 *Measure for Measure*, 3.1.119–20.

24 See Introduction, page 9; and Terence Hawkes, op. cit., p. 3 and passim.

25 John W. Velz, '"Gracious Silence" in Shakespeare', in *The Shakespeare Newsletter*, Summer 2002, pp. 31, 34, 36.

26 Interview with the author, 14 July 1999.

27 *The Tempest*, Epilogue, lines 1–3; see Derek Longhurst, '"You base football-player!":
Shakespeare in contemporary popular culture', in Graham Holderness, op. cit., p. 70.

28 Anne Righter, Introduction to *The Tempest* (Penguin, 1968), p. 50.

Acknowledgements

The author and publisher wish to thank the following for their permission to reprint copyright material:

'Shakespeare "especially dear" to Nazis', 'Wilhelm Shakespeare', 'Shakespeare as "Germanic Poet"'. Reproduced with permission of the *Evening Standard*.

Tom Stoppard and Marc Norman, *Shakespeare in Love*; Tom Stoppard, *Rosencrantz and Guildenstern are Dead*. Reproduced with permission of Faber and Faber Ltd.

Michael Billington, 'Henry V' (© *The Guardian* 2003); St John Ervine, 'An old Clo'man' (© *The Observer* 1927); 'Pass Notes no 915' (© *The Guardian* 1996); Jonathan Romney, 'Al Pacino playing Richard III' (© *The Guardian* 1996); Judith Mackrell, 'Unholy force' (© *The Guardian* 1998); Judith Mackrell, 'Modern lovers' (© *The Guardian* 1998); 'Pass Notes 9/8/2000' (© *The Guardian* 2000); John Mullan, 'The Serpent' (© John Mullan 2003); Gregory Doran, 'The Antidote to Shakespeare' (© Greg Doran 2003); Gary Taylor, 'Cry Havoc' (© Gary Taylor 2003); Nicholas Hytner, 'Guardian Review' (© Nicholas Hytner 2003). Reproduced with permission of *The Guardian*.

David Nathan, 'Is The Merchant of Venice anti-Semitic?' Courtesy of the *Jewish Chronicle*.

Jonathan Bate, *The Genius of Shakespeare*. Reproduced with permission of Macmillan UK.

Alfred Jarry, *The Ubu Plays* (trans. Cyril Connolly and Simon Watson Taylor). Reproduced by permission of Methuen Publishing Limited. Translation © Cyril Connolly and Simon Watson Taylor.

Patrick Stewart, 'Playing Shylock'. Reproduced with permission of the *Morning Star*.

Chris Moss, 'Prince of the barrio', *The Guardian*, 1999. Reproduced with permission of Chris Moss.

Francesca T. Royster, 'Cleopatra as Diva: African-American Woman and Shakespearean Tactics', in Marianne Novy (ed.), *Transforming Shakespeare: Contemporary Women's Re-visions in Literature and Performance*. Reproduced with permission of Palgrave Macmillan.

Steven Berkoff, 'Perchance to Act' © Steven Berkoff 1989. Reproduced with permission of Rosica Colin Limited.

Lisa Jardine, 'The Age of Manly Tears' (© *Telegraph* Group Limited 1997); 'Shylock as hero' (© *Telegraph* Group Limited 1934); John Simpson, 'Mirjana Markovic' (© *Telegraph* Group Limited 2001). Reproduced with permission.

Fig. 23. Reproduced with permission of the Belgrade Theatre, Coventry.

Fig. 7, Fig. 10. Reproduced with permission of The Bridgeman Art Library.

Fig. 5. Reproduced with permission of the British Film Institute.

Fig. 9. By permission of the Folger Shakespeare Library.

Fig. 11. Reproduced with permission of John Haynes.

Fig. 15. © 2003 Kunsthaus Zürich. All rights reserved.

John Taylor (attd), *William Shakespeare*; Fig. 17. By courtesy of the National Portrait Gallery, London. Fig. 1 (courtesy 20th Century Fox), Fig. 2 (courtesy Miramax Films), Fig. 4 (courtesy Renaissance Productions), Fig. 8 (courtesy Peter Rogers Productions), Fig. 13 (courtesy Bayly/Pare Productions), Fig. 16 (courtesy Columbia Pictures Corp.), Fig. 18 (courtesy Miramax), Fig. 19 (courtesy Columbia Pictures), Fig. 22 (courtesy Touchstone Pictures), Fig. 24 (courtesy All Arts). Reproduced with permission of the Ronald Grant Archive.

Fig. 6 (© Malcolm Davies, Shakespeare Birthplace Trust), Fig. 14 (© Joe Cocks Studio Collection, Shakespeare Birthplace Trust), Fig. 20 (© Reg Wilson Collection, Royal Shakespeare Company), Fig. 21 (© Malcolm Davies, Shakespeare Birthplace Trust). Reproduced with permission of the Shakespeare Centre Library.

Fig. 3. Reproduced with permission of the Victoria and Albert Museum.

Fig. 12. Reproduced with permission of National Museums Liverpool (The Walker).

Although every effort has been made to contact copyright holders, there are instances where we have been unable to do so. If notified, the publisher will be pleased to acknowledge the use of copyright material in future editions.

Index

(Entries marked in **bold italics** refer to numbers in the colour plates)